EX LIBRES

CHRIST AND SATAN

An Old English Poem

Edited with introduction, notes, and glossary
by
MERREL DARE CLUBB

ARCHON BOOKS
1972

Library of Congress Cataloging in Publication Data

Christ and Satan.
  Christ and Satan, an old English poem.

  (Yale studies in English, v. 70)
  Reprint of the 1925 ed.
  Thesis—Yale University.
  Bibliography: p.
  I. Clubb, Merrel Dare, 1897-   ed. II. Series.
PR1630C6 1972   829'.1   71-179569
  ISBN 0-208-01127-7

First published 1925
Reprinted with permission of
Yale University Press, Inc.
in an unaltered and unabridged edition
as an Archon Book
by The Shoe String Press, Inc.
Hamden, Connecticut 06514

Printed in the United States of America

PATRI · MEO

QUI

NON · SOLUM · JUVENTUTEM · MEAM

SUSTENTAVIT · INSTITUITQUE

SED · ETIAM · MENTEM · ET · COR

OPTIMO · EXEMPLO · CONCITAVIT

HAS · PRIMITIAS · LABORIS

D. D. D.

PREFACE

The poem which is the subject of this edition has not heretofore been completely and separately edited. This fact has disposed the editor to adopt a policy of which some, who believe that editorial matter should be restricted to the very minimum, may be inclined to disapprove. But since the textual and literary problems presented by *Christ and Satan* have elicited widely different views, the editor did not think it advisable merely to offer a new set of opinions, without making specific reference to those of previous scholars.

No pains have been spared to render accurate the text of the poem. It has been collated three times with a rotograph of the manuscript, and a final collation has been made since the text was in page-proof. Anything approaching a diplomatic reprint of a poetical text so obviously imperfect was, of course, out of the question; but I have refrained as much as possible from altering the reading of a manuscript which, as the variants show, has been rather excessively emended.

I wish to express my sincere gratitude to Professor Albert Stanburrough Cook for his kindly interest throughout the progress of my work upon this edition, as well as for much valuable counsel and aid in the printing. My thanks are also due in large measure to Professor Robert J. Menner, under whose guidance the actual writing was done. I am obliged to Mr. Rudolph Willard for permission to use his transcripts of the homilies of the Vercelli Book. To my wife I am grateful for generous assistance in preparing the original copy, and in reading the proof.

A considerable portion of the expense of printing has been borne by Yale University and by Miami University.

Oxford, Ohio,
May, 1925.

CONTENTS

INTRODUCTION

MANUSCRIPT. TITLE

Christ and Satan comprises the latter portion of MS. Junius XI, preserved in the Bodleian Library at Oxford. This is a small parchment folio, containing 229 written pages. It measures 12¾ inches in height, and 7¾ in breadth. The writing covers, on an average, 9⅛ by 5½ inches. The margin at the bottom is twice as deep as that at the top. There are 27 lines to the page, whereas the first part of the book was ruled on the scale of 26 lines. All the pages are completely filled with writing, with the two following exceptions: the lower half of page 229 is vacant, and the same portion of page 225 contains a curious unfinished design. According to Stoddard,[1] the present binding of oak boards covered with vellum dates from about 1450-1475. There is evidence that two folios have been cut out, one between pages 216 and 217, the other between pages 222 and 223. Stoddard thinks that a cut on page 212 indicates the loss of a folio before page 213, and that the folio which formed the other half of the leaf (if such there were) would have come between pages 228 and 229. This third loss has been doubted. At any rate, there is no break in the sense in any

---

[1] 'The Cædmon Poems in MS. Junius XI,' *Anglia* 10. 157-167. Stoddard's article contains the most exhaustive external description of the whole manuscript. See also the 'Account of Cædmon's Metrical Paraphrase of Scripture History, an Illuminated Manuscript of the Tenth Century,' by Henry Ellis, in *Archæologia* 24. 329-335; and Westwood's *Palæographia Sacra Pictoria*. The scholars who have discussed the Junius MS. have almost wholly confined their attention to the first part, because, first, it is a much better specimen of calligraphy, and, secondly, it contains the very interesting series of drawings illustrating the *Genesis*. These may be seen in facsimile in *Archæologia, loc. cit.*, and Kennedy's *The Cædmon Poems*.

of the three cases, so that the missing folios were probably left vacant for future illustration. Afterwards, since parchment was a valuable commodity, some one may have cut them out. The manuscript is comparatively well preserved. There are no illegible passages, and only pages 224 and 225, which face each other, have been blurred to any extent. The poem begins at page 213 and ends at page 229. It is preceded in the MS. by three others: the *Genesis, Exodus,* and *Daniel.* Of all four, only the *Genesis* bears a title (and this by a later hand). Because of the change in subject-matter, between the two sections, from the Old Testament to the New, which was accompanied, moreover, by a change in scribes, and as a result of a literal interpretation of the rubric at the end, 'Finit Liber II. Amen,' *Christ and Satan* was for long described as the 'Second Book of Cædmon.' (Hickes spoke of it as the 'additament.') Grein[2] was the first to apply to it the name accepted for the present edition. Wülker,[3] following the more recent theory as to the unity of the piece, affixed the following titles at lines 1, 366, and 665: 'Die Klagen der Gefallnen Engel,' 'Christi Höllenfahrt, Auferstehung, Himmelfahrt, und Kommen zum Jüngsten Gericht.'

We know nothing of the history of the Junius MS. before the middle of the seventeenth century, when Francis Dujon, known as Junius, published in Amsterdam a fairly exact reprint of it in Old English type.[4] He informs us that James Ussher, Archbishop of Armagh, had given him the manuscript. William Somner also consulted it for his *Dictionarium Saxonico-Latino-Anglicum* (1659). Upon Junius'

---

[2] *Bibliothek der Angelsächsischen Poesie,* 1857.
[3] In his revision of Grein's *Bibliothek,* 1894.
[4] *Cædmonis Monachi Paraphrasis Poetica Genesios ac præcipuarum Sacræ paginæ Historiarum, abhinc annos MLXX. Anglo-Saxonicè conscripta, et nunc primùm edita à Francisco Junio F. F. Amstelodami . . . Typis et sumptibus Editoris. MDCLV. 4°. 106 + 10 pp.*

death in 1677, it came, with the rest of his collections, into the possession of the Bodleian.

Earlier scholars generally assigned the manuscript as a whole to the tenth century. Ellis, Stoddard, the editors[5] of the Palæographical Society's facsimiles (see Series 2, Plates 14, 15), and Blackburn[6] date it about the year 1000, or the early eleventh century. Keller,[7] whose study of the writing of dated documents puts him in a position to give an especially trustworthy verdict, decides for the last decades of the tenth, evidently without distinguishing chronologically the two 'books.' He places it somewhat later than the Exeter Book and the Vercelli Book (i. e., after 970-980 A. D.).[8] This will do very well for Book I, but Keller can not have studied Book II very minutely, since he does not seem aware that more than one scribe shared in it, whereas there are actually three.[9]

In dating a poetical manuscript, one must remember that a scribe working from a literary exemplar is more likely to exhibit archaic features than would the same scribe in writing legal documents. Keller mentions so-called high *e*'s in Book II. In the work of the first scribe, they do occur, but two facts are to be noticed. First, these *e*'s are of an especially archaic and unpleasing variety (*ᶜ*), and look as if made to order; and, in the second place, the scribe soon tired of aping this particular feature. There are roughly 14, 8, and 3 high *e*'s on the first three pages taken in order.[10] On the basis of Keller's own criteria, the more important of which are

[5] E. A. Bond, E. M. Thompson, G. F. Warner.

[6] *Exodus and Daniel*, Introduction, p. vii.

[7] *Angelsächsische Palaeographie (Palaestra, Vol. 43)* 1. 39.

[8] See Keller's article entitled 'Angelsächsische Schrift' in Hoops' *Reallexikon der Germanischen Altertumskunde*.

[9] His notion that there are dotted *t*'s in Book II cannot be substantiated. A few *t*'s look as though supplied with dots, but the dots are really metrical points.

[10] On the imitativeness of the first scribe, see below, p. xix, note 25.

mentioned in the course of the following paragraphs, it is
evident that the writing of Book II is later than that of
Book I; but probably there was less than a generation
between them, so that the manuscript of Book II can be
dated about 1000 A. D.[11]

All three scribes[12] avoid the high *e* (with the exception
noted above); they avoid also both the round *s* and the high
s (ſ), employing the 'insular' *s* (ᚱ) almost exclusively.
They never use the three-stroke *a*. The terminations of the
short vertical strokes are never pointed, whereas those of the
long strokes are often blunt in the writing of scribes B
and C, but sometimes extravagantly long and pointed, sometimes blunt, in that of A. A and C make no distinction
between *d* and *ð* except in the lateral stroke. A uses only
the straight-line *y* (dotted only once, and that by the Corrector). B begins by imitating the *y* with outward bending
shanks (ᛉ), but suddenly, at the top of page 225, he drops
this for the straight form, which he employs consistently
thereafter. He usually dots his *y*. Both A and B curiously,
for about a page (pages 215 and 217), imitate what Keller
calls the West Saxon *g*, the lower stroke of which is con-
tinued to form a complete loop.

The first scribe, who copied pages 213-5, to use Keller's
characterization, writes a round, very irregular hand. Many
of his individual letters are graceful, but the *tout ensemble*
is unpleasing to the eye. His most distinctive letter is *a*,
for which he uses the minuscule *a*, similar to the modern
small Roman. The second scribe wrote the bulk of the
poem, stopping with page 228. Toward the end, that is,

[11] Thorpe (*Metrical Paraphrase of parts of the Holy Scriptures in
Anglo-Saxon*, p. VII) inferred from the character of the transcription that *Christ and Satan* was taken down from oral dictation. Groschopp ('Das Angelsächsische Gedicht "Crist und Satan,"' *Anglia*
6. 266) showed that this theory was impossible.

[12] For convenience, I shall speak of them as A, B, and C in the
following discussion.

from the middle of page 227 to the middle of page 228, he seems to have tried to economize both space and time. Most of the lines in this section look very cramped, and abbreviations are much more frequent than usual. B's hand is very easy to read, and much more regular than A's. Some of his pages on the whole are very pleasing in appearance; yet the form of his letters is quite plain, so that his style must be ranked rather lower than that of the scribe of Book I. He is much more careful than A in confining his use of ð to the medial and final positions. The third scribe is responsible for only half a page. He uses a blunter pen, and writes uniformly. His work is a considerable improvement on A's.

I can see very little apparent chronological difference in the writing of these three scribes,[13] none of such importance as is evident between the work of the two scribes of the Beowulf MS.[14]

The first six (except the fourth) of the twelve sections into which the text is divided are numbered with small Roman numerals. In eight cases, a plain large capital marks the beginning. There is one ornamental capital somewhat similar to those of Book I, which were formed by various combinations of a strange sort of monster. On three occasions, the space for the capitals is left vacant. The points

[13] See below, p. xix, note 25, on the way they treat the dialect of their copy.

[14] There is some difference of opinion concerning the quality of the transcription. Dietrich, in his note on line 479 (*Zs. f. D. Alt.,* Vol. 10) and elsewhere, lays to the inexactness of the poet, not to the incompetence of the scribes, the lines which make sense, but are metrically confused. Wülker (see his note on 729) considers that either poet or scribes might be guilty; while Holthausen (*Anglia Bb.* 5. 234) and Graz (*Eng. Stud.* 21. 19) argue that the transcription, instead of the poet, is at fault. Except possibly with regard to the last portion of the poem, I believe that these last-mentioned scholars are nearer the truth. It seems probable to me, however, that the corruption of the text took place in an intermediate MS., not in the work of our three scribes.

of division, in eleven instances out of twelve, correspond to
rather definite pauses in the progress of the poem. Only
the sixth is superfluous, and even this marks a separate para-
graph. The twelfth section, however, needs to be broken up
into two parts at line 665. The first eleven sections range
in length from 31 to 77 lines, or from three-fourths of a
page to over one and one-half pages of manuscript. (The
twelfth contains 135 lines, and covers two and one-half
pages.) This orderly but unequal distribution of material is
against Henry Bradley's theory[15] that the numbered sections
in *Christ and Satan* correspond, as he thinks they do in the
Genesis and the *Exodus*, 'to the separate sheets of an earlier
MS.' Bradley continues: 'I myself think it very likely that
a critical examination of the text might render it probable
that the sheets were approximately equal in the number of
verses that they contained.' Such a critical examination
would have to pursue a truly Procrustean policy of ampu-
tating and stretching.

    Two or three hypotheses offer possible explanations of the
way in which the manuscript of *Christ and Satan* came to
form a part of the Junius codex. First, it could have been
written as a continuation of Book I. Thus Stoddard thinks
that agreement in size and form between the two sections
warrants the belief that the book which was bound in the fifteenth century was a single manuscript, of the same size as
in the eleventh century. Blackburn amplifies this view. He
is of the opinion 'that the book was originally intended for
the first part only, that this was left unfinished, . . . the
work of the scribe being . . . interrupted before he had filled
the book, and that the pages left unwritten at the end were
afterwards utilized by other scribes for writing the second
poem.' This is very plausible. But, granted that the two
sections were written at the same place, it is not impossible

---

[15] 'The Numbered Sections in Old English Poetical MSS.,' *Pro-
ceedings of the British Academy*, 1915-6, p. 179.

that the size of parchment used, and the width of the upper
and lower margins (which are the only features in which
Books I and II agree), should be more or less fixed quanti-
ties in a given scriptorium; so that similarity in such matters
need not imply that two manuscripts belonged originally to
the same book, even though they came in course of time
to be bound together. Besides, a later scribe who knew
Book I, and intended to add our poem to it as Book II, could
easily imitate such externalities. There is one additional
clue. The rotograph shows on every leaf that the manuscript of *Christ and Satan* has been folded from top to
bottom in the middle after it was written, whereas I have
been able to discover indications of such folding in none of
the facsimiles of the *Genesis*. If this should be corroborated
by an examination of the manuscript of Book I itself, Blackburn's explanation would have to be given up. It seems
clear, however all this may be, that at some later time in the
eleventh century the two sections were treated as one book,
because there are traces in the *Genesis* of the hand of the
Late West Saxon Corrector who was so active in *Christ and
Satan*.

The scribes use little punctuation, properly speaking. A
has a few semicolons, and B also on one page. The end of
the sections is marked by a simple period, a semicolon, two
periods, or a period and a dash. After line 365 stand a colon
and a dash. Capitals occur sporadically, and are as likely as
not to be used in the wrong place. The mark most consistently and accurately employed is the metrical point, indicating
the pause between hemistichs. It is found pretty regularly
throughout, except for a space of fifteen lines following line
280, and is rarely misplaced. In many instances it has been
added by the Corrector, who also distinguished the cæsural
pause by a check, beginning with line 51. He omits this
last for two or three long periods, and often places it at the
end-pause. Abbreviation is confined chiefly to the Tironian
sign ⁊ , for *and* (the full form is never found), ˜ over vowels

for *m,* and 🄟 for *þæt.* *Wǣt, þoñ, scās, æft* are isolated forms
for *wæter, þonne, sanctas,* and *æfter.*

Blackburn's notes[16] on the use of accent-marks in the
Exodus hold equally good for *Christ and Satan.* These
marks are very frequent (190 in the first 250 lines), and
seem to come from more than one hand. In by far the
majority of instances, the accent chances to have been placed
on a long syllable, but this does not prove that it was intended
for a sign of length. It is more probable that it indicates
syllables which seemed to the writer or reader to be emphatic
in metre or sense.

A fourth person, in addition to the three scribes, had a
hand in giving the manuscript its final form, namely, a corrector.[17] His chief work consisted in changing the vowels
of the text to the normal Late West Saxon form; but he
by no means does this in a thorough-going manner, and his
activity falls off decidedly after line 125, where the second
scribe, who did most of the normalizing himself, begins to
write.[18] The Corrector also occasionally has a suggestion to
offer in passages of which the meaning is dark. His corrections are usually written in the space between the lines, but
alterations of the letters, or even of whole words, of the text
are found. Sometimes they take the form of alternative
readings, and there are a very few explanatory glosses. He
often joins, by means of lines, syllables which belong
together, or separates others by large commas. The addi-

---

[16] *Op. cit.,* pp. xiv-xviii.

[17] Sievers (*Zs. f. D. Alt.* 15. 456) thinks the Corrector's writing
apparently contemporary with that of the scribes; Wülker (*Bibliothek*) considers it somewhat later; Frings (*Zs. f. D. Phil.* 45. 219-
221), for phonological reasons, assigns the Corrector to the time of
Ælfric. He is probably not far removed from the time of the MS.
There are a few corrections which seem to be in a hand different
from that of the regular corrector.

[18] For an account of the phonology and inflection of the Corrector's
modifications of MS. readings, see Frings' article in *Zs. f. D. Phil.*
45. 220-1.

tions which the Corrector made cause no trouble; but he also made a number of erasures, which either obscure the phonology of the text or deprive us of the original reading, at the same time offering a substitute which is of questionable value. There is no indication whatever that he worked from any other copy, even from the probably faulty one which the scribes had used. His few attempts at elucidation or restoration, some of which are acceptable, are quite obvious, and most of his changes are unnecessary. Cosijn,[19] indeed, describes him as worthless. Frings,[20] however, inclines to regard most of his emendations affecting the sense or syntax of the poem as real improvements. They often are, when judged by the standards of rigorous normality, but there is no reason to suppose that they restore the original readings. Frings lists the following lines as containing changes which are not 'superfluous': 29, 89, 95, 97, 107, 120, 214, 217, 236, 331, 389, 437, 476, 588, 682, 687, 693, 711. It has seemed to me that only those in 95, 120, 236, 389, 437, and 682 are of any value in establishing the text, although some of the others are not exactly superfluous.

LANGUAGE

Groschopp's investigation of the language of *Christ and Satan* was the first which was extensive enough to be at all significant.[21] The value of his conclusions, however, is

[19] *Beitr. zur Gesch. der D. Spr. und Lit.* 21. 23.
[20] *Op. cit.,* pp. 219-220.
[21] Hickes described the dialect of the 'Cædmonian' poems as Dano-Saxon, by which he meant the language of Northumbria after the Danes had corrupted it. See his *Thesaurus Linguarum Vett. Septentrionalium* (1703), p. 133; also his letter to Bishop Nicolson (quoted by Thorpe, pp. IX, X), and Wanley's *Catalogus,* p. 77. Thorpe took issue with Hickes; he believed the poems to be in 'pure Saxon,' except for some orthographic peculiarities in the second book (*Cædmon's Metrical Paraphrase of parts of the Holy Scriptures in*

diminished by the fact that he was apparently not aware of the existence of a Mercian dialect, alongside of West Saxon, Kentish, and Northumbrian. Since the distinctive features of the last of these three are absent, he explained the variations from standard West Saxon, many of which he admitted were to be found also in Northumbrian, as chargeable to Kentish scribes. He believed the original version to have been West Saxon, which original version was derived in turn from a long Northumbrian poem.[22] In the same year (1883), Kühn said it seemed certain to him that the extant text, with its mixed dialect, had been recast from a Mercian original.[23]

Kühn's opinion on the dialect, with slight modification, was substantiated in Frings' admirable and exhaustive study.[24] On the basis of the grammars of Bülbring and Sievers, Frings showed conclusively that the language of *Christ and Satan* was originally a Mercian-Northumbrian border dialect,

---

Anglo-Saxon (1832), p. IX). Bouterwek listed a number of peculiarities in the language of *Christ and Satan,* which he said remind one of Northumbrian; but he admitted that indubitable characteristics of that dialect can be only rarely pointed out (*Cædmon's des Angelsachsen Biblische Dichtungen* (1848-54), p. CCXXXIV).

[22] *Das Angelsächsische Gedicht 'Crist und Satan'* (reprinted in *Anglia* 6. 248-276). In 1885 Sievers supported Groschopp's Kentish hypothesis. Accepting *iū* in 107, Sievers scanned the line with primary accents on *iū* (instead of *āhte*) and *ealles,* and concluded that we have here an instance of an alliteration possible only in Kentish, *i (g): ea.* He also singled out *styde,* 197, as a Kentish form. Sievers' general theory of the poems in Junius XI is as follows: 'Ich glaube, die ganze sammlung ist in Kent oder dessen nachbarschaft zusammengebracht worden, für einzelne der gedichte auch direkt kentischer ursprung nachzuweisen' (see *Beitr. zur Gesch. der D. Spr. und Lit.* 10. 195-9).

[23] *Uber die Angelsächsischen Gedichte von Christ und Satan,* pp. 38-42. Brandl characterized the poem as of Anglian origin in his *Geschichte der Altenglischen Literatur,* in Paul's *Grundriss der Germanischen Philologie* (1908) 2. 1045.

[24] 'Christ und Satan,' *Zs. f. D. Phil.* 45. 216-237.

that is, that it occupied an intermediate position between the Rushworth Gloss to Matthew and the Vespasian Psalter on the one hand, and the Rushworth Gloss to Mark, Luke, and John, the Lindisfarne Gospels, and the Durham Ritual on the other. He neatly disposes of Sievers' two isolated Kenticisms, and explodes Groschopp's notion that the original was in the West Saxon dialect, and that the non-West Saxon forms were to be assigned to the scribes, by a single observation: there are in the text quite a considerable number of West Saxon and especially Late West Saxon characteristics, several of which are certainly later than many of the non-West Saxon peculiarities. Hence it is the West Saxon rather than the non-West Saxon forms which must have derived from the scribes—just the reverse of Groschopp's view. Frings believes that the scribes had the Anglian original before them, and there is surely no ground for any other conclusion.[25] Having shown that the original dialect cannot have been Kentish, Frings also excludes the assumption of an intermediate Kentish version. The only apparently certain Kentish form in *Christ and Satan* is *seondon*, found in 104 and 709 (see Sievers-Cook, *Grammar of Old*

---

[25] This does not exclude the possibility of intermediate Anglian transcriptions, however.

Frings' summary of the different policies which the three scribes pursue in their treatment of the text may well be given in his own words: 'Der erste schreiber bemühte sich vergebens, den ihm vorliegenden anglischen originaltext in ein glattes spätws. umzuschreiben; er brach daher ab [mit v. 125]; dem zweiten schreiber gelang die umschrift wesentlich besser; und erst der dritte hielt sich wieder treuer an die vorlage [in v. 711-733]. Der spätws. korrector sah sich daher namentlich in v. 1-125 zu verhältnismässig zahlreichen änderungen gezwungen.' In regard to this characterization, the only doubt which arises is whether it is necessary to assign failure to achieve a smooth Late West Saxon rendering as the cause of the first scribe's breaking off at line 125. His work is so imitative, that is, in an easy-going way, that one must doubt whether he had any well-defined purpose of consistently Saxonizing his text at all.

English, 427, n. 2, 3).[26] In 709 it is an emendation for
seond, offered by the Corrector. Whether Frings is right
in considering dissyllabic *seondon* in 104 open to suspicion
because burdensome to the line, or not, in any case it would
be rash to affirm the existence of a Kentish intermediary on
the basis of one doubtful form, which, for convenience'
sake, we may lay to the first scribe.

The second scribe by his normalizing, and the Corrector
by his erasures, have considerably obscured the original dialect (i. e., a rather distinct type of Anglian) ; but because of
the first scribe's imitativeness, and the fact that the poem
does not seem to have gone through many stages of transmission, that dialect is represented about as consistently, and
in proportionally as great an abundance of forms, as is the
original speech of any other Old English poem of equal
length which has come down to us in a West Saxon version.[27]

The phonological peculiarities which constitute the chief
body of evidence regarding the dialect of *Christ and Satan*
are presented below in *résumé* for convenience of reference.[28]

[26] See also Heidemann, 'Die Flexion des Verb. Subst. im Angelsächsischen,' *Archiv* 147. 33 ff.

[27] The age of the dialect, and the evidence it presents in regard to
the unity and date of the poem, will be reserved for treatment under
those general topics.

[28] This sketch is based upon the comprehensive study made by
Frings. It makes no pretensions to completeness or originality,
though the editor has ventured to disagree with a very few of
Frings' conclusions. He has also slightly changed the arrangement,
presenting the normal WS. phenomena before those of the other
dialects. Although the references to lines in which a given phenomenon is to be found are usually by no means complete, references have
been given, wherever possible, to at least one line in each of the three
parts, in order to emphasize the linguistic unity of the original version.
The developments noted begin, for the most part, with the West
Germanic, not the Old English sounds. The sign > is used for
'becomes,' 'appears as.' Unless otherwise specified, a given phenomenon is characteristic of WS., or at least is to be found in that
dialect, and hence is of no value in determining the original dialect
of the poem.

VOWELS OF STRESSED SYLLABLES

WG. ă in a closed syllable when not influenced by the sounds of adjacent syllables usually becomes *æ*. A few cases of Mercian *e* are found (e. g., *gefestnade*, 3; *scref*, 26; *hrefnan*, 500; *gefregn*, 526).

ă before nasals > both *a* (*gelamp*, 24; *land*, 213; *gelamp*, 478; *sang*, 663; *mancynnes*, 668; *handum*, 706) and *o* (*song*, 45; *moncynnes*, 64; *lond*, 215; *hondum*, 540; *stondað*, 620; *hondum*, 680A; *gong*, 708).

a before *l* + cons. > *ea* (*wealdend*, 125; *ealdor*, 373; *ealle*, 385; *gewealde*, 687) and *a* (Anglian, etc.) in *ymbhaldeð*, 7; *waldendes*, 396; *alne*, 702.

ă before *r* + cons. > *ea* (*bearn*, 10; *þearle*, 421; *wearð*, 711) and Anglian *a* (*forwarð*, 21; *swarte*, 640; *swarta*, 704).

ă before *h* > *ea* (*leahtrum*, 263; *geseah*, 7:6) and *e* (*esle*, 681).

i-umlaut of ă + *l* + cons. = Anglian *æ* in *wælm*, 30; *e* (Saxon patois and Kentish) in *welme*, 39; and LWS. *y* in *hylle*, 338, 433, 717, and *syleð*, 292.

i-umlaut of ă + *r* + cons. = Anglian *æ* in *wærgðu*, 89; *āwærgdan*, 416; *e* (Anglian, etc.) in *underne*, 1; *edcerres*, 451; *cer*, 698; and LWS. *y* in *āwyrgda*, 316; *cyrre*, 538; *āwyrgda*, 676.

ă after palatals > *ea* (*sceal*, 48; *gesceafta*, 442); *æ* (Anglian, etc.) in *gescæft*, 139; and *e* (Anglian, etc.) in *gescefta*, 203, 584; *gesceft*, 664; when affected by *i*-umlaut > LWS. *y* (*scypend*, 57; *scyppend*, 535); and *e* (Anglian, etc.) in *sceppendes*, 106.

u-umlaut of ă = Anglian *ea* (*eaples*, 411).

ĕ in a closed syllable not influenced by sounds of adjacent syllables > *e* (*swegles*, 23; *selde*, 663) and Anglian *æ* (*rægnas*, 11; *swægles*, 124[?]).

self(a) is spelled with *e* in 9, 648; with LWS. *y* in 218, 306, 441, 545; and with non-WS. *eo* in 22 cases.

ĕ before *r* + cons. > *eo* (*eorðan*, 16; *eorlas*, 478; *geornor*, 705); *e* (through Anglian 'leveling') in *wercum*, 48. *e* remains unbroken in *tōwerpan*, 85.

ĕ before *h* + cons. > *i* in *six*, 15; *riht*, 207, 347, 688.

ĕ after palatals > *i, y* (*gife*, 572, 646; *gylp*, 254; *bescyrede*, 343), and *e* (Anglian, etc.) in *sceldbyrig*, 309.

u-umlaut of ĕ = *eo* in *meotod*, 2, 401, 697 (Anglian, etc.; cf. WS. *metod*, 668); WS. *heolstres*, 101; *geseotu*, 602 (Anglian, etc.); after *w* and before *r*, we have *eo* in *weorulde*, 211 (Anglian, Kent.); *weoroda*, 564; *o* in *woruld*, 59; *e* in *werud*, 33.

o/a-umlaut of ĕ = *eo* (Anglian, Kentish) in *spreocan*, 78; *beoran*, 158, 206; *feola*, 160; *ongeotan*, 301; *feola*, 477; Anglian *ea* (*teala*, 557, 733); unumlauted, *fela*, 402, 497 (WS.).

ĭ is usually retained; LWS. *y* appears, e. g., in *hym*, 70; *syndon*, 150; *synd*, 358; *fyrndagum*, 463.

ĭ before *r* + cons. > Anglian *eo* (*beornende*, 158; *beorneð*, 414); affected by *i*-umlaut > *i* (*āfirde*, 67; *wirse*, 24); and *y* in *wyrse*, 125.

u- and *o/a*-umlaut of ĭ = *eo* (*cleopað*, 616); *eo* (Anglian, etc.) in *leomu*, 155; *neoman*, 198; *hleonade*, 433; *weotod*, 692.

i-umlaut of ŭ usually = *y* (*āfylled*, 100; *yfeles*, 374; *myntest*, 689); LWS. (occasionally Anglian) *i* is also found in *drihten*, 47; *hihte*, 643; *drihten*, 665.

ā > WS. ǣ in *dǣdum*, 156; *blǣd*, 414; *nǣre*, 676; and ē (of other dialects) in *nēdran*, 102; *begēton*, 474; *ēðm*, 704. *Nēh*, 339, is either LWS. or Anglian.

i-umlaut of *ai* = ǣ (*ǣhte*, 87; *mǣndon*, 386; *lǣhte*, 716); and ē (usually described as Kentish, but this ē occurs before dentals also in Mercian; see Bülbring, *Elementarbuch*, § 167, and Luick, *Hist. Gram. d. Engl. Sprache*, § 187) in *clēne*, 7, 18; *gedēlde*, 19; *hēlende*, 54; *gelēdde*, 88.

au before *c, g, h* > *ēa* (*hēah-*, 29; *ēagum*, 390, 718) ;
Anglian or LWS. *ē* (*hēhseld*, 208; *hēhenglas*, 601;
ēgum, 728) ; and Anglian *ǣ* in *þǣh*, 265.
i-umlaut of *au* = *ī, ȳ* (*līge*, 325; *gelȳfdon*, 416) ; *ē* (Anglian,
etc.) in *hēran*, 54; *bēgde*, 381 ; *lēg*, 715.
OE. *ēo* before a guttural > *ēo* (*lēoht*, 28, 367) ; and the
exclusively Anglian *ī* (*līht*, 68, 361, 679; *sīc*, 275).
i-umlaut of *iu* = *ȳ, ī* (*lȳhteð*, 105; *gelīhtan*, 431), and
Mercian *ēo* (also Kentish) in *ðēostræ*, 38; *dēore*, 82,
543.

VOWELS OF INFLECTIONAL SYLLABLES

For a list of lines in which *æ* is used for weak *e*, see Introduction, p. lix, n. 100.
Earlier *un*, instead of *on, an*, as the ind. plur. pret. ending,
occurs in *sceolun*, 30, 41 ; *gesawun*, 718.
The tense-stem of the second weak conj. is usually either *-od-*
or *-ad-*, but weakened *-ed-* is found in 25, 280, 320, 534,
620.

CONSONANTS

u is twice used for *f* (*seolua*, 13, 712).
On *d* for *ð* in MS. *sīdas* see note on 189ᵇ.
Gecȳdde, 200, for *gecȳðde* is LWS.
h instead of *c*, in the word *ac*, is found in this proportion,
8:6. Sievers notes *ah* as a characteristic of Northumbrian, though it is found in the other dialects.
Later *h* for final *g* occurs in *āstāh*, 549, 563; *beorh*, 682;
āstāh, 682; *g* is retained in *āstāg*, 717, 730.
g > *i* in *eisegan*, 36 (either Northumbrian or Kentish).
g omitted in *menio*, 476 (late), and LWS. *middaneard*, 165,
272.
Initial *h* is omitted in *reðre*, 99; *nīgan*, 208; *insīðgryre*, 456;
gerēaw, 489; *rēam*, 717. See Sievers, *Gram.* 217, n. 2.
It is inorganic in *hrefnan*, 500.

Gemination has not yet taken place in *ātre,* 79; *nēdran,* 102; *tūdor,* 659; whereas it is found in *āttre,* 40, 129, 163, 318; *ǣrror,* 151, 299; *nǣddran,* 337, 412; *hlūddre,* 601.

All the relevant inflectional variations from the normal WS. are mentioned in the notes, and need not be repeated here. Some examples are listed under Vowels of Inflectional Syllables. All of these variations confirm the Anglian character of the original text.

SOURCES AND LITERARY RELATIONS

To lay as large a foundation of fact as possible upon which to base discussion of the more difficult problems of unity, date, and authorship, it will be well at this point to try to determine what are the sources from which the underlying conceptions of *Christ and Satan* are drawn, and in what relation it stands to other Old English poetry. The following investigation will fall naturally into three sections, in accordance with the threefold division in the subject-matter of the poem.[29]

In any strict sense of the word, the laments of the fallen angels in lines 1-365 cannot be said to have a source. The story of their fall had developed gradually on the basis of a few scattered Biblical passages, with accretions from Jewish apocryphal writings, especially the Enochic literature. Gregory the Great (whose fondness for demonology is easy to discover) in his thirty-fourth homily on the Gospels, and in his elaborate allegorical comments on all the Biblical verses which could be conceived to have the slightest reference to the subject, gave the story a systematic and definitive form, which, with some modification to be ascribed to the

---

[29] The structural outline of *Christ and Satan,* which will be found in the pages just preceding the notes, will, it is hoped, be of assistance to the reader in locating the various sections of the text mentioned hereafter.

genius of Milton, has come to stand on an equal footing among the western nations with many of the Scriptural narratives. But the Latin Fathers were, in general, too much occupied with the theological aspects of the story, and the moral edification to be derived from it, to evolve any such dramatic conception of the state of mind of the apostates themselves, in the various phases of their existence, as we find presented in *Christ and Satan* 1-365. Avitus of Vienne introduces a speech of Lucifer in which he deplores his lost glory,[30] but it is in the defiant spirit of *Genesis B,* not the plaintive tone of *Christ and Satan.* Aldhelm, on the other hand, seems to have been slightly more impressed with the pathos of the fallen Lucifer's situation. His language in describing the contrast between Lucifer's present degradation and former preëminence verges upon the sympathetic:

> Lucifer idcirco deserto climate cæli
> Nigra satellitibus stipatus Tartara farsit;
> Cælicolas ista prostravit belva[31] superbos,
> Qui prius angelica fulserunt luce corusci,
> Sedibus et superis florebant sorte beata:
> Tertia stellarum rueret dum portio præceps,
> Lucida bis tantum manserunt sidera sursum.[32]

And the three lines (quoted in the note to lines 34 ff.) which Lucifer speaks in the riddle, *Lucifer,* are still nearer the tone of the Old English poem.[33]

[30] *De Originali Peccato* 89 ff. (ed. Peiper, pp. 214-5) ; tr. by Guizot, *History of Civilization* (tr. Hazlitt, 2. 152-3).

[31] I. e., Superbia.

[32] *De Virginitate* 2741-7 (ed. Ehwald) ; the passage occurs in what is often called *De Octo Principalibus Vitiis* (296-302).

[33] Pitman, *The Riddles of Aldhelm* (*Yale Studies in English* LXVII*), p. 48.

On this slender basis Abbetmeyer (*OE. Poetical Motives derived from the Doctrine of Sin,* p. 18) makes Aldhelm not only the originator of the conception of a lamenting Satan, but also ascribes to him the authorship of the first vernacular 'plaint.' As Brown remarks in his review of Abbetmeyer (*Mod. Lang. Notes* 19. 223) : 'If we must have a name to conjure with, Aldhelm may do as well as another.'

Abbetmeyer believes that from such passages as a beginning there evolved a cycle of 'Plaints of Lucifer.' First
came the early portion of *Genesis A,* which narrates the story
of the fall of the angels; next, the laments of *Satan* 1-365,
also lines 454-6, and, in spirit, lines 665-733; and finally,
the long dialogue between Guthlac and the demons in *Guthlac
A* 529-656. Then there are 'incidental allusions to the Fall
in the manner of the plaints' in *Andreas* 1185-94, 1376-85;
Elene 759-771, 939-952; *Christ* 558 ff. [in reality only 561-5
are involved], 1520 ff. [to line 1549; compare also the
phraseology of lines 1613-34]; *Juliana* 418-424; *Prayers* 4.
54-7 [not extended enough to be relevant].[84] The phraseology of *Judith* 112-7 also seems to have been influenced by
that of some of the passages enumerated above.[85]

[84] *Op. cit.,* pp. 16-19.

[85] Carleton Brown points out that the parallels which Abbetmeyer
lists between *Christ and Satan* and *Genesis A* are extremely slight,
'only such as might be expected where two authors are narrating the
same incident.' In *Genesis A* there is hardly a hint of lamentation
on the part of the apostates. The verbal correspondences between
Genesis A and the whole of *Christ and Satan* are so few, so scattered,
and generally so insignificant as to make it doubtful whether there
was any vital relationship at all between the two poems, even though
both treat the themes of the Creation, the fall of the angels, and
the fall of man. The poet, or poets, of *Satan* may well have read
Genesis, but almost the only traces of familiarity with it to be discovered are in such mere tags as 2[b] (see *Gen.* 950), 117[b] (1840), 122[a]
(930), 189[b] (905), 24[b], etc. (28), 501 (1719). Of course, many of
the conceptions in the two poems are the same, but that was only to
be expected. The similarities in diction between *Satan* and the two
remaining so-called Cædmonian poems, *Exodus* and *Daniel,* and also
the *Beowulf,* are negligible.

Grüters, whose theory is that portions of the OS. *Genesis* and
Heliand were dependent on OE. poems, believes the following four
parallels, which have no equivalents in the rest of the OE. corpus,
prove that a connection subsists between *Genesis B* and *Christ and
Satan.* He is unable, however, to make up his mind as to the exact
details of the relation (see his *Über einige Beziehungen zwischen
Altsächsischer und Altenglischer Dichtung,* pp. 33-4). His parallels

By far the most important literary relationship of *Christ and Satan* 1-365 is its connection with *Guthlac A* 529-656. Abbetmeyer was the first to make this clear. In the *Vita Sancti Guthlaci*, when the devils threaten that they will drag the saint with them into hell-fire, pretending that God has given them power over him, he merely replies:[36] 'Wā ēow þēostra bearnum and forwyrde tūddre, gē syndon dūst and acsan and ȳsela; hwā sealde ēow earman, þæt gē mīn āhton geweald on þās wītu tō sendanne? Hwæt, ic hēr eom andweard and gearu, and bīdige mīnes Drihtnes willan; for hwon sceolon gē mid ēowrum lēasum bēotingum mē egsian?' In the poem the demons' threats and Guthlac's replies are expanded to above a hundred lines, the phraseology of which throughout is strongly reminiscent of the laments in *Christ and Satan*, and in some lines necessitates the assumption either of direct borrowing of one poem from the other, or of indebtedness on the part of both to some common source.

(which happen to fall within *Sat.* 1-365) are: *Sat.* 81-2 : *Gen.* 261 (cf. also 340) ; *Sat.* 55 ff., 22 ff. : *Gen.* 280 ff. (note esp. 283[b]) ; *Sat.* 179-185 : *Gen.* 296-300; *Sat.* 150-2 : *Gen.* 356-8. There are a few more possible correspondences between the two poems taken as wholes: *Sat.* 29 : *Gen.* 739 *(hēahgetimbro); Sat.* 32[a] : *Gen.* 793[a]; *Sat.* 192-3 : *Gen.* 746[b]; *Sat.* 260[a] : *Gen.* 407[a]; *Sat.* 282 : *Gen.* 621 *(womcwidas,* which is not found elsewhere) ; *Sat.* 341-2 : *Gen.* 374-5; *Sat.* 456 : *Gen.* 718; *Sat.* 634[a] : *Gen.* 697; *Sat.* 705-7 : *Gen.* 345-6. Wülker, by expressly dating *Christ and Satan* later than *Genesis B,* seems to imply that the former may have been influenced by the latter *(Gesch. der Eng. Litt.* I. 59). Yet this may be drawing an inference he did not intend to suggest. At any rate, if either of the poems exerted any influence on the other in these rather unimportant passages, I think it much more probable that the OE. poem affected the OS. than *vice versa.* The conception of the personality of Satan in *Genesis B* is so striking that it seems hardly possible that, if the OE. poet knew the poem well enough to borrow phrases from it, he should have been able to resist letting some traits of the OS. characterization slip into his own; but there is not the slightest hint of such a thing having occurred.

[36] I quote the OE. version (chap. 5).

The poet of the *Guthlac* has written a dialogue of some
dramatic power; but since the phrases which are common to
the two poems in several instances have much more point in
their setting in *Christ and Satan* than in the *Guthlac*, there
can be little doubt that the author of the *Guthlac* borrowed
either from *Christ and Satan* or from a common original, not
the author of the latter directly from the former.

The following are the most important parallels:[37]

Christ and Satan		*Guthlac*
22	Ðūhte him on mōde	635	Wēndun gē and woldun
	þæt hit mihte swā,		wiþerhycgende,
	þæt hīe wēron seolfe		þæt gē Scyppende
	swegles brytan,		sceoldan gelīce
	wuldres waldend.		wesan in wuldre.
	Him ðær wirse gelamp,		Ēow þær wyrs gelomp,
	ðā hēo in helle		ðā ēow se Waldend
	hām staðeledon,		wrāðe bisencte
	ān æfter ōðrum		in þæt swearte sūsl,
	in þæt atole scref,		þær ēow siððan wæs
	þær hēo brynewelme		ād inǣled. . . .
	bīdan sceolden	643	þæt gē wærnysse
	sāran sorge;		brynewylm hæbben,
	nales swegles lēoht		nales blētsunga.
	habban in heofnum.		
22[b]	þæt hit mihte swā.	548	hit ne meahte swā.

---

[37] In presenting this list of parallels and the others which come
further on, I do not aim at completeness, but have tried to select only
such lines as might have at least a modicum of significance for the
literary problems which we must attempt to solve. Mere rows of
identical kennings and alliterative epic formulas are of little assistance
in ascertaining date, authorship, and the like. Most of the parallels
given in the Introduction have been gathered independently by the
editor, though, of course, many of them have been printed before, in
one connection or another, in the studies of Groschopp, Kühn,
Merrill and McClumpha, Abbetmeyer, and Grüters.

Christ and Satan		*Guthlac*	
28	nales swegles lēoht habban in heofnum hēahgetimbra, ac gedūfan sceolun in ðone dēopan wælm.	554	Nū þū in helle scealt dēope gedūfan, nales Dryhtnes lēoht habban in heofonum, hēahgetimbru, seld on swegle.
31	niðær undẹr nessas in ðone neowlan grund.	535	niþer under næssas nēole grundas.
49	bættran hām.	626	tō þām betran hām.
65	firenfulle.	532	firenfulra (not found in the 'Cædmonian' or Cynewulfian poetry).
128	fȳrlēoma . . . āttre geblonden.	640	ād inǣled āttre geblonden.
160	firna herde.	522	synna hyrdas.
190	þā hē gehēned wæs.	569	sē ēow gehȳnde
192	þā hē God bedrāf in þæt hāte hof.		and in hæft bidrāf.
254	Þis is īdel gylp þæt wē ǣr drugon ealle hwīle.	633	for þām oferhygdum, þe ēow in mōd āstāg þurh īdel gylp ealles tō swīðe.

It will be noticed that all but one of the passages in *Christ and Satan* lie between lines 22 and 193. There are also a few correspondences between lines 1-365 and *Guthlac A*, exclusive of lines 522-656:

108	. . . gebīdan hwæt mē Drihten God dēman wille.	349	Forðan ic gebīdan wille þæs þe mē mīn Dryhten dēmeð.
120ᵃ	hēan and earm.	425	hēan and earm.
139	on þā beorhtan gescæft.	749	in þā beorhtan gesceaft.
206	Beoran on brēostum blīðe geþōhtas.	770	berað in brēostum beorhtne gelēafan.

The conceptions and turns of expression similar to those in the sections of *Christ and Satan* and *Guthlac A* just discussed, which are to be found in the lines cited from the *Juliana, Elene,* and *Andreas,*[38] since they occur in dialogues between saints and devils, may possibly be derived from the *Guthlac* directly, rather than from 'Plaints of Lucifer' or from *Christ and Satan.* Abbetmeyer's hypothesis that *Christ and Satan* 1-365 evolved from a cycle of plaints, which in turn go back to one prototype, is quite plausible. However, though we may grant a common original for *Guthlac* 529-656 and *Christ and Satan* 22-193, Part I of the latter poem is itself really the only piece of evidence which might indicate the existence of such a cycle; and Part I in its entirety could have been framed by the repetition and elaboration of the *leitmotif* furnished by the poem which was also the source of *Guthlac A* 529-656, just as well as by piecing together several laments already at hand. It seems possible to account for the facts of relationship within the group of poems which we have discussed, on the basis of ordinary literary borrowing.

Up to the beginning of the first exhortation at line 194, the similarities between *Christ and Satan* and the poems of the Cynewulfian school (with the exception of those in the connected passages listed above[38]) are very few. The following are the only significant ones:

> *Christ and Satan*
>
> 47 herigað Drihten   *Chr.* 429   wē hine dōmhwate
>   wordum and wercum.   dǣdum and wordum
>   hergen holdlice.
>
> 49 bīdan in bendum.   *Chr.* 147   (*Harr.* 88)   bidon in
>   bendum.
>
> 82 hefde mē drēam mid
>   Gode.   *Chr.* 1637   āgan drēam mid Gode.

---

[38] See above, p. xxvi.

Christit and Satan

97 ic eom fāh wið God. *An.* 1188 (cf. *Beow.* 811) eart
                                                ðū fāg wið God.
156 Nū ic eom dædum fāh, *Rood* 13 and ic synnum fāh,
     gewundod mid wommum.   forwunded mid wom-
                                       mum.
                            El. 1242 Ic wæs weorcum fāh,
                                       synnum āsæled.

In the last 170 lines of the first part of *Christ and Satan,*
in which the tone of exhortation becomes more apparent, the
diction and phraseology is rather more reminiscent of the
Cynewulfian poetry. The exhortations which are scattered
throughout the first two parts should be compared especially
with those in *Exodus* 531-547; *Guthlac A* 753-790; *Christ*
746-778, 1579-1694; and also with the passages at the end
of the *Elene, Phœnix,* and *Dream of the Rood,* in which the
joys of heaven, the pains of hell, or the terrors of Doomsday,
are depicted. The following parallels will show with what
poems lines 194-365 are most nearly related :

Christ and Satan

210 behōfað . . .   *Chr.* 1077 Ðonne bēoð bealde
     þæt him wlite scīne   þā þe beorhtne wlite
     þonne hē ōðer līf   Meotude bringað.
     eft gesēceð.   1581 Hē his sāwle wlite
                                             georne bigonge.
                               848 Is ūs þearf micel
                                             þæt wē gæstes wlite . . .
                                             georne biþencen.

217 Crīste gecwēmra.   *Jul.* 259 Crīste gecwēme.
                               El. 1049   "   "

233 wē [in] wuldres wlite   *Pr* 16 in wuldres wlite
     wunian mōston.   wunian mōtan.
                               Ph. 609 hȳ in wlite wuniað
                                             wuldre bitolden.

248 strang and stīðmōd.   *Rood* 40 strang and stīðmōd.

Christ and Satan

260	grimme grundas.	*Chr.* 1527	on grimne grund.
293	uppe mid englum, ēadigne dream.	*Chr.* 661	uppe mid englum ēce staþelas.
314	drēama drēam.	*Chr.* 580 *Ph.* 658	drēama drēam. " "
317	þæt hē Heofencyninge hēran ne wolde.	*El.* 367	hū gē Heofoncyninge hȳran sceoldon.
329	þǣr hēo oft fægerne folgað hæfdon uppe mid englum.	*Chr.* 390	Habbaþ folgoþa cyst mid Cyninge.
333	þǣr is wōm and wōp wīde gehēred.	*An.* 1554	Þǣr wæs wōp wera wīde gehȳred.
349	Nis nǣnig swā snotor nē swā cræftig nē þæs swā glēaw . . . þæt āsecgan mæge, etc.	*Chr.* 219	Nis ǣnig nū eorl under lyfte secg searoþoncol tō þæs swīðe glēaw þe þæt āsecgan mæge, etc.
357	bringað tō bearme blōstman stences wyrta wynsume.	*Ph.* 542	stīgað tō wuldre wlitige gewyrtad mid hyra weldǣdum.
		658	hī Dryhtne tō giefe worda and weorca wynsumne stenc in þā mǣran gesceaft Meotude bringað.
		194, 529	wyrta wynsume.

There is little evidence that the poet in 1-365 was drawing from Latin documents, either Scriptural, apocryphal, or patristic. There is but one instance (in 306-9) of what sounds like quotation, and even there the poet probably quoted from memory. However, the imagery employed, and also the general conceptions of the section, though they sometimes appear as if introduced or connected somewhat inconsequentially, are of such a nature that one should be wary of making *a priori* assumptions that the first part was written in an early time when 'extreme simplicity, directness, and rude passion' prevailed,[39] or taken down 'from the lips of an uneducated poet whose knowledge of sacred history and Christian doctrine came from what he had "heard with the hearing of the ear." '[40]   It is at least as probable that this part was composed by a man who possessed a fair stock of theological knowledge.   The faults which make lines 1-365 seem illogical at times are not due to lack of knowledge, but either to lack of architectonic power in the poet, or to peculiar circumstances in the evolution of the poem.[41]   If this caution is to be observed with regard to the first part, in which the poet had to draw largely on his imagination, we shall find it even more necessary to remember in considering the literary relations of the second part.

Hickes[42] and Kühn[43] were of the opinion that the apocryphal *Gospel of Nicodemus* was the source of the first section of lines 366-664.[44]   It may be granted that the poet could

[39] Brooke, *Hist. Early Eng. Lit.*, p. 326 and note 1.

[40] Bradley, 'The "Cædmonian" Genesis,' in *Essays and Studies* 6. 10-1.

[41] See below, the discussion of the unity of *Christ and Satan*.
I have also found in writing the commentary that many features which have been thought to indicate illiterateness, illogicality, or indebtedness to popular Teutonic conceptions, are either to be laid to faulty transcription, or can be otherwise explained by a reinterpretation of the text, or by adducing illustrative passages from religious literature.

[42] *Thesaurus* I. 133-4.

[43] *Op. cit.*, pp. 11-15. In the same year, Groschopp expressed the opinion that the poet had neither the Bible nor *Nicodemus* before him (*op. cit.*, p. 262).

[44] Although it is unnecessary to attempt a full account of the development of, or a bibliography of the literature on, the tradition of the 'Descensus Christi ad Inferos' (called in early English the 'Harrowing of Hell'), a brief sketch may be found of some service. The most specific of the New Testament passages which seem to point to

have known the 'gospel,' but he certainly never draws from it directly; hence it must be classed among the ultimate sources. Abbetmeyer[45] seems to favor a view previously suggested by Ten Brink,[46] to wit, that lines 366-664 may be a fragment of an exposition 'of the second article, or even of the whole Creed.' Ten Brink's second and more acceptable suggestion,[47] which underlies recent discussions of the sources, renders unnecessary the assumption that there is any conscious reference to the Creed, in spite of the fact that each of the sentences of the Creed which mention the events in Christ's life subsequent to the Crucifixion is represented by a section in the poem. (Even though these events are all represented, there is much additional matter interspersed between them.) According to Ten Brink's second view, it is 'quite possible that this fragment [?] is a homily for Easter

a belief that Christ descended to preach to the dead (according to later views, merely to liberate the righteous) is 1 Pet. 3. 19-20. However, many other verses, both in the narrative and epistolary books, of which the exact import was not so clear, were held to refer to such an event. See Mt. 27. 52 (all Biblical references are to the Vulgate); Jn. 5. 25; Acts 2. 24, 31; Rom. 10. 7; Eph. 4. 9; Phil. 2. 10; Col. 1. 20. The Descent was also thought to be prefigured in the following Old Testament passages: Ps. 15. 10; 23. 7 ff.; 85. 13; 106. 10-4; Isa. 42. 7; 45. 2; Hos. 6. 1-3; 13. 14; Zech. 9. 11. The details of the story, however, were most thoroughly worked out in the second part of the *Gospel of Nicodemus,* which bears the separate title, *Descensus Christi ad Inferos,* and which exists in three separate versions, two Latin and one Greek. The *Descensus* has been assigned by scholars variously to the third, fourth, or fifth centuries. To patristic literature I shall cite only three references which are of special interest for *Christ and Satan:* Epiphanius, *Homilia II in Sabbato Magno (Patr. Gr.* 43. 451 ff.); Pseudo-Augustine, *Sermo* CLX *(Patr. Lat.* 39. 2060); Eusebius (Alexandrinus?), *Sermo de Confusione Diaboli* (Latin version edited by E. K. Rand, *Mod. Phil.* 2. 261-278; pp. 277-8 contain a condensed and inconsequential account of the events after Christ's death).

[45] *Op. cit.,* p. 12.
[46] *Early Eng. Lit.* 1. 87-8.
[47] *Ibid.,* p. 87, n. 4.

Sunday, bereft only of its beginning, and with contents similar to the prose homily in the *Blickling Homilies'* (i. e., the seventh of the collection).[48]   Förster[49] believes that a Latin homily based upon (or possibly a lost version of) the 160th Pseudo-Augustinian sermon, eked out by the entire story of the Descent as it must have been told in the unmutilated work of which only a fragment is preserved in the *Book of Cerne*,[50] is not only the original of the seventh Blickling homily, but also the source of the version of the Harrowing in *Christ and Satan,* the Old English *Harrowing of Hell,* lines 84 ff., and the Mercian *Martyrology,* p. 50 (Herzfeld's edition). The connection between these works is indubitable.

Grau pushes the theory still further:[51] 'Setzt man in die 7. Blicklinghom. statt der erhaltenen fassung des zweiten teiles die der älteren Hattonpredigt ein, so erhalten wir einen text, von dem ich nicht anstehe zu behaupten dass er bezw. seine (lat.) vorlage quelle von Christ und Satan 2 gewesen ist.' Grau thinks with good reason that the second part of the seventh Blickling homily, as we have it, has been abbreviated. The account of the Last Judgment breaks off suddenly after the enumeration of the signs of the seven last days. Since there are many similarities in the phraseology with which these signs are described in *Bl. Hom. 7* and the homily of MS. Hatton 116, Grau believes that the latter portion of the Blickling homily originally resembled that of the Hatton homily, which contains a complete version of the Last Judgment, and a brief description of the joys of heaven, as well as a short exhortation.

[48] Brandl also thinks that the poet used as a source some Latin homily similar to the Blickling Paschal homily. See Paul's *Grundriss* 2. 1046.

[49] *Archiv für das Studium der Neueren Sprachen* 116. 306.

[50] *The Prayer Book of Aedeluald the Bishop, commonly called the Book of Cerne,* ed. Kuypers, pp. 196-8.

[51] *Quellen und Verwandtschaften der Älteren Germanischen Darstellungen des Jüngsten Gerichtes,* pp. 194-6.

It is altogether probable that some homily similar to those
mentioned above furnished a model for many of the structural features of *Christ and Satan* 366-664. However, that
homily must have been very different from either the Pseudo-
Augustinian, Hatton, or Blickling homily, if it was in any
very vital sense a source of the section as a whole; for there
are only four lines in the poem in which any of these has
left clear verbal traces, namely, in the words with which
Eve's address to Christ is introduced,[52] and in her offering
her supplication to him in the name of her daughter Mary.[53]
Here the borrowing is almost literal, and would seem to be
immediate, whereas elsewhere in *Christ and Satan* the similarities with the homilies are only of a general sort. I give
below the order of events which a homily such as Grau has
reconstructed would present, so that, by comparison with the
Structural Outline of the poem, the reader may decide
whether the homily should be considered a direct source:
Christ descended to the earth to save mankind. After the
Jews had laid many plots against him, he suffered death on
the cross, and went to harry hell. The devils express their
terror at his approach. Then, after the captives give vent
to their joy, comes the 'harrowing.' All the captives except
Adam and Eve being released, each one of the first pair indi-
vidually prays for mercy, and is liberated. When the Lord
had plundered hell of its spoil, he came forth from the tomb,
showed his wounds to the disciples, and thereafter ascended
to heaven, and sat down at the right hand of the Father.
After the signs of the seven days have been given, the Judgment scene follows. The benediction of the redeemed and
the malediction of the damned are quoted. Finally, there is
a description of the bliss of heaven, based on the Apocalypse,
and the homily ends with an exhortation. It should be kept
in mind that such a condensed *résumé* as this tends to emphasize the similarity with the poem, since most of the events

[52] 408-9; see note on 408ᵇ.   [53] 438-440; see note.

just listed are at least represented in it. I do not mean to dispute the evident fact that *Christ and Satan* owes much in its organization to such homiletic synopses. But the poet omits or treats very cursorily several features of the narrative as told in the composite homily, and presents much more frequently events, or even whole scenes, not mentioned there (e. g., the reference to Judas' announcement to the captives of Christ's approach, Christ's address to the liberated patriarchs in heaven, the scene in Galilee, Pentecost, and the fate of Judas). Therefore we need not assume that any special homily was the source of lines 366-664. The parallels which Grau draws between the Judgment scene in MS. Hatton 116 and that in *Christ and Satan* are so vague as to be against the dependence of the poem on the homily.

Although the poet may have referred to the text of the Bible once or twice, it is not probable that he was drawing directly from books in lines 366-664. Indeed, some of the store of reading upon which he drew does not seem to have been very fresh. However, there is every reason to believe that he had a fair general acquaintance both with the Bible and with other religious literature. His learning does not appear to have been perfectly digested, but he could not, with any propriety whatever, be described as simple or unlearned.

The following lines contain the most important resemblances in phraseology between the second part of *Christ and Satan* and other Old English poems:

Christ and Satan	*Genesis A*
630 wērige gāstas.	90 wērige gāstas.
369 wrōht onstalde.	911, 932 wrōhte onstealdest.
	Daniel
507, 555 Drihtnes dōmas.	32, 745 Drihtnes dōmas.
	Beowulf
641 fǣhðe and firne.	137, 879, 2480 fǣhðe and fyrene.
631 helle hæftas	163 hwyder helrūnan
hwyrftum scrīþað.	hwyrftum scrīþað.
432 wið earm gesæt.	749 wið earm gesæt.

Christ and Satan	Guthlac A
463 fēond geflēmed.	107 Fēond wæs geflȳmed.
442 ēce Ordfruma ealra gesceafta.	610 ēcne Onwealdan ealra gesceafta.
581 Dæleð dōgra gehwæm . . .	654 þær is riht Cyning
help and hǣlo hæleþa bearnum.	help and hǣlu hæleþa cynne.
460 Hōfon hine mid him handum hālige.	702 hōfon hine hondum.
405 fēond oferfohten.	775 fēond oferfeohtað.

Guthlac B

564 Þā cōm wolcna swēg hālig of heofonum.	1256 ðā cwōm lēohta mǣst hālig of heofonum. (Cf. also *An.* 88.)

Christ

495 Fērde tō foldan þurh fǣmnan hād.	92 fǣmnan hād. 444 ācenned wearð þurh clǣnne hād.
581 Dæleð dōgra gehwæm Drihten weoroda . help and hǣlo hæleþa bearnum.	427 his forgifnesse gumum tō helpe dǣleð dōgra gehwām Dryhten weoroda.
657 Cyning in cestre.	578 Cyning on ceastre.
490 [þæs] carcernes clom ðrōwade.	735 in carcerne clommum gefæstnad. (Cf. also *An.* 130.)
637 clom and carcern.	
620 Þonne stondað þā forhtan . . . 801 Þǣr sceal forht monig bēoð beofigende hwonne him Bearn Godes dēman wille.	on þām wongstede wērig bīdan hwæt him æfter dǣdum dēman wille. (Cf. *Jul.* 706-7.)
607 hlūd gehēred.	So 492, 835, 949.
602 ofer burga geseotu.	1240 ofer burga gesetu.

Christ and Satan	*Christ*
640 stǣleð [fēondas] fǣhðe and firne.	1374 on þæt frǣte folc firene stǣleð (note context).
472 ic ēow þurh mīne mihte geworhte, Ādām ǣrest, etc.	1380 Hwæt! ic þec, mon, mīnum hondum ǣrest geworhte.
489 Þa mē gerēaw þæt mīn handgeweorc [þæs] carcernes clom ðrōwade.	1415 ðā mec ongon hrēowan, þæt mīn hondgeweorc on fēonda geweald fēran sceolde.
628 Āstīgað . . . in þæt wītehūs.	1536 gefeallað . . . on wītehūs. (Cf. also *Gen.* 39.)
494 tō wrece gesette.	1602 tō wrace gesette.
556 Ūs is wuldres lēoht torht ontȳned.	1673 wuldres lēoht torht ontȳned.
567 tō þām hālgan hām.	1675 tō þām hālgan hām. (So *An.* 1683.)

Compare also *Chr.* 466-7 with *Sat.* 558-562; 491-4 with 564-5; 531-2 with 580; 727 with 549; and 928-930 with 568-9.

	Andreas
584 hē āna is ealra gescefta Wyrhta and Waldend.	324 hē is Cyning on riht Wealdend and Wyrhta wuldorþrymmes, ān ēce God eallra gesceafta. (Cf. 700-3.)
556 Ūs is wuldres lēoht torht ontȳned, þām ðe teala þenceð.	1611 Ēow is wuldres lēoht torht ontȳned, gif gē teala hycgað.
661 Swā wuldres Weard wordum herigað þegnas ymb Þēoden.	871 Ūtan ymbe Æðelne englas stōdon, þegnas ymb Þēoden

Christ and Satan	*Andreas*
(Cf. 235-6.)	þūsendmǣlum,
	heredon. . . .

Phœnix

412 þurh nǣddran nīð.	413 þurh nǣdran nīþ.
459 in þā mǣran burh	633 in þǣre mǣran byrig
(= heaven).	(= heaven).
624 tō þǣre mǣran byrig.	
499 hū hēo mē dēaðes cwealm . . .	642 hē dēaþes cwealm . . .
hrefnan mihten.	ræfnan sceolde.
560 ǣr hē in þā mǣran ge-	660 in þā mǣran gesceaft
sceaft . . .	(= heaven)
bringan wolde	Meotude bringað, etc.
hāligne gāst.	
	Dream of the Rood
549 hē on bēame āstāh.	40 gestāh hē on gealgan
	hēanne.
	(Cf. also 34 and *Chr.*
	1492.)
662 Þǣr is þrym micel.	139 þǣr is blis mycel.

The striking thing about these lists is the evidence they
offer for a fairly close relationship between *Christ and Satan*
366-664 and the poems written or influenced by Cynewulf.
That so many poems of such an ambitious nature should be
indebted to a single unfinished one is hardly conceivable.
Hence, the obligation must be assigned to *Christ and Satan.*
The similarities in diction, however, do not adequately measure the general resemblance of the poem, beginning from
line 190,[54] with the Cynewulfian poems. Wherever, in the
latter, there occur extended exhortations, or passages describing the bliss of heaven or the torments of hell (often in connection with the Judgment Day), one is sure to recognize an
affinity in conception and tone between these passages and

[54] See p. xxxi.

those in *Christ and Satan* which treat the same themes.   This
may be verified, by way of example, in the last one hundred
lines of the *Christ,* where there are not very many verbal
correspondences with *Christ and Satan.*

The third part of the poem, which recounts Christ's temptation, is incomplete, and is broken by a lacuna of several
lines, at the very least.   For the temptation proper, the poet,
as was often the case in Part II, would seem to have
depended upon his well-stocked, but not especially accurate,
memory of Gospel story.   I have been able to discover
nothing analogous to the long episode which follows the
actual temptation.   Christ bids the tempter make a complete
survey of hell, that he may realize the absolute supremacy of
his adversary, and the tempter obeys the command.   It is
just possible that the poet took his hint from a sentence in
the Blickling homily on the temptation,[55] but, until some
more adequate source is proposed, we must credit to the
poet's own genius the conception as well as the execution of
this, one of the two or three most remarkable passages in the
poem.

The verbal similarities, in the case of a section of sixty-
eight lines, which treats a subject not found in other Old
English poems, naturally cannot shed much light on the
problems presented by the poem as a whole.

Christ and Satan

675, 690 Þā him andswarode	*An.* 202, 343, 510 Him ðā ond- swarude
ēce Drihten.	ēce Dryhten.
688 riht cyning.	*Gu.* 654 ryht Cyning.
692 þē is sūsl weotod.	*An.* 889 Þām bið wræcsīð witod.
	951 is þē gūð weotod.
	1365 þē synd wītu þæs grim weotud.

[55] Page 31 (quoted in the note on 691 ff.).

Christic and Satan

696 sorga mǣste.   *Chr.* 1082 sorga mǣste.
                                        (Cf. also *Chr.* 1209;
                                        Gen. B 364.)
705 Wāst þū þonne þē geor-
        nor.   *Beow.* 821 wiste þē geornor.
                        An. 932 wāst nū þē gearwor.
                        El. 945 wīte ðū þē gearwor.
715 se wonna lēg.   *Beow.* 3115 wonna lēg.
731-2 ongunnon...reordian. *An.* 469 Ongan ðā reordigan.

Significant parallels with the 'Cædmonian' poetry are con-
spicuously absent. The only possible echo is *wið God
wunne,* 705 (cf. *Gen.* 77; *Ex.* 514), but similar phrases
occur also in the *Beowulf, Christ,* and *Genesis B.*

UNITY AND GENESIS

One question must now be met squarely before we can discuss the date and authorship. Is *Christ and Satan* one, two,
or three poems, or is it a collection of fragments? W. D.
Conybeare was the first to apply the word 'fragments' to the
poem.[56] He describes Book II as 'introduced by several

[56] John J. Conybeare, *Illustrations of Anglo-Saxon Poetry,* edited
by his brother William Daniel Conybeare (1826), p. 189. Thorpe
repeats this: 'In the second book, we find little else than a series of
unconnected fragments.' He thinks it singular that neither by the
scribe nor by Junius are they noticed as fragments (p. VII, note).
Thomas Wright held the 'latter folios of the manuscript of Cædmon'
to be 'nothing but the stringing together of such passages of the
original as the scribe could at the moment recall to memory' (*Essay
on the State of Literature and Learning under the Anglo-Saxons,* p.
24). Ettmüller suggests a bibliographical explanation of the present
state of the poem: Book II is full of gaps; probably there were at
the very first several independent poems on the Descent which were
collected in one book; only after the dropping out of several leaves
did these come to be considered a single poem (*Handbuch der
Deutschen Litteraturgeschichte,* p. 135; see also *Scopas and Boceras,*
p. XIV).

long harangues of Satan and his angels, . . . so little connected with the sequel or with each other, and so inartificially thrown together, as rather to resemble an accumulation of detached fragments than any regular design.' Rieger first suggested that *Christ and Satan* is composed, not of an indefinite number of fragments, but of a very small number of independent poems (in his opinion, two).[57]

In 1877, Ten Brink[58] propounded a theory later accepted by Kühn,[59] Sievers,[60] Wülker,[61] and Bentinck Smith.[62] He considered each of the three parts (1-365, 366-664, 665-713) to be a separate poem[63]—the first part complete, the second preserved in a fragmentary state, the third a single fragment. Possibly each of the last two belonged to a greater whole. These, after they had been mutilated, were 'appended as a connected whole to the *Fallen Angels* in the existing manuscript.' The first part shows the Old English tendency to variation applied to the larger proportions of a poem. Kühn gave, in support of this threefold division, lists of phrases for the Deity, the devils, man, hell, saying, seeing, going, and also other phrases which occur more than once in

---

[57] *Zs. f. D. Phil.* 7. 6: 'Der Satan schliesst vielmehr mit v. 365, und mit dem folgenden beginnt ein gedicht von ähnlichem inhalt und ähnlicher anlage wie Cynewulfs Christ.' Ten Brink, Wülker, and Bentinck Smith all echo this comparison with the *Christ,* which, however, is pertinent only in a very general sense.

[58] *Gesch. der Engl. Litt.* (1877). My references are to the English translation (1883). *Christ and Satan* is discussed on pp. 86-8 of Vol. 1.

[59] *Über die Angelsächsischen Gedichte von Christ und Satan.*

[60] *Beitr. z. Gesch. der D. Spr. und Lit.* 10. 499.

[61] *Grundriss z. Gesch. der Ags. Litt.,* p. 131, note; *Gesch. der Engl. Litt.* 1. 59. Wülker, as stated above, also makes a threefold division of the text in the *Bibl. der Ags. Poesie.*

[62] *Cambridge Hist. Eng. Lit.* 1. 53.

[63] Ziegler also (*Der Poetische Sprachgebrauch in den sogen. Cædmonschen Dichtungen,* p. 174) speaks of *Christ and Satan* as 'three poems.'

each of the first two parts.[64]   These lists are practically
worthless as evidence, because no allowance is made for the
unequal length of the three sections, or for the differences in
subject-matter.   Naturally, for example, the numerous
phrases descriptive of hell in lines 1-365 will not be largely
represented in lines 366-664, in which hell is by no means so
important as in the former section.   Kühn brushes aside the
verbal similarities between the parts, by saying that many of
them are found in other poems, and that they are too few to
disprove his thesis.   He points out what no one would think
of disputing, that 1-365 are prevailingly lyric in tone and
repetitious in style, whereas 366-664 and 665-733 are epic, the
last section being further distinguished by its lack of exhortation.   The metrical statistics which Kühn presents, without
considering either their relevancy or the possibility that the
differences they show might in certain instances have some
relation to the subject-matter of the three parts, are altogether inconclusive with regard to the question of unity.

In the same year (1883) that Kühn's dissertation appeared,
Groschopp proposed still another theory.   Groschopp was
impressed by two facts concerning *Christ and Satan*.   On
the one hand, there are indisputable links connecting the three
parts, in spite of their differences in tone; on the other hand,
the poem seemed to him full of gaps, errors, and inconsistencies in the contents, derangements in the metre, and disorder
in the structure.   (He was especially disturbed by the position of the Temptation scene, coming as it does after the
Ascension, and, for that matter, after Doomsday.)   To
obtain an explanation of the genesis of the poem which would
harmonize these conflicting characteristics, Groschopp felt
driven to this conclusion: 'In Crist und Satan reste einer
einzigen grösseren dichtung vorliegen, die ein restaurator

[64] Balg followed this same unsatisfactory method in trying to prove
that the four poems of the Junius MS. are by different authors (*Der
Dichter Cædmon und seine Werke*).

unter einfügung eigener sätze und anschauungen versucht hat, wider zu einem ganzen zu vereinigen.'[65] Only fragments of the *quasi-Heliand,* and these not very long, lay before the restorer. Groschopp makes of this well-meaning person a veritable scapegoat, who bears away all the sins and deficiencies of our extant text—'So lassen sich, wie ich glaube, alle ungereimtheiten nach inhalt und form erklären'[66]—truly a comfortable hypothesis. There is, however, absolutely no evidence for the existence of the larger poem, and the fact that we possess homilies which contain much the same sort of concatenation of the events of Christ's *'post mortem* life' as is found in Part II (the only section of the poem which even *seems* to point to a Gospel harmony, such as the *Heliand*) renders unnecessary the assumption that we have in *Christ and Satan* fragments of a larger whole. Moreover, a considerable proportion of the inconsistencies, and much of the apparent disorganization of the poem, would not have seemed so serious to Groschopp if he had tried to be more sympathetic, and less literal, in interpreting the text itself. Groschopp's theory, as he developed it, has appealed only to Brooke[67] among later writers.

Abbetmeyer[68] accounts for the poem by a genetic theory. Most of the first and older portion developed gradually, as a cycle of 'Plaints of Lucifer,' from one original vernacular

---

[65] *Op. cit.,* p. 252.

[66] P. 260.

[67] Brooke points out a convenient division of Part I into three sections, the breaks coming after lines 224 and 315. As he says, these sections end 'with three similar hymns of praise' (more properly speaking, with three exhortations). Brooke's interpretation of this division is unconvincing: 'They are like three lays, into which a Scôp might divide his one subject, to be sung on three separate evenings; and such may have been the form of Cædmon's religious songs. The others, too [i. e., Parts II and III], may be separate *Cantatas,* within a general paraphrase of the history of redemption' (*op. cit.,* p. 326, note; p. 329).

[68] *Op. cit.,* pp. 10-2, 16-9.

plaint. Because of the close connection which they show with
Guthlac A, Satan 1-224 should be considered to have been
originally a distinct poem, 'as it were, growing out of' the
first part of *Genesis A*. Within this section the three monologues spoken by the same *fire-breathing* demon (75-125,
126-159, 160-189) are independent variants of the same
theme, intended to be recited by themselves. For the rest of
Part I, Abbetmeyer accepts Brooke's division into three
large sections at lines 224 and 315. In these, the original
plaint (varied, of course) was made the basis of pious exhortation. It was also used to set off the Descensus story in
lines 444-456. Regarding the composition of the poem as a
whole, Abbetmeyer says: 'It would seem that *Sat.* 366-664
did not originally belong to the same cycle as the other *Sat.*
poems. . . . In [the] original draft, the *descensus* section
was presumably of the same length as the other parts.[69] In
the course of time, this topic received numerous amplifica-
tions from various sources, among others, as has been shown,
from *Gen. A* and *Sat.* 1-365. When once this theme pre-
dominated, the remaining sections would be regarded as, in a
way, an exhortation, and thus the whole poem, *Sat.* 366-664,
was embodied in our manuscript as a parallel or variant of
Sat. 1-224, 225-315, 316-365.' The third part, lines 665-733,
is a homily on the temptation of Christ, placed in our manuscript not 'because it treated of Christ, but because it
described some of the sufferings of Satan; for these form
the real subject of the *Sat.* poems.' The closing lines seem
to be the beginning of another plaint of the demons.[70]

[69] This is extremely doubtful. Compare the preponderance of the
theme of the Descent in *Bl. Hom.* 7, and the Pseudo-Augustinian
homily. The comparison that may be drawn between *Christ and
Satan* and the homilies vitiates Abbetmeyer's whole conception of the
way Parts I and II were put together.

[70] Abbetmeyer supplements his theory with another suggestion (p.
19): 'In *Sat.* 1-365 we may have a collection and arrangement of
Plaints made for the purpose of dramatic recitation. A priest

Abbetmeyer has done a valuable service in tracing the origins of the story of the fall and the laments of the apostates, and especially in indicating the relation of *Christ and Satan* to *Guthlac;* but one cannot help agreeing with Brown in regard to the worth of his exposition of the structure of the former poem: 'In such an elaborate process of scissoring and re-arranging as Dr. Abbetmeyer has undertaken, the chances of arriving at the original components of the poem are, of course, extremely slight.'[71]

Of late, the tendency has been to revert to the theory that the poem is one.[72] Graz examined the verse with far greater thoroughness than Kühn had done, and came to the conclusion that the metrical characteristics of *Christ and Satan* were distinctly in favor of unity.[73] In 1902, Barnouw, on the basis of his investigation of the article and weak adjective, declared it unified.[74] The most plausible defense of the unity of *Christ and Satan* is that by Brandl.[75] He says: 'Das ganze ist ein versuch, das erlösungswerk nach den grundsätzen des gefolgschaftswesen darzustellen.' In the second part he sees the happy service of Christ presented as a contrast to the wretched life which Satan and his fellows

probably recited the introduction and exhortations, some other ecclesiastic or some layman might take the role of Satan, and a choir the parts of Satan's followers. Practically the same material later makes up some of the Miracle Plays.' This is interesting enough as pure speculation.

[71] *Mod. Lang. Notes* 19. 223.

[72] About midway between the theory of multiplicity and that of unity stands the view of Ebert (*Allgem. Gesch. der Lit. des Mittelalters im Abendlande* 3. 255) : because of the close relation of the two parts in content, language, and style, Part I is to be considered an independent introduction to Part II; Part III is a fragment of another poem.

[73] *Metrik der sog. Cædmonschen Dichtungen*, pp. 72, 73.

[74] *Textkritische Untersuchungen nach dem Gebrauch des Bestimmten Artikels und des Schwachen Adjectivs in der Ae. Poesie*, p. 108.

[75] *Op. cit.*, p. 1046.

lead in hell, as depicted in the first part. The third part relates the only direct conflict which, according to the Bible, took place between the Redeemer and the leader of hell. Brandl remarks the similarity between *Christ and Satan* and the seventh Blickling homily, mentioning in particular the fact that in the homily, as in the poem, before the entrance to Limbo is burst open, the devils hold an anxious consultation.

After his thorough study of the language, Frings[76] was of the opinion that, from the grammatico-metrical standpoint, no argument can be brought against the conclusion that the poem is by one author. Because the original Anglian text lay before the scribes, the theory that the poem could have been put together in the West Saxon transcription from fragments, by either one or several poets, is excluded. This is incontrovertible, but Frings' study can throw no light upon the question whether the poem could have been put together in the Anglian original itself, from fragments by one or more Anglian poets.

In the light of the facts of literary relationship, as well as of the discrepant opinions just reviewed, it would be rash to attempt to give a categorical answer to the question, 'Is *Christ and Satan* a single, unified poem?' It is, however, impossible to belittle the elements of unity in the whole. They are such as can not be completely accounted for by the simple assumption of a restorer of fragments. Brandl has clearly expressed one element of unity, in the contrast between the blessings to be obtained by becoming a faithful thane in the *comitatus* of God and Christ, and the miseries incurred by the members of the *comitatus* of Satan. Others have noted the contrast drawn throughout the poem, but especially in Parts I and III, and in the passages descriptive of heaven in Part II, between the torments of hell and the joys of heaven. Grein, by his title, *Christ und Satan*, sug-

---

[76] *Op. cit.*, pp. 235-6.

gests that the figures of Christ and Satan are set over against each other, and that the poem is built around the struggle between these two adversaries. Not only is such a struggle set forth in the accounts of the Descent and Temptation, but it underlies the whole of Part I, in which Christ is represented both as the creator of the universe and the object of Satan's hatred, the being against whom his revolt is particularly directed. It is to be noted, also, that the character of Satan and his relation to his followers are exactly the same in Part III as they were in Part I. The differences in style which have been supposed to exist between the three parts are either imaginary, or are to be explained by the fact that the lyric, epic, and didactic *genres* have been blended in one poem, each presiding over its own more or less unified sections. The first part, in which the elegiac prevails, is not unnaturally very repetitious; for the subject, Satan's loss of heavenly bliss and present misery, is limited in scope. The second part, which is narrative, is, as we should expect, more straightforward. (It is far from innocent of repetition, however.)

The verbal resemblances point very decidedly toward unity. I list first those phrases which are found in all three divisions.[77]

---

[77] The more obvious kennings and alliterative formulas are omitted. Parallels found only in *Christ and Satan* are distinguished by the asterisk. However, I have not run down some of the others, so that there may be a few more unique parallels than I have indicated.

I	II	III
26 in þæt atole scref.	419 in ðis hāte scref.	727 geond þæt lāðe scræf.
73 geond þæt atole scref.	633 in þæt sceaðena scræf.	
129 " " "		
28 nales swegles lēoht	449 Nalles wuldres lēoht	692 þē is sūsl weotod
habban in heofnum,	habban mōton,	geara tōgegnes,
hēahgetimbra,	ah in helle grund.	nalles Godes rīce.
ac gedūfan sceolun		
in ðone dēopan wælm.		
73 earme ǣglēcan.	448 earm āglǣca.	713 earm ǣglēce.
	579 " "	
98 helle duru.	So 380, 467.	So 723.
126 se wērega gāst.	630 wērige gāstas.	731 þā wērigan gāstas.
219 Drihten Hǣlend.	So 576.	So 683.

These are neither numerous nor especially significant.
But that there should be as many as there are is surprising.
I now list the parallels between Parts I and II, I and III, II
and III, in order.

I	II
*20 Ādām ǣrest,	473 Ādām ǣrest
and þæt æðele cyn.	and þæt æðele wīf.
41 sūsel þrōwian.	395 atol þrōwian.
42 nalles wulres blǣd habban.	508 habbað wuldres blǣd.
	593 þǣr is wuldres blēd.
46 þǣr nū ymb ðone Ēcan	552 secgan Drihtne þanc
æðele stondað	dǣdum and weorcum.
heleð ymb hēhseld,	661 Swā wuldres Weard
herigað Drihten	wordum herigað
wordum and wercum.	þegnas ymb Þēoden.
(Cf. 220.)	
49 bīdan in bendum.	414 beorneð in bendum.
54, 364 Hǣlende hēran.	So 595, 645.
63 Segdest ūs tō sōðe.	430 Segdest ūs tō sōðe.
70 hæfdon hym tō hyhte.	643 him tō hihte
335 nabbað [h]ē tō hyhte.	habban sceoldon.
*87, 117, 254, 279	454 atol tō ǣhte.
eall (ēðel) tō ǣhte.	
*102 in ðissum neowlan genipe.	446 in þæt neowle genip.
180 in þis neowle genip.	
*103, 157 wītes clom.	444 wītes clomma.
	453 wītes clom.
105 dimme and deorce.	455 dimne and deorcne.
116 swā hē ǣr dyde.	525 swā hē ǣr dyde.
123, 142, 293, 330	391, 591 uppe mid englum.
uppe mid englum.	
127 ealle ætsomne.	526 ætsomne ealle.
128 fāh in fyrnum.	479 fēond in firenum—
	fāh is ǣghwǣr.
141, 253 wuldres lēoht.	So 449, 556, 617, 650.

I		II	
161	atol ǣglǣca, ūt of helle.	579	earm ǣglǣca innon helle.
*162,	343 wītum wērig(e).	428, 449	wītum wērig(e).
169	mid handum ... gerǣcan.	437	rǣhte þā mid handum.
184,	305 Meotode cwēman.	655	Meotode cwēmaš.
190	hwearf þā tō helle.	400	hwearf þā tō helle.
217	Crīste gecwēmra.	596	Crīste cwēman.
230	Nū is gesēne.	441	nū is gesēne.
232	Drihtnes mihtum.	605	þurh Drihtnes miht.
*235	sang ymb seld.	663	sang æt selde.
236	þūsendmǣlum.	509, 569, 632	þūsendmǣlum.

Only 3 times elsewhere, in *Ex., An., Jud.*

*237	wunodon on wynnum.	508, 593	wuniaš (wunaš) in wynnum.
		556	in wynnum wunian.
243	dōgra gehwilcne.	581	dōgra gehwǣm.
258	Cyning of cestre.	657	Cyning in cestre.
281	Him wæs Hǣlend God wrāš geworden for womcwidum.	428	swylce him Wuldor- cyning for onmǣdlan eorre geworden.
		452	Seoššan him wæs Drihten wrāš geworden.
288	ūp tō englum.	625	ūp tō englum.
295	beorhte scīnaš geǣlige sāwle.	652	And ymb þā weallas wlitige scīnaš
309	sōšfæste men . . . scīnaš in sceldbyrig.		engla gāstas and ēadige sāwla.
316	se āwyrgda wrāše geþōhte þæt hē, etc.	371	[Þā] Sātānus swearte geþōhte þæt hē, etc.
*320	wīde geond windsele wēa cwānedon.	386	wīde geond windsele wordum mǣndon.
322	swylce onǣled.	421	þearle onǣled.

I

341 hāte onǣled. (Cf. 40, 97.)

327 nalles ūp þanon.

346 nergendne Crīst.

*359 Fæder mancynnes . . .
hīe gesegnað
mid his swīðran hond.

361 lǣdað tō līhte
þǣr hī līf āgon.

II

634 And nō seoððan
þæt hīe ūp þonan.

570 nergende Crīst.

615 And hēo gesēnað
mid his swīðran hond
Cynincg alwihta.

589 Laðað ūs þider tō
lēohte . . .
þǣr wē mōton, etc.

I

30 ac gedūfan sceolun
in ðone dēopan wǣlm.

*80 in wītum word[e] indrāf.

*111 dēofla menego.

*153, 357 brōhton tō bearme.

181 āworpen of worulde.

*185, 336 wēan and wītu.

III

670 in helle gedēaf.

731 wordum in wītum.

730 dēofla mænego.

672 Brōhte him tō bearme.

669 þe ǣr āworpen wæs
of heofonum.

715 wēan and wītu.

II

368, 614, 651 Godes rīce.

390 ēagum gesāwon.

454 egsan gryre.

544 hē mid hondum
Hǣlend genōm.

559 fēowertig daga.

628 āstīgað nū, āwyrgde,
in þæt wītehūs.

III

693 Godes rīce.

718 ēagum gesāwun.

728 egsan gryre.

680A Þā hē mid hondum
genōm.

667 fēowertig daga.

691 Gewīt þū, āwyrgda,
in þæt wītescræf.

Taken together, these parallels are by no means so few as Kühn would lead us to suppose,[78] and there is a respectable number of them which do not appear in other poems. In

[78] *Op. cit.*, p. 26.

liv *Introduction*

short, a much stronger case can be made out for the unity than for the multiplicity of *Christ and Satan*. Yet we must account for the presence in the poem, both of elements that are certainly among the sources of *Guthlac A,* which scholars agree in placing either early in Cynewulf's career or before him, and of others which are either echoes or actual borrowings from poetry assigned to Cynewulf's later period or to his imitators.

The present editor's hypothesis concerning the evolution of *Christ and Satan* is as follows. The poem is essentially the work of one poet. This poet's first intention was to compose a narrative poem on the events in the history of Christ after his crucifixion, similar in general to the synthetic works exemplified in the seventh Blickling homily. Of course, Christ's descent into hell was the most stirring incident in the series, and the poet's imagination was kindled by it.[79] He wished to make it as dramatic as he could. By presenting the dialogue between Eve and the Saviour, and the speech of Christ to the liberated patriarchs in heaven, which have no real counterparts in the typical accounts of the Harrowing, he strengthened the latter part of the episode. For his introduction to it, the poet saw possibilities in another sort of material. The terror of the devils in anticipation of Christ's assault upon their realm was expressed in speeches of moderate length, both in the *Gospel of Nicodemus* and in the Blickling homily. But the poet thought he could work in the story of the fall of the evil angels, and introduce certain laments of theirs which would show the contrast between their original glory and their present (and impending greater) degradation—such laments as he was familiar with in another poem or (possibly) collection of poems.[80]

[79] As was that of the Blickling homilist. The Harrowing of Hell takes up almost one-half of the extant homily.

[80] The portion of *Christ and Satan* which seems most certain to have been taken more or less directly from another poem (or other poems) on the woes of Lucifer is that between lines 20 and 193.

By these means he could give a more elaborate background for his great scene. The laments were originally set in the period immediately, or not long, after the fall, and had already been drawn upon by the poet of *Guthlac A* to enrich his dialogue between the saint and the demons. It is not impossible that the poet of *Christ and Satan* knew *Guthlac A;* at least the similarities in phraseology, in sections not concerned with devils and hell,[81] seem to indicate some very slight relation between the two poems.

The poet, however, did not succeed in remodeling his extraneous material so that it joined neatly to the episode of the Descent. He was carried away by this new theme; added other laments, and even a description of the devils' condition written in the third person (316 ff.) ; and was led into long didactic passages exhorting his readers to choose the service of God, and escape the torments inflicted upon the devils for their rebellion; with the result that he wrote in Part I what is almost an independent poem. Moreover, the relation between the characters Christ and Satan had so taken hold of his imagination that he could not refrain from returning to it again in the third part, in spite of the necessity, under which this laid him, of committing a gross anachronism. The idea of confronting the two great adversaries with each other, and representing Satan as becoming finally conscious of the enormity of his crime and its punishment, and of subjecting him to the reproaches and taunts of his own followers, in order that his complete overthrow and isolation might become apparent, was too tempting to be renounced.[82]

---

[81] See p. xxix.

[82] The manuscript gives only very slight evidence that the account of the Temptation was even to be considered a distinct section of the poem; not even a small capital introduces line 665, which begins in the middle of a MS. line without a break. A small capital *s* had just been used in 661. The presence of this capital might indicate that the new section should begin at 661, instead of at 665, and such a

Old English poets have never been commended especially for their constructive ability, and hence the lack of articulation and centralization so evident in *Christ and Satan* need not prejudice us against the conclusion that the poem is the product of a single molding spirit. Moreover, since the clearly unfinished state of the poem makes it probable that the present transcription derives (possibly through one or more intermediary copies) from an unimproved first draft, we cannot be certain that the poet might not have succeeded, if he had tried to bring to completion his evidently expanding design, in more perfectly adapting his material, and in reforming the proportions of his piece.

AUTHORSHIP AND DATE

Junius, who is credited with attaching the name of Cædmon to the poems in MS. Junius XI, was not very positive in his attitude concerning their authorship. He merely says that, since they correspond in style, genius, and argument to what we learn from Bede's account (*Hist. Eccl.* 4. 24), when he refers to them hereafter, he will use the name of Cædmon.[83] He later calls his edition 'Cædmonis Monachi Paraphrasis Poetica.'[84] Groschopp was the last scholar who, on

division is about as good as the one which has always been accepted without comment.

[83] *Observationes in Willeramum*, p. 248.

[84] Hickes, Junius' pupil, says that Junius ascribed (*inscribit*) the poems to Cædmon, but did not definitely assign them to him (*non adjudicat*). Hickes believed the whole collection to have been written by an imitator of Cædmon in the tenth century, but that Book II was later than Book I (*Thesaurus* I. 133). Thorpe, with the qualification that due allowance must be made 'for such interpolations, omissions, and corruptions of the original text as Cædmon . . . may be supposed to have suffered at the hands of ignorant transcribers,' reverted to the theory of Cædmonian authorship, which he affirmed more definitely than Junius had done. However, of the second book he says, 'As the orthography used in this part of the poem is less pure,

the basis of independent investigation, felt prone to assign *Christ and Satan* to Cædmon. Because of its 'simple and popular' style of presentation, he considered the poem (that is, the longer original poem, from the fragments of which, according to Groschopp, the extant *Christ and Satan* was put together) among the earliest specimens of Anglo-Saxon poetry which have come down to us, and believed that it is possibly one of Cædmon's. Yet he was of the opinion that it was not at all related to the *Genesis, Exodus,* and *Daniel.*[85] Brooke,[86] Bentinck Smith,[87] and Bradley,[88] overemphasizing the rudeness and simplicity in form and content, echo the same opinion with slight variations.[89]

Grein omits before the title, *Christ und Satan,* the word 'Cädmons,' which he had prefixed to the titles of the other three poems of Junius XI,[90] and in his grammar says that

and the language less grammatical, than in the first part, it is perhaps to be considered as less ancient' (see pp. VIII, XII).

Ettmüller opposed Junius' and Thorpe's opinions, on the grounds that the language is Saxon of the ninth century, the style epic, not didactic, and the author possessed of much knowledge of 'rebus civilibus' and various other learning, all of which facts are in disagreement with Bede's account. See *Scopas and Boceras,* p. XIII.

[85] *Op. cit.,* pp. 264-5.

[86] *Op. cit.,* pp. 326-330.

[87] *Loc. cit.*

[88] *Essays and Studies* 6. 10-1.

[89] Bouterwek is very vague: 'Cædmon's poems' are of varying worth, and neither by one poet nor of one time (p. CXL); had Hickes recognized in the linguistic peculiarities of Book II the Northumbrian dialect, he would hardly have been averse to assigning it to Cædmon. Yet Bouterwek is not wholly certain that the dialect of Book II is Northumbrian (p. CCXXXIV).

Dietrich (*Zs. f. D. Alt.* 10. 311, 367) merely says that the author of the second book is much inferior to that of the first, and that the language of Cædmon is not so old as that of *Beowulf* and Cynewulf.

Of Book II, Morley (*English Writers* 2. 95) assigned only the 'Temptation fragment' to Cædmon.

[90] *Bibl. der Ags. Poesie.*

Christ and Satan is less likely than these three to rest upon a Cædmonian original.[91]   Ten Brink believed that his three poems probably had different authors, and that there can hardly remain any doubt that they 'belong to a much later period than the Old Testament poems.'   He dates them at the end of the ninth century, or the beginning of the tenth.[92] Wülker[93] agreed with Ten Brink concerning the authorship. He dated the three poems before 950, but after *Genesis B*.[94] From the use of the definite article and weak adjective, the value of which as an exact criterion of chronology has been seriously doubted, Barnouw dated *Christ and Satan* at 880 A. D., contemporary with the *Elene* and *Azarias*.[95]   Later (in 1914) he expresses this opinion: 'In an Old English poem of a time which still remembered the first years of Christianity, a Satan who lamented, but did nothing, would be unimaginable.'[96]   Grau had felt somewhat similarly: 'Ich muss gestehen, dass ich eine literarische behandlung der person des Satans . . . in der frühzeit, etwa der Cynewulfs, für gänzlich unmöglich halte. Diese periode beschäftigt sich nur mit der einfachen, grossen lichtgestalt des himmels-königs Christus. Die komplizierteren probleme des Crist und Satan hätten in der zeit des eben überwundenen heiden-tums m. e. keinen anklang gefunden.'[97]   Brandl, who also depended chiefly on the article-adjective test which Barnouw

[91] *Kurzgefasste Ags. Grammatik*, p. 8.

[92] *Op. cit.*, pp. 88, 376. Kühn also assumes three authors, and assigns the poems to a relatively late period (pp. 35-8, p. 28).

Balg (*Der Dichter Cædmon und seine Werke*) affirmed that the poems of MS. Junius XI are by seven authors, and that none of them could be assigned with certainty to Cædmon. (Balg believed that the *Genesis, Exodus,* and *Daniel* contained long interpolations, but did not challenge the unity of *Christ and Satan*.)

[93] *Grundriss z. Gesch. der Ags. Litt.*, p. 131, n. 1.

[94] *Gesch. d. Eng. Litt.* I. 59.

[95] *Op. cit.*, p. 230.

[96] *Anglo-Saxon Christian Poetry*, pp. 24 ff.

[97] *Op. cit.*, p. 196.

had employed, placed the poem shortly after Cynewulf,[98] whereas Richter specified the latter half of the eighth century.[99] A few apparently archaic spellings made a relatively early date, about 750, seem most acceptable to Frings.[100]

The theory that Cædmon had any share in the authorship of *Christ and Satan* should be abandoned. It is doubtful whether any one would have thought of assigning this poem to him had it not been appended in the MS. to three other poems which seemed to correspond to Bede's list of that poet's works. The fact that it treats certain New Testament subjects which Bede reported that Cædmon versified would hardly by itself have prompted scholars to connect it with Cædmon's name. If *Christ and Satan* had been bound up in the Vercelli Book, it might never have been mentioned in connection with Cædmon. The similarities it presents with the two poems which are generally considered most likely to preserve some of the work of the 'first English poet,' namely, *Genesis A* and *Daniel,* are insignificant.

In seeking an appropriate date we have plenty of leeway— from ca. 680 to ca. 950 A. D. Evidently no one set of the

[98] *Loc. cit.*

[99] *Chronologische Studien zur Angelsächsischen Literatur,* pp. 34-5, 101.

[100] See *op. cit.,* p. 233. Frings points out that in one case breaking has not taken place (*tōwerþan,* 85), but isolated cases of the same phenomenon are found in Rushworth[1] (*āwerþ, werþe*), which is not a relatively early text. *Sīdas* (for *sīðas*), 189, which Frings considers an example of a very old spelling, is probably a scribal error (see the note on this line). The use of *æ* for the weak vowel *e* in 31, 38, 53, 141, 182, 361, and 733, in a North Anglian text, is inconclusive as a criterion of age. Forms similar to most of these occur sporadically in later documents, and in two or three of the lines cited, *æ* has been produced by the Corrector's addition of *e* to *a* as a quick and inconspicuous method of emending (so probably in 38 and 361, and certainly in 141 and 182). Such scanty and doubtful evidence is of no validity. Besides, all but two of these archaic-looking spellings are found between 20 and 193, so that they might be assigned to the older poem from which the poet borrowed.

criteria which have been used can be trusted alone. I can see no reason why an early date must be accepted. The literary relations of the poem would indicate a time after the close of the period of Cynewulf's literary activity, that is, after, roughly, the last decades of the eighth century, or the beginning of the ninth.[101] On the other hand, the arguments for a relatively late date (i. e., after 850) are wholly inconclusive. Clearly the article-adjective test may point in either of two directions (compare Barnouw with Brandl), and deductions from the *Zeitgeist* depend on subjective impressions. Besides, the character of the presentation and characterization has been adduced as final proof both of Cædmonian authorship, which would push the poem back to the end of the seventh century, and of the latest datings (compare Groschopp, Brooke, and Bradley with Grau and Barnouw). It does not seem that what we know of the poem would warrant assigning a more precise period for the composition of *Christ and Satan* than 790-830 A. D.

[101] See Cook, *Elene, Phœnix, and Physiologus,* p. xiii.

CHRIST AND SATAN

TEXT

THE TEXT

Abbreviations are expanded without notice, except that those which are unusual are mentioned in the variants. Emendations are enclosed in square brackets. Italics indicate change in the order of letters. Underscoring marks letters or words offered as emendations by the Corrector. Erased letters are not printed in the text unless the erasures can be assigned with absolute certainty to the Corrector, or unless their absence renders the meaning doubtful. Probably by far the greater number of the erasures were made by the Corrector, but it is preferable to print the forms as they have been preserved, rather than try to decide in every case who is responsible for the change. Wülker's text is full of inconsistencies in the treatment of these erasures. The numbering of the lines first used by Grein and Wülker has been retained. The numbers of lines which are not included in Grein's numbering are given as, e. g., 680 A. In the right-hand margin from 366 to 733 will be found Wülker's numberings of Parts II and III.

Insignificant normalizations by later editors are omitted from the variants. Unless otherwise specified, the Corrector's alterations there recorded were made by the addition of letters above those letters they were intended to replace. The interrogation-mark indicates that an emendation was put forward with some diffidence. The letter *n.*, after an abbreviation standing for a scholar's name, means that the emendation or suggestion was proposed in a note.

ABBREVIATIONS

B.[1] Bouterwek (text).
B.[2] Bouterwek (notes).
Br. Bright ('Jottings').
C. The Corrector.
Cs. Cosijn (*Anglosaxonica*).
D. Dietrich (*Zs. f. D. A.* 10).
E. Ettmüller.
G.[1] Grein (*Bibliothek*).
G.[2] Grein (*Sprachschatz*).
G.[3] Grein (*Germania* 10).
GK. Grein-Köhler (*Sprachschatz*).
Gz. Graz (*Beiträge*).

H.[1] Holthausen (*Indog. Forsch.*).
H.[2] Holthausen (*Anglia Bb.* 5).
J. Junius.
K. Kock (*Jubilee Jaunts and Jottings*).
S.[1] Sievers (*Zs. f. D. A.* 15).
S.[2] Sievers (*Rhythmik*).
T. Thorpe.
W. Wülker (*Bibliothek*).
Wms. Williams.
Wnrs. Wieners.

CHRIST AND SATAN

Þæt wearð underne   eorðbūendum
þæt Meotod hæfde   miht and strengðo
ðā hē gefestnade   foldan scēatas.
Seolfa hē gesette   sunnan and mōnan,
5   stānas and eorðan,   strēam ūt on sǣ,
wæter and wolcn,   ðurh his wundra miht.
Dēopne ymblyt   clēne ymbhaldeð
Meotdd on mihtum,   and alne middangeard.
Hē selfa mæg   sǣ geondwlītan,
10 grundas in [g]eofene,   Godes āgen Bearn;
and hē ārīman mæg   rægnas scūran,
dropena gehwelcne;   daga enderīm
seolua hē gesette   þurh his sōðan miht.
Swā se Wyrhta   þurh his wuldres Gāst
15 serede and sette   on six dagum
eorðan dǣles,   [and] ūpheofon,

Page 213 *of MS.*—*Wülker gives as the title: Die Klagen der Gefallnen Engel.*—1ᵃ *MS.* ð *of* wearð *partly over an erased* þ.—1ᵇ *MS.* e *erased after* eorð-; *J., T., E.* eorðebuendum; *B.*¹ eorðe buendum; *B.*² *as MS.*—2 *C.* hĩ (him) *after* meotod *above the line.*—5 *J., T., B.¹, E.* uton; *Cs.* and utsæ (?).—6ᵃ *MS.* wæt; *T., B.*¹ sæwæter; *C.* wolcen; *Edd. except J.* wolcen.—6ᵇ *E.* wuldra.—7ᵃ *MS.* ymblyt; *J., T., B.¹, E., G.², G.³, W.* ymblyt; *G.*¹ yðmyð; *H.*² ymbhwyrft; *Br.* ymblyhte.—7ᵇ *G.², G.³, Gs., Br.* dene; *H.*² dēre (?); *Cs.* dryhten *for* dene (?); *GK.* derne (?); *T. n.* uphaldeð (?); *E.* uphealdeð.—9 *MS.* se *changed to* sæ *by a later hand* (*S.*¹).—10 *MS.* heofene; *C. changes the final* e *to* o *and adds* n *above the line; J., T., B.¹, E.* heofene; *S.*¹ *thinks* heofenen *the original reading; W.* heofenen; *G.¹, Gs., Cs.* geofene.—11 *B.*² rægnscura.—14 *B.*² *for* swa se, wise (?); *H.*² wyrhta eac.—16ᵃ *T. n.: should grammatically be* dalas; *B.¹, Br.* dælas; *E.* dalas; *G.*¹ dǣles.—16ᵇ *MS., J., T., G.¹, W.* up on heofonum; *T. n.: error for* and upheofon, *or* upheofonas; *B.*¹ upon heofonas; *E., Cs., Br.* and upheofon.

[and] hēanne holm.   Hwā is þæt ðe cunne
orðonc clēne   nymðe ēce God?

_ Drēamas hē gedēlde,   duguðe and geþēode:
20 Ādām ǣrest,   and þæt æðele cyn,
engla ordfruman,   þæt þe eft forwarð.
Ðūhte him on mōde   þæt hit mihte swā,
þæt hīe wēron seolfe   swegles brytan,
wuldres waldend.   Him ðǣr wirse gelamp,
25 ðā hēo in helle   hām staðeledon,
ān æfter ōðrum,   in þæt atole scref,
þǣr hēo brynewelme   bīdan sceolden
sāran sorge;   nales swegles lēoht
habban in heofnum,   hēahgetimbra,
30 ac gedūfan sceolun   in ðone dēopan wælm,
niðær under nessas   in ðone neowlan grund,
grēdige and gīfre.   God āna wāt
hū hē þæt scyldige werud   forscrifen hefde.

17ᵃ *MS.* henne; *scribe adds* a *above the line; J., T., B.*¹, *W., Cs.*
heanne; *MS.* holme; *E., G.*¹ heahne holm; *H.*², *Br.* and heanne;
W. n. agrees that we should have holm; *Cs.* ofer holme (?) *or* heahe
holmas (??); *Br.* holm.—18ᵃ *C., T., B.*¹, *E., G.*¹ *change to* clæne;
*G.*¹ *n.* clænne (?); *C. vel* buton (*over* nymðe).—19ᵃ *C., T., B.*¹, *E.,*
*G.*¹ gedælde.—19ᵇ *T. n.· error for* geteode. creavit; *E.* geogoðe, *if*
emendation is necessary; Gz., Br. geogoðe.—20ᵃ *G.*¹ Adame; *G.*²
Adam; *E.* ærest scop.—21ᵃ *E.* ordfruma.—21ᵇ *J.* misreads ꝥ te; *B.*¹
þætte; *C.* forwearð; *T., B.*¹, *E., G.*¹ forwearð.—22ᵃ *C.* heom.—23ᵃ
C. alters to wæron (æ *from* e) sylfe.—23ᵇ *Gz., Wnrs.* bryttan.—24ᵇ
*G.*¹ þæs *for* ðær; *G.*² þær; *MS.* wise; *C. adds* ors *above* ise; *T.,*
*B.*¹, *E.* wors; *G.*¹, *Gz.* wirse; *W.* wirs; *C.* gelomp.—25 *E.* hie on.—
27ᵃ *E.* hie; *B.*² hie on.—27ᵇ *MS.* sceoden; *scribe adds* l *above the*
line; C. writes o *above the second* e; *E.* sceoldon.—28ᵇ o *canceled*
and then erased between e *and* g *of* swegles.—29ᵃ *Second* b *of* habban
added above by scribe.—29ᵇ *MS., J., T., B.*¹, *E., G.*¹, *W.* heahgetim-
brad; *B.*² heahgetimber; *G.*¹ *n.* heahgetimbra (?); *H.* (*Angl.* 44.
354) heahgetimbru *or possibly* heofnes heahgetimbrum.—30 *E., G.*¹,
W., Cs. sceoldun.—31ᵃ *J., E., G.*¹ niðer under; *B.*¹, *T., W.* undær.—
32 *C.* (*W.*) grædige.—33ᵃ *Scribe adds* ge *to* scyldi *above line.*—33ᵇ *C.*
alters to hefde; *E.* hæfð; *W.* hæfde.

Cleopa[ð] ðonne se alda ūt of helle,
35 wriceð wordcwedas, wēregan reorde,
eisegan stefne: 'Hwǣr cōm engla ðrym,
þe wē on heofnum habban sceoldan?
Þis is ðēostræ hām, ðearle gebunden
fæstum fȳrclommum; flōr is on welme,
40 āttre onǣled. Nis nū ende feor
þæt wē sceolun ætsomne sūsel þrōwian,
wēan and wērgu, nalles wulres blǣd
habban in heofnum, hēhselda wyn.
Hwæt! wē for Dryhtene iū drēamas hefdon,
45 song on swegle sēlrum tīdum,
þǣr nū ymb ðone Ēcan æðele stondað,
heleð ymb hēhseld, herigað Drihten
wordu[m] and wercum; and ic in wīte sceal
bīdan in bendum, and mē bættran hām
50 for oferhygdum ǣfre ne wēne.'
Ðā him andsweradan atole gāstas,

34 *MS.* cleopad; *Edd.* cleopað; *C.* ealda.—35 *Scribe adds* word *above* cwed-.—36 *D.* egesan.—37 *MS.*, *Edd.* ða þe.—38 *MS.* þe *erased before* ðeostræ; *J. (in Errata)* se ðeostræ; *MS. first had* ðeostra; æ *looks a little like C's work; E., G.*¹ þeostre.—40 *G.*¹, *B.-T. Sup.* is.—41ª *Cs.* we ætsomne.—41ᵇ *Gz.* susl.—42ª *MS., J., T., B.*¹, *E., W.* wergum; *B.*² mid wergum; *D., G.*², *Cs.* wergun (*Cs.: i. e.,* wergung); *G.*¹ wergung; *Frings and Unwerth, PBB. 36. 559,* wergum (= wergm); *Sperber, PBB. 37. 148-9, Wms.* an (on) wergum; *Sievers, PBB. 37. 339, GK.* wērgu.—42ᵇ *MS.* nelles; *scribe cancels first* e, *writes* a *above it; J.* wuldræs (wulres *in Errata*); *E., W.* wuldres; *G.*¹ wuldres leoht.—44ᵇ dreamas *begins page* 214.—46 e *of* ecan *from* æ *by erasure.*—47ª *First* e *of* heleð *seems to have been altered to* æ, *probably by C.; T., E., B.*¹, *G.*¹ hæleð; *MS.* ym; b *above and between* y *and* m *has been erased; scribe added* b *after* ym *and above line.*—48ª *MS.* wordun; *Edd.* wordum; *C.* wiorcum.—49ᵇ *MS.* bættran; b *erased; scribe (probably) had put a dot under a of* æ; *Edd.* bættran; *MS.* for *canceled after* bættran.—51 *MS.* 7 sweradan.

swarte and synfulle,   sūsle begrorene:
'Þū ūs gelǣrdæst   ðurh lyge ðīnne
þæt wē Hēlende   hēran ne scealdon.

55   Ðūhte þē ānum   þæt ðū āhtest alles gewald,
heofnes and eorþan,   wǣre hālig God,
Scypend seolfa.   Nū earttū sceaða[na sum]
in fȳrlocan   feste gebunden.
Wēndes ðū ðurh wuldor   ðæt þū woruld āhtest,

60   alra onwald,   and wē englas mid ðec.
Atol is þīn onsēon!   habbað wē alle swā
for ðīnum lēasungum   lȳðre gefēred.
Segdest ūs tō sōðe   þæt ðīn sunu wǣre
Meotod moncynnes;   hafustū nū māre sūsel.'

65   Swā firenfulle   fācnum wordum
heora aldorðægn   [a]n reordadon
on cear[i]um cwidum.   Crīst hēo āfirde,
drēamum bedēlde.   Hæfdan Dryhtnes līht
for oferhygdum   ufan forlēton;

70   hæfdon hym tō hyhte   helle flōras,
beornende bealo.   Blāce hworfon

52ᵃ *C.* swearte.—52ᵇ *MS., J., T., B.*¹ begrorenne; *E., W.* begrorene;
D. begrowene (?); *G.*¹ *accepts* begrowene; *H.*², *Sievers (in note on
Cs.)* behrorene; *Cs.* susl begnornedon.—54ᵃ *C., E., G.*¹ hælende.—54ᵇ
C. sceoldon.—57ᵃ *Wnrs.* scyppend.—57ᵇ *MS.* nu eart tu earm sceaða;
possibly a letter erased after earm; *J.* ðu earm 7 sceaða; *T., E., G.*¹,
*W. as MS.; B.*¹ earmsceaða; *G.*¹ *n.* sceaða earm (?); *Br.* nu, sceaða,
eartu, *or* nu eartu, sceaða earma; *MS. after* sceaða *letters are erased,
which were spaced thus* : :   : : : *(see note); W. n.:* ne wyrn *or the
like erased.*—58 *B.*² fyre locum.—59 *E.* worulda.—63 *C. alters first* e
of segdest *to* æ; *E.* sægdest.—64ᵇ *E., G.*¹ hafas; *Gz.* susl.—66 *MS.*
unreordadon; *E., B.*² onreordadon; *G.*², *K. (Plain Points and Puzzles,
p. 24)* an reordadon.—67ᵃ *MS., J., T., E., B.*¹, *G.*¹, *W.* cearum; *S.*²
(p. 456) cearigum; *H.*² ceargum; *Gz.* cwiðdun; *Cs.* cearium.—68ᵃ
C. erased e *of* bedelde *and added* æ *above; T., E., B.*¹, *G.*¹ bedælde.—
68ᵇ *C. erased* i *of* liht, *added* eo *above; T., E., B.*¹, *G.*¹ leoht.—69ᵇ
C. forlæten *by altering* e *and* o; *Edd.* forleten.—71ᵇ *C.* hweorfon; *E.,
G.*¹ hwurfon; *B.*¹, *E., H.*² blāce; *G.*¹ blāce.

scinnan forscepene, sceaðan hwearf[e]don,
earme æglēcan, geond þæt atole scref,
for ðām anmēdlan þe hīe ǣr drugon.

II

75   Eft reordade   ōðre sīðe
fēonda aldor.   Wæs þā forht agēn,
seoððan hē ðes wītes worn gefēlde.
Hē s[p]earcade, ðonne hē spreocan ongan,
fȳre and ātre; ne bið swelc fǣger drēam
80 ðonne hē in wītum word[e] indrāf:
'Ic wæs iū in heofnum hālig ængel
Dryhten dēore; hefde mē drēam mid Gode,
micelne for Meotode, and ðēos menego swā some.
Þā ic in mōde mīnum hogade
85 þæt ic wolde tōwerpan wulres lēoman,
Bearn Hēlendes, āgan mē burga gewald
eall tō ǣhte, and ðes earme hēap
þe ic hebbe tō helle hām gelēdde.

72ᵇ *MS., Edd.* hwearfdon; *S.²* (*p. 316*), *H.²*, *Gz.*, *Cs.* hwearfedon.—
74 *MS.* medlan; *C.* (? *scribe*) *adds an* above.—76ᵇ *MS., J., T., B.¹,*
E., W. forworht; *G.¹, Gz.* forht; *G.¹ n.* þy forhtor gen(?); *Cs.*
forhtra gen; *Wms.* forworhta gen.—77ᵃ *C. erased* e *of* ðes, *added* æ
above; Edd., except J., W. ðæs.—78ᵃ *MS. at first* swearcade; *scribe*
changes c *to* t; *J., T., B.¹, W.* sweartade; *E. n.:* perhaps spearcade;
G.¹, Cs. accept spearcade.—78ᵇ *MS.* ðoñ.—79ᵃ *C., Edd.* attre.—79ᵇ
MS. n *of* ne *made from* h *by erasure; J.* he.—80ᵃ *D.* inwitum.—80ᵇ
MS., Edd. word; *H.¹* word[gid]; *Br.* þa (*or* þas) word; *K.* word =
word[e]; *H. (Angl. Bb. 30. 2)* þæt, þa, *or* þas word; *E.* indræfeð;
B.² utadraf; *Gz. (Metrik)* in adraf; *Gz. (Beiträge)* ut adraf *or* ut
þorhdraf.—82 *C. puts a dot under* e *of* dryhten, *adds* e *at end; J.,*
T., B.¹ dryhtene; *E., G.¹* dryhtne.—85ᵃ in *or the like erased after* ic;
C. towiorpan; *G.¹* toworpan.—85ᵇ *Edd. except B.* wuldres.—86 *C., E.*
hælendes; agan *begins p.* 215; *C., G.¹* geweald.—87 o *of MS.* ðeos
looks as if erased; Edd. ðeos.—88 *C. alters second* e *of* geledde *to* æ;
E. gelædde.

89–90   Wēne þæt tācen sutol þā ic āseald wes on wærgðu,
         niðer under nessas in ðone neowlan grund.
         Nū ic ēow hebbe tō hæftum hām geferde
         alle of earde.
                      'Nis hēr ēadiges tīr,
         wloncra wīnsele, nē worulde drēam,
95   nē engla ðrēat; nē wē ūpheofon
         āgan mōten. Is ðes atola hām
         fȳr onǣled. Ic eom fāh wið God.
         Ēce æt helle duru dracan eardigað
         hāte on reðre; hēo ūs helpan ne magon.
100   Is ðes wālica hām wītes āfylled;
         nāgan wē ðæs heolstres, þæt wē ūs gehȳdan magon
         in ðissum neowlan genipe. Hēr is nēdran swēg,
         wyrmas gewunade. Is ðis wītes clom

89ª *C., Edd. except Junius* wene ge; *GK.* socen *for* tacen (?).—
89ᵇ *MS.* and wærgðu þa ic of aseald wes; *J.* wærg ðu; *T.* of-aseald;
*n.: several ll. wanting; B.*¹ *gap of more than one hemistich after* wærgðu; *E.* tacen, teonfulle gastas/swutol—wæs/; *G.*¹ teon—wærgðu/; *G.*¹
Wms. þa ic of swegle; *W.* wærgðu . . ./þa ic of . . . a. w./;
*H.*¹ þa ic aseald wes of swegles wlite; *Cs.* of swegle adrifen and
asæled wæs; *Wms.* wærgðu gesyne.—91ª *C. cancels* e *of* nessas, *writes*
æ *above; T., B.*¹, *E., G.*¹ næssas.—91ᵇ ðone *from* ðonne.—92ᵇ *MS.*
gefærde, a *erased; C.* geferede; *J., T., B.*¹, *G.*¹ gefærde; *W., Wms.*
gefærede.—93ª *C. (possibly another man), T., G.*¹ ealle.—93ᵇ *T. n., G.*¹,
Cs. eadigra.—94ª *C.* wynsela (a *by alteration*); *Trautmann in Wnrs.*
wynsele (*because* winsele *is a false 'dehnwort'*).—95ª e *of* engla *from*
æ *by erasure; Edd. except E.* ængla.—95ᵇ *Cs.* nu *for* ne (?); *C.,*
Edd. except J. ne we; *C.* upp-.—96ª *C., Edd. except J.* agan ne m.—
96ᵇ ðes *made by writing tall* s *over erasure of* os.—97ª *MS.* fyre (? e
added by another corrector); *Edd. except J.* fyre.—98 *MS.* e *of* ece
from æ; *W.* æce; *H. (Eng. Stud. 27. 205) omits* ece; *E.* dura; *Gz.,*
Wnrs. duru helle.—99 *E., G.*¹, *Gz.* hreðre; *C.* hy.—100 *MS.* ðes
from ðæs; *J.* ðæs.—101ª n *of* nagan *over erased capital.*—101ᵇ *G.*¹
behydan; a *of* magon *from* æ.—102ᵇ e *of* her *and* sweg *from* æ.—
103 *B.*² gewuniað; is þis witehus / clommum feste g.; *E., G.*¹, *Wms.*
þes.

feste gebunden.   Fēond seondon rēðe,
105   dimme and deorce.   Ne hēr dæg lȳhteð
for scedes scīman,   Sceppendes lēoht.
'Nū āhte gewald   ealles wuldres;
þær ic mōste in ðeossum atolan   ēðele gebīdan
hwæt mē Drihten God   dēman wille,
110   fāgum on flōra.   Nū ic fēran cōm
dēofla menego   tō ðissum dimman hām.
Ac ic sceal on flyhte   and on flyge ðrāgum
earda nēosan,   and ēower mā,
þe ðes oferhȳdes   ord onstaldon.
115   'Ne ðurfon wē ðæs wēnan,   þæt ūs Wuldorcyning
æfre wille   eard ālēfan,
ēðel tō æhte,   swā hē ær dyde,
ēcne onwald;   āh him alles gewald,
wuldres and wīta,   Waldendes Sunu.
120   Forðon ic sceal hēan and earm   hweorfan ðȳ wīdor,
wadan wræclāstas,   wuldre benēmed,
duguðum bedēled,   nænigne drēam āgan

uppe mid englum,   þęs ðe ic ǣr gecwæð
þæt ic wǣre seolfa   swegles Brytta,
125   wihta Wealdend.'   (Ac hit him wyrse gelomp!)

III

Swā se wērega gāst   wordum sǣde
his earfoðo   ealle ætsomne,
fāh in fyrnum   (fȳrlēoma stōd
geond þæt atole scræf   āttre geblonden) :
130   'Ic eom limwæstmum   þæt ic gelūtian ne mæg
on þyssum sīdan sele,   synnum forwundod.
Hwæt! hēr hāt and ceald   hwīlum mencgað;
hwīlum ic gehēre   hellescealcas,
gnornende cynn,   grundas mǣnan
135   niðer under næssum;   hwīlum nacode men
win[d]að ymb wyrmas :   is þes windiga sele
eall inneweard   atole gefylled.
'Ne mōt ic hihtlicran   hāmes brūcan,
burga nē bolda,   nē on þā beorhtan gescæft
140   ne mōt ic ǣfre mā   ēagum starian.
Is mē nū wyrsa   þæt ic wuldres lēoht
uppe mid englum   ǣfre cūðe,
song on swegle,   þǣr Sunu Meotodes

123ᵃ e *of* englum *made from* æ *by erasure; Edd. except E.* ænglum.
—123ᵇ *J., T., B.¹, E., G.¹* þæs; *W.* þes.—124ᵇ *First* e *of* swegles *from*
æ *by erasure; Edd. except E.* swægles.—125ᵃ *C. writes the letters*
ihta wealdend *over erasure; S.¹ thinks the second scribe wrote them;
the word under* wihta *was clearly* waldend.—125ᵇ c *of* ac *from* h *by
erasure; E., G.¹, Cs.* me *for* him; *C.* gelamp.—126 Swa *begins page*
216, *which is the first page written by the second scribe.*—130 *G.¹* lim
wæstmum; *G.² combines.*—132ᵃ *J., T., B.¹, E., G.¹* Hwæðer; *S.¹, W.*
Hwæther; *H.²* Hwæt! her; *G.¹* cald.—132ᵇ *B.²* me swencgeð.—133
E., G.¹, W. helle scealcas.—134 *C., T., B.¹, G.¹* gnorniende.—136 *MS.,
Edd.* winnað; *T. n.: error for* windað (?); *C., T., B.¹, E., G.¹*
ymbe.—141 *C. alters* a *of* wyrsa *to* æ; *T., B.¹, W.* wyrsa; *E.* wirse;
G.¹ wyrse.

habbaðˈ ēadige bearn   ealle ymbfangen
145 seolfa mid sange.   Nē ic þām sāwlum ne mōt
[ðe of eorðan cumað]   ænigum sceððan
būtan þām ānum   þe hē tō āgan nyle;
þā ic mōt tō hæftum   hām geferian,
bringan tō bolde   in þone biteran grund.
150 Ealle wē syndon   ungelīce
þonne þe wē iū in heofonum   hæfdon ǣrror
wlite and weorðmynt.   Ful oft wuldres [swēg]
brōhton tō bearme   bearn Hǣlendes,
þǣr wē ymb hine ūtan   ealle hōfan,
155 leomu ymb Lēofne,   lofsonga word,
Drihtne sǣdon.   Nū ic eom dǣdum fāh,
gewundod mid wommum;   sceal nū þysne wītes
beoran beornende   in bǣce mīnum,   [clom
hāt on helle,   hyhtwillan lēas.'
160 Þā gȳt feola cwī[ð]de   firna herde,
atol ǣglǣca,   ūt of helle,
wītum wērig.   Word spearcum flēah
āttre gelīcost,   þonne hē ūt þorhdrāf:
'Ealā Drihtenes þrym!   ēalā duguða Helm!
165 ēalā Meotodes miht!   ēalā middaneard!
ēalā dæg lēohta!   ēalā drēam Godes!

144ᵃ *MS.* eadigne; *so J., T., B.¹, E., G.¹, W.; B.²* habbeð eadige,
bearn, ealle; *Gz.* eadge.—145 *E., G.¹* seolfan; *G.³* seolfa.—146-7 *T.,*
B.¹ a hemistich missing after nyle; *E.* earmum atolum þe—nyle; *G.¹*
eadigra ænigum; *G.³, Gz.* þara æfæstra ænigum; *W. a hemistich*
missing before ænigum; *Barnouw (Textkrit. Untersuch., p. 104)*
suggests þe up of eorðan cumað *or* þe up to eðle (earde) cumað, *to*
fill gap in 146.—147ᵇ *T., B.¹* toagan; *G.¹, Cs.* agen; *G.³* agan; *S. (in*
note on Cs.) þe hē agan nyle (?).—152 *G.¹, H.², K.* wuldres sweg.—
153ᵇ *K.* bearne (?).—155 *B.²* leoðu *for* leomu.—160 *MS.* cwide,
herede; *C. vel* cwidum; *J., T., B.¹, E., G.¹, W.* cwide; *Rieger, Lese-*
buch, G.³, S.² (p. 456), Gz. cwiðde; *Rieger* heorde; *G.³, S.², Cs.* herde
(= hirde); *Gz.* hirde; *B. (Glossary), E.* herede (herian); *D.* harede.
—163 *C., T., B.¹, E., G.¹* þurh-.—166 o *of* leohta *made from* d; *J.*
leohða; *T., B.¹* dægleohta.

ēalā engla þrēat! ēalā ūpheofen!
ēalā þæt ic eam ealles lēas ēcan drēames,
þæt ic mid handum ne mæg heofon gerǣcan,
170 nē mid ēagum ne mōt ūp lōcian,
nē hūru mid ēarum ne sceal æfre gehēran
þǣre byrhtestan bēman stefne;
ðæs ic wolde of selde Sunu Meotodes,
Drihten ādrīfan, and āgan mē þæs drēames gewald,
175 wuldres and wynne— mē þǣr wyrse gelamp
þonne ic tō hihte āgan mōste.
Nū ic eom āscēaden fram þǣre scīran driht,
ālǣded fram lēohte in þone lāðan hām.
'Ne mæg ic þæt gehicgan hū ic in ðǣm becwōm,
180 in þis neowle genip, [n]ī[ð]synnum fāh,
āworpen of worulde. Wāt ic nū þā
þæt bið alles lēas ēcan drēamas
sē ðe Heofencyninge hēran ne þenceð,
Meotode cwēman. Ic þæt morðer sceal
185 wēan and wītu and wrace drēogan,
gōda bedǣled, iūdǣdum fāh,
þæs ðe ic geþōhte ādrīfan Drihten of selde,
weoroda Waldend; sceal nū wreclāstas
settan sorhgceari, sī[ð]as wīde.'

---

167 *Edd. except W.* upheofon.—170 *C.* g̃ *(erased) after* up.—172
byrhtestan *begins p.* 217; *C.* byman.—173 *Gz., Wnrs.: a monosyllable
lost before* sunu.—175^b *G.*¹ þæs (?); *Rieger, Gz.* þæs.—176^a *G.*¹
ic ær; *Br.* þone þe.—176^b *H.*², *Gz.* habban *for MS.* agan.—179^b *G.*¹
n. þæm = þeam, *vapor; Rieger in* þone ðæm; *D.:* hof *or* ham
lost (?); *Gz.* þæt ham (*or in* hæft); *MS.* w *of* becwom *canceled*
(? *by C.*); *Edd.* becwom.—180 *MS.* mid synnum; *B.*¹, *G.*¹, *Rieger,
W., Gz.* niðsynnum; *T. gap of two hemistichs after* genip; *E. reads*
nearowe gebunden—genip / seoc *and* sorhfull mid—fah.—181^a *G.*¹,
Rieger, Gz. wuldre.—181^b *C.*, *Edd. add* ꝥ (þæt) *after* ic.—182^b *C.*
changes to ęcan dreamæs; *W. accepts; J., T., B.*¹, *G.*¹ dreames.—184
MS. morðre; *T. n.:* þæs morðres *required* (?); *E. accepts* þæs
morðres; *G.*¹, *W.* þæs morðre; *Rieger* þæs morðer; *K.* þæt morðor.
—189^a *C., Edd. add* g *to* ceari.—189^b *MS.* sidas; *Edd.* siðas.

[IV]

190   Hwearf þā tō helle   þā hē gehēned wæs,
       Godes andsaca;   dydon his gingran swā,
       gīfre and grǣdige,   þā hē God bedrāf
       in þæt hāte hof   þām is hel nama.
       Forþan sceal gehycgan   hæleða ǣghwylc
195   þæt hē ne ābelige   Bearn Waldendes;
       lǣte him tō bysne   hū þā blācan fēond
       for oferhygdum   ealle forwurdon.
       Neoman ūs tō wynne   weoroda Drihten,
       up[p]e ēcne gefēan,   engla Waldend.
200   Hē þæt gecȳdde   þæt hē cræft hæfde,
       mihta miccle,   þā hē þā mænego ādrāf,
       hæftas of ðǣm hēan selde.   Gemunan wē þone
       hālgan Drihten;
203–204 ēcne mid al[l]a gescefta   cēosan ūs eard in wuldre
205   mid ealra cyninga Cyninge,   sē is Crīst genemned;
       beoran on brēostum   blīðe geþōhtas,
       sibbe and snytero,   gemunan sōð and riht,
       þonne wē tō hēhselde   nīgan þencað,
       and þone Anwaldan   āra biddan.
210   Þonne behōfað   sē ðe hēr wunað

191 *C. vel* some; *G.*[1] swa some.—192 *C., T., B.*[1]*, E., G.*[1]*, W.* hig; *J.* hie.—195 e *of* abelige *from* æ *by erasure; Edd. except E.* abǣlige; *E.* abelge.—198 *C. vel* niman.—199 *MS., Edd.* upne.—200[a] *B.*[1]*, E., G.*[1]*, W.* gecȳde.—200[b] *MS., J., T., B.*[1]*, W.* mægencræft; *E., G.*[1]*, H.*[2]*, Gz. omit* mægen.—202 *Gz.* heahan.—203-4 *MS., Edd.* ecne in wuldre mid alra; *B.*[1] wuldra; *E.* ecne in wuldre ealdor; heran we þone ælmihtigan / mid—gescæfta mænego; ceosan, etc./; *B.*[1] (*as* 204[a]) eorðan ceosan; *B.*[2]*, G.*[1] ordfruman ceosan; *D.* ealdre (*or* ealdor) ceosan (?); *T. gap of a hemistich (W. a word) before* ceosan; *H.*[2] or (*or* ord) ceosan (?); *Gz., Kaluza (Eng. Stud. 21) print* ecne in wuldre—wuldre *as an expanded line.*—205 *S.*[2] (*12. 476*), *Cs.* cyning *for* cyninge.—208 *C.* hnigan (h *in margin*); *Edd.* hnigan.—209[a] *MS.* þonne (*first* n *partly erased*); *C. vel* ealwaldan; *T., B.*[1]*, E., G.*[1] alwaldan.—209[b] *C. changes to* arǣ; *Edd.* ara.—210 se *begins p.* 218.

weorulde wynnum þæt him wlite scīne
þonne hē ōðer līf eft gesēceð;
fǣg[e]re land, þonne þēos folde sēo,
is wlitig and wynsum; wæstmas scīnað
215   beorhte ofer burgum.   Þǣr is brāde lond,
hyhtlicra hām in heofonrīce,
Crīste gecwēmra.   Uta cerran þider
þǣr hē sylfa sit, sigora Waldend,
Drihten Hǣlend, in ðǣm dēoran hām;
220   and ymb þæt hēhsetl hwīte standað
engla fēðan and ēadigre;
hālige heofenþrēatas herigað Drihten
wordum and weorcum.   Heora wlite scīneð
geond ealra worulda woruld mid Wuldorcyninge.

V

225   Þā gēt ic furðor gefregen fēond ondetan;
226–227   wæs him eall ful strang wom and wītu.   Hæfd[e]
Wuldorcyning
for oferhigdum ānforlǣten.
Cwæ[ð] eft hraðe ōðre worde:

---

211 *E.* weorulda; *B. (Glossary)* wlitescīne.—213ª *MS., J., T., B.*[1]
fægre; *C.* ·s· (*scilicet* ?) mycele *above* fægre; *T., B.*[1] mycele fægre;
E., G.[1]*, W.* mycele fægerre; *so S.*[2] (*p. 499*); *Gz.* fægerre.—213ᵇ *E.*
folde is / þær wlitig; *T., B.*[1] folde / seo is; *G.*[1]*, W.* folde seo:/ þær
is.—214ª *C.* ·s· þær *above* is; *Gz., Wnrs.* omit þær is.—215 *K.* bradre.
—216 *MS.* n *erased after* hyhtlicra; *J.* hyhtlicran.—217ᵇ *C. adds* on
above ut, *connects* a *by dashes with* cerran *on the next line of MS.;*
Edd. uton acerran.—220 *C. adds* e *to* ymb.—221 *Edd.* eadigra.—222
MS. haligre, r *erased; J.* haligre.—224 *H.*[2] wuldorcyning.—225 ·v·
in margin before þa; *MS., J.* feonda; *T.* feond (*in note: for*
feondas); *B.*[1] feondas; *G.*[1] feonda bearn /; *W.* feonda . . . /; *H.*[1]*,*
Gz. feonda mænigu.—226ª *G.*[1] unriht ondetan; *H.*[1]*, Gz.* yfel ondetan;
W. . . . . ondetan; *T., B.*[1] *gap of a hemistich after* strang.—226ᵇ *MS.,*
Edd. hæfdon.—229ª *MS., Edd.* cwædon.—229ᵇ *C. vel* oðrum wordum
(*so T., B.*[1]*, G.*[1]*, W.*).

230 'Nū is gesēne þæt wē syngodon
uppe on earde.   Sceolon nū æfre þæs
drēogan dōmlēase gewinn Drihtnes mihtum.
Hwæt! wē in wuldres wlite wunian mōston,
þær wē hālgan Gode hēran woldon;
235 and him sang ymb seld secgan sceoldon
þūsendmælum.   Þā wē þær wæron,
wunodon on wynnum, gehērdon wuldres swēg,
bēman stefne.   Byrhtword ārās
engla Ordfruma, and þæm Æþelan tō
240 hnigan him sanctas.   Sigetorht ārās
ēce Drihten, ofer ūs gestōd,
and geblētsode bilewitne hēap
dōgra gehwilcne, and his se dēora Sunu,
gāsta Scyppend.   God seolfa wæs
245 eallum andfeng þe ðær ūp becōm,
and hine on eorðan ær gelēfde.
    'Þā ðæs ofþūhte þæt se Þēoden wæs
strang and stīðmōd.   Ongan ic þā steppan forð
āna wið englum,· and tō him eallum spræc:
250 "Ic can ēow lǣran langsumne rǣd,
gif gē willað mīre mihte gelēfan:
uta oferhycgan Helm þone micclan,
weroda Waldend, āgan ūs þis wuldres lēoht

---

230 *C. adds* ge *before* syngodon; *T., B.*[1], *G.*[1], *W.* gesyngodon.—232
S.[2] (*12. 467*) domleas; *Gz.: omit* gewinn.—233 *C. in after* we (*above
line*); *T., B.*[1], *G.*[1], *W.* we in.—236ᵃ *T. gap of a hemistich before*
þusend-; *B.*[1], *G.*[1] þegnas ymb þeoden þusendmælum /; *W. . . . . . .*
þusendmælum.—236ᵇ *MS.* þær wunodon; *C.* wæron *above line after*
þær; *J., T., B.*[1], *G.*[1] *omit* wæron; *B.*[1], *G.*[1] þa we þær wunodon—sweg
(*for* 237).—238 *B.*[2] byrht weard; *Cs.* burgweard.—239ᵇ *MS., Edd.*
and to þæm æþelan; *H.*[1], *Gz. as in text.*—240ᵃ *MS.* scās.—243 *Cs.*
gehwilce.—245 *Cs.* andfenge *or* andfengea.—246 *C.* gelyfde.—247 *G.*[1],
W. þa me.—250 eow *begins p.* 219.—251ᵃ w *erased after* gif; *C., Edd.*
minre (n *possibly by scribe*).—251ᵇ *Scribe cancels* a *of MS.* mihta,
writes e *above it; J.* mihta.—252ᵃ *C., Edd.* utan.

eall tō ǣhte." Þis is īdel gylp
255   þæt wē ǣr drugon   ealle hwīle.

VI

'Ðā gewearð ūsic   þæt wē woldon swâ
Drihten ādrīfan   of þām dēoran hām,
Cyning of cestre.   Cūð is wīde
þæt wreclāstas   wunian mōton,
260   grimme grundas.   God seolfa him
260 A   rīce haldeð;   hē is āna [riht] Cyning,
þe ūs eorre gewearð,   ēce Drihten,
Meotod mihtum swilc.
     'Sceal nū þēos menego hēr
licgan on leahtrum,   sume on lyft scacan,
flēogan ofer foldan—   fȳr bið ymbūtan
265   on ǣghwylcum,   þǣh hē uppe sēo.
Nē mōt hē þām sāwlum   þe ðǣr sēcað ūp
ēadige of eorþan   ǣfre gerīnan;
ah ic be hondum mōt   hǣþenre sceal[e]
grīpan tō grunde,   Godes andsacan.
270   Sume sceolon hweorfan   geond hæleða land
and unsibbe   oft onstyrian
monna mǣgðum   geond middaneard.
Ic hēr geþolian sceal   þinga ǣghwylces

---

256 *MS.* þ *in margin as indication for capital.*—259 *G.¹, W.* þæt
we.—260-1 *MS., J., T., B.¹, G.¹, W.* he is ana cyning; *G.¹, W.* grimme—
haldeð *as one line; S.²* (12. 477) *assumes gap of 2 hemistichs after*
haldeð; *as another possible arrangement, S.²* omits ece drihten *and
prints as one line* he—gewearð / ; *Gz.* rice—cyning (= 260A) *with*
riht *for* ana; *Cs.* he is an riht cyning; *G.¹, W.* he is—drihten / ; *T.,
B.¹ give* 260-261 *as in MS.*—262 *B.², D., G.¹, W.* mihtum swið.—263 *C.*
sceacan.—265 *B.¹, G.¹* þeah.—266 *G.¹* mot ic.—267 *C., Edd.* gehrinan.—
268 *MS.* sceal; *T. n.: perhaps* hæþene scealcas; *B.¹, G.², W.* hæðenne
scealc; *G.¹* hondum mæg hæþenra sceal.—273 *Gz.* þinga æghwilc *or*
gehwylces.

(in ðæ[m] bitr[an bryne]   beala gnornian,
275   sīc and sorhful)   þæs ic seolfa wēold,
þonne ic on heofonum   hām staðelode.
Hwæðer ūs se Ēca   æfre wille
on heofona rīce   hām ālēfan,
ēðel tō æhte,   swā hē ær dyde?'
280   Swā gnorned[e]   Godes andsaca,
hāt on helle.   Him wæs Hælend God
wrāð geworden   for womcwidum.
Forþon mæg gehycgan   sē ðe his heorte dēah,
þæt hē him āfirre   frēcne geþōhtas,
285   lāðe leahtras,   lifigendra gehwylc.
Gemunan symle on mōde   Meotodes strengðo;
gearwian ūs tōgēnes   grēne stræte
ūp tō englum,   þær is se ælmihtiga God.
And ūs befæðman wile   Frēobearn Godes,
290   gif wē þæt on eorðan   ær geþencað,
and ūs tō þām Hālgan   helpe gelēfað;
þonne hē ūs nō forlæteð,   ah līf syleð
uppe mid englum,   ēadigne drēam.
Tæceð ūs se Torhta   trumlicne hām,
295   beorhte burhweallas;   beorhte scīnað
gesælige sāwle,   sorgum bedælde,

---

274 *MS., J.* bitres in ðæs beala; *T., B.*[1] *as MS.; they print* bitre—
gnornian *as one hemistich with gap of a hemistich thereafter; T. n.:
perhaps* bitre in þas bealu; *G.*[1] bitre in þæs brynes beala; *W.* ðæs . . .
beala; *H.*[1]*, Gz.* bitre in ðæs brandes; *Trautmann in Wnrs.* bæles
beala.—275 *C.* seoc *(by changing* i *to* e *and writing* o *above); Edd.
except J.* seoc.—278 *Gz.* heofonrice.—279 *MS., J., T.* eðle; *T. n.:
error for* eðel; *B.*[1]*, G.*[1]*, W.* eðel.—280 *MS., Edd.* gnornedon, andsacan.—281 *MS., Edd.* hate.—287 *Gz. (Metrik)* gierwan.—288 *Gz.*
omits *god.—291 MS.* gelefað; *scribe cancels* a *and writes* e *above it;
Edd.* gelefað.—294 torhta *begins p. 220.—295 Rieger (Zs. f. D. Ph.
7. 18) thinks the line corrupt; H. (Eng. Stud. 37. 205)* blāce *for first*
beorhte.

þǣr hēo [wīde]f[e]rð wunian mōten
cestre and cynestōl.   Uton cȳþan þæt!
dēman wē on eorðan ǣrror lifigend!
300 Onlūcan mid listum locen Waldendes,
ongeotan gāstlice: ūs ongēan cumað
þūsend engla, gif þider mōton,
and þæt on eorðan ǣr gewyrcað.
Forþon sē bið ēadig se ðe ǣfre wile
305 mān oferhycgen, Meotode cwēman,
synne ādwǣscan; swā hē sylfa cwæð:
'Sōðfæste men, sunnan gelīce,
fǣgre gefrætewod, in heora Fæder rīce
scīnað in sceldbyrig.' Þǣr Sceppend seolf
310 hēo befæðmeð, Fæder mancynnes,
āhefeð holdlice in heofones lēoht,
þǣr hēo mid Wuldorcyninge wunian mōton,
314 āgan drēama drēam mid Drihtne Gode,
315 āwa tō aldre, ā būton ende.

[VII]

Ēalā hwæt se āwyrgda wrāðe geþōhte
þæt hē Heofencyninge hēran ne wolde,
Fæder frēfergendum. Flōr āttre wēol,

---

297 *MS., Edd. except G.*¹ æfre forð; *G.*¹, *Gz.* wideferð.—299 *Gz.*
ær; *MS., Edd.* lifigendon /; *K.* lifigend / onlucan.—300 *G.*¹ onlucan.—
302 *G.*¹, *W.* gif we.—305 *G.*¹ oferhycgan.—309ᵃ *Gz.* sceldbyrg.—309ᵇ
MS., Edd. þær heo; *H.*² *omits* heo; *J., T., B.*¹ sceppend / seolf.—310
*G.*¹ *n., Wnrs.* friðe befæðmeð (?); *H.*² heo befæðmeð; *nes of*
mancynnes *written above line.*—312 *S.*² (*12. 476*), *H.*² wuldorcyning;
Gz. wuldrc-.—313 *MS., J.* awa to aldre agan dreama dream mid
drihtne gode a to worulde; *Edd. as in MS. with the following exceptions:* *T. gap of a hemistich after* aldre; *B.*¹ aldre unswiciende; *G.*¹
agan sceolon /; *W.* agan . . . /; *H.*¹ agan æfre, fægre, *or* wynne;
Gz. as in text.—315 *Rieger* (*Zs. f. D. Ph. 7. 18*), *H.*² buton ende
forð; *MS.* n *of* ende *expanded to width of 2 letters.*—316 *Space left
for capital;* e *written at left edge of page.*

     hāt under hæftum; hrēo[p]an dēofla,
320 wīde geond windsele wēa cwānedon,
     mān and morður: wæs ðǣr[e] menego þǣr
     swylce onǣled; wæs þæt eall full strong.
     Þonne wæs heora aldor, þe ðǣr ǣrest cōm
     forð on fēþan, fǣste gebunden
325 fȳre and līge; þæt wæs fǣstlic þrēat.
     Ēc sceoldon his þegnas þǣr gewunian
     atolan ēðles, nalles ūp þanon
     gehēran in heofonum hāligne drēam,
     þǣr hēo oft fǣgerne folgað hæfdon
330 uppe mid englum. Wǣron þā alles þæs,
     gōda, lēase; ah nymþe gryndes [ād]
     wunian [ne] mōten and þone wērigan sele,
     þǣr is wōm and wōp wīde gehēred,
     and gristbitung[c] and gnornung[c] mecga.
335 Nabbað [h]ē tō hyhte nymþe [hāt] and cyle,
     wēan and wītu and wyrma þrēat,
     dracan and nǣddran, and þone dimman hām.
     Forðon mihte gehēran sē ðe æt hylle wæs
     twelf mīlum nēh þæt ðǣr wæs tōða gehēaw,

---

319 *MS., J., T., B.*[1], *G.*[1] hreowan; *G.*[3], *W., K.* hreopan; *G.*[1] deoflu.—320[a] *Scribe adds* d *of* windsele *above; J.* winsele.—320[b] *T., B.*[1], *G.*[1], *W.* wea-cwanedon; *H.*[2] wea cw-; *K.* wean.—321 *MS.* ðær; *T. n.:* ðær *apparently error for* seo; *B.*[1] seo; *G.*[1], *W., K.* ðære.—322[a] *G.*[1], *W.* swyðe.—322[b] *B.*[2] æled *for* eall.—324 *J. prints* fætse, *but corrects in Errata.*—325 *G.*[1] *n.* þrea (?), þræd (?).—326[a] *Gs., Wnrs.* sceoldon ec; *B. translates* ec '*ewig.*'—331 *MS., J.* leas; *C., other Edd.* lease; *B.*[2] (*p. CCXXXIV*) *thinks* goda *stands for* godan. —331[b] *MS.* ah nymþe gryndes; *C. underlines (cancels?)* ah; *K. omits; G.*[1] gryndes bealu; *W. n.* grynde *or* grundas *possible; K.* grundas an.—332 *T., B.*[1], *G.*[1], *W.* ne moten.—334 *MS., J., T., B.*[1], *G.*[1], *W., Gz.* gristbitunge and gnornunge; *H.*[2] gristbitung and gnornung; *Gz. omits first* and *and* mecga; *Cs. as in text; T. n.: several ll. wanting after* mecga.—335[a] *MS., J., T., B.*[1] we; *B.*[2], *G.*[1], *W.* hie *for* we.—335[b] *MS., J., T., B.*[1], *G.*[1], *W.* cycle and fyr; *Gz.* hat and cald; *em. Cs.*—336 þreat *begins p.* 221.

340   lūde and gēomre.   Godes andsacan
      hweorfan geond helle   hāte onǣled
      ufan and ūtan   (him wæs ǣghwǣr wā),
      wītum wērige,   wuldres bescyrede,
      drēamum bedǣlde.   Hēofon dēop gehygd,
345   þā hēo on heofonum   hām staðelodon,
      þæt hīe woldon benǣman   nergendne Crīst
      rodera rīces.   Ah hē on riht gehēold
      hīred heofona   and þæt hālige seld.
         Nis nǣnig swā snotor   nē swā cræftig
350   nē þæs swā glēaw   nymþe God seolfa
      þæt āsecgan mǣge   swegles lēoman,
      hū [scīma] þǣr   scīneð ymbūtan
      Meotodes mihte   geond þæt mǣre cynn
      (þǣr habbað englas   ēadigne drēam,
355   sanctas singað) : þæt is se seolfa God.
      Þonne bēoð þā ēadigan   þe of eorðan cumað,
      bringað tō bearme   blōstman stences,
      wyrta wynsume,   þæt synd word Godes.
      Þonne hīe befæðmeð   Fæder mancynnes,
360   and hīe gesegnað   mid his swiðran hond;
      lǣdað tō līhte,   þǣr hī līf āgon
      ā tō aldre,   ūplicne hām,
      byrhtne burhstyde.   Blǣd bið ǣghwǣm

340 *C., Edd.* hlude; *H. (Eng. Stud. 37. 205; see Rieger, Zs. f. D. Ph. 7. 29)* geomre and hlude.—341 *J.* hweorfon.—346 *J.* nergende.— 349ᵃ *Gz. (Metrik)* nis nan.—349ᵇ *G.¹* sundorcræftig; *H.¹, Gz.* searo-cræftig.—350 *Gz.* gleaw and wis.—352 *MS., J., T., B.¹* hu sunnu; *T. n.: error for* sunne; *G.¹* hu scir sunnu; *W.* hu . . . sunnu; *H.¹, Gz.* scima *for* sunnu; *Cs.* hu scir sunna (*or* sunu?).—355 *MS.* se *erased before* seolfa; *MS., J., T., B.¹, G.¹, W.* seolfa for god; *H.²: omit* for (?); *H. (Eng. Stud. 51. 181)* for seolfan gode.—356 *T. n.: consider-able hiatus after* cumað.—357 *G.³* stencas (?).—358 *Scribe makes* a *of* wyrta *from* e; *Edd.* wyrte.—361 *C. alters to* lædæð; *T., W.* lædæð; *G.¹* lædeð.—363ᵃ *C., T., B.¹, G.¹* beorhtne, -stede.

þǣm ðe Hǣlende hēran þenceð,
365 and wel is þām ðe þæt [wyrcan] mōt.

[VIII]

Wæs þæt encgelcyn ǣr genemned
Lūcifer hāten, 'Lēohtberende,'
on gēardagum in Godes rīce.
Þā hē in wuldre wrōht onstalde,
370 þæt hē oferhȳda āgan wolde. 5
[Þā] Sātānus swearte geþōhte
þæt hē wolde on heofonum hēhseld wyrcan
uppe mid þām Ēcan. (Þæt wæs ealdor heora,
yfeles ordfruma.) Him þæt eft gehrēaw
375 þā hē tō helle hnīgan sceolde, 10
and his hīred mid hine [in] īn[ð]o geglīdan,
Nergendes nīð; and nō seoððan
þæt hī mōsten in þone ēcan andwlitan [sēon]
būton ende.
Þā him egsa becōm,
380 dyne for Dēman, þā hē duru in helle 15
bræc and bēgde. Blis wearð monnum

---

364 C. hyran.—365 MS., Edd. ðe þæt mot; D. wyrcan mot (?);
H.² mot fon; Gz. omits 365.—366 W. before 366 prints the title:
*Christi Höllenfahrt, Auferstehung, Himmelfahrt, und Kommen zum
Jüngsten Gericht; T. n.: gap after genemned.—369 C., T., B.¹, E.,
G.¹ add e to wroht; C. onstealde.—370 Cs. for oferhyde agan (or
eawan or æfnan?) wolde.—371ᵃ MS., J., T., B.¹, E., G.¹, W. omit þa;
H.¹ Satanus seolf; Gz. þær Satanus; Br. þa, þæt, or se Satanus.—
371ᵇ T. gesohte; B.¹ gesohte—wolde /; E. sw. searwum geþohte.—
373 E. wið.—374 MS. ordfruman; Edd. ordfruma.—376ᵇ MS. into
geglidan; E. in to henðo; G.¹, W. in to g.; Gz. (Metrik) heonon to
g.; Cs. him to gesiðum; K. in hatunge geglidan; H. (Anglia Bb.
30. 4) in hete geglidan or glidan.—377ᵃ Cs. in þæt nearwe nið.—377ᵇ
D. wæs siððan.—378 T. n.: andwlitan error for onwlitan; E. andwlitan sceawian; H.² andwlitan seon; Gz. (Metrik) eagum wlitan;
Br. transposes thus: andwlitan mosten.—379 E., G.¹, Cs. a buton.—
380 Gz. omits in.

þā hī Hǣlendes   hēafod gesāwon.

Þonne wæs þām atolan   þe wē ǣr nemdon

· · ·

385   þā wǣron mid egsan   ealle āfyrhte,   20
wīde geond windsele   wordum mǣndon:
'Þis is stronglic   nū þes storm becōm,
Þegen mid þrēate,   Þēoden engla.
Him beforan fēreð   fǣgere lēoht
390   þonne wē ǣfre ǣr   ēagum gesāwon,   25
būton þā wē mid englum   uppe wǣron.
Wile nū ūre wītu   þurh his wuldres cræft
eall tōweorpan.   Nū ðes egsa cōm,
dyne for Drihtne,   sceal þes drēorga hēap
395   ungēara nū   atol þrōwian.   30
Hit is se seolfa   Sunu Waldendes,
engla Drihten.   Wile uppe heonan
sāwla lǣdan,   and wē seoððan ā
þæs [he]reweorces   hēnðo geþoliað.'
400   Hwearf þā tō helle   hæleða bearnum,   35
Meotod þurh mihte;   wolde manna rīm,
fela þūsenda,   forð gelǣdan
ūp tō ēðle.   Þā cōm engla swēg,
dyne on dægrēd: hæfde Drihten seolf
405   fēond oferfohten.   Wæs sēo fǣhðe þā gȳt   40
open on ūhtan,   þā se egsa becōm.

---

382 gesawon *begins p.* 222; *J.* he.—383 *T. n.: gap of several ll.
after* 383; *B.*¹, *W. gap of one line; E. supplies as* 384 fagum folce
forht geworden; *G.*¹ fagum folce ferhð geaclod.—385 *Gz. (Metrik),
Wnrs.* wæron þa.—386 *MS., J.* winsele; *C., other Edd.* windsele.—
387ᵃ *E.* stronglic strið.—387ᵇ *B.*² styrne *for* storm.—389 *MS., J., W.*
fæger; *C., T., B.*¹ *add* e *to* fæger; *E., G.*¹, *S.*², *H.*², *Gz.* fægerre.—
397 *G.*¹, *Gz.* up. —399ᵃ *MS., J., T., E., G.*¹, *W., H.*² yrreweorces; *B.*¹
yrre weorces; *Gz.* herweorces; *Clark Hall* yrreðweorh.—399ᵇ *E. n.*
earfoðu *for* henðo; *H.*² ermðo *for* henðo.—400 *Scribe adds* to *above
line.*

Lēt þā ūp faran ēadige sāwle,
Ādāmes cyn.

And ne mōste Ēfe þā gȳt
wlītan in wuldre ǣr hēo wordum cwæð:
410 'Ic þē ǣne ābealh, ēce Drihten,   45
þā wit Ādām twā eaples þigdon
þurh nǣddran nīð, swā wit nā ne sceoldon.
Gelǣrde unc se atola, sē ðe ǣfre nū
beorneð on bendum, þæt wit blǣd āhton,
415 hāligne hām, heofon tō gewalde.   50
Þā wit ðæs āwærgdan wordum gelȳfdon;
nāmon mid handum on þām hālgan trēo
beorhte blǣda— unc þæs bitere forgeald
þā wit in þis hāte scræf hweorfan sceoldon,
420 and wintra rīm wunian seoððan,   55
þūsenda feolo, þearle onǣled.

'Nū ic þē hālsige, heofenrīces Weard,
for þān hīrede þe ðū hider lǣddest,
engla þrēatas, þæt ic ūp heonon
425 mǣge and mōte mid mīnre mǣgðe.   60
And ymb þrēo niht cōm þegen Hǣlendes
hām tō helle; is nū hæftum strong,
wītum wērig, swylce him Wuldorcyning
for onmǣdlan eorre geworden.

407[a] *T., B.[1], W.* upfaran; *G.[1] hyphenates.*—407[b] *C. (possibly scribe) alters* e *of* sawle *to* a; *E.* sawla.—408 efe *produced* (? *by C.*) *by altering* æfre; *T. n.: context requires* ac *for* and; *B.[1], E.* ac.—409[a] *T. n.:* wuldre *apparently error for* wulder; *B.[1]* wulder; *E., G.[1]* wuldor; *G.[3]* wuldre.—409[b] heo *formed by addition of* o *to* he (? *by C.; S.[1] thinks by scribe*).—412 *J.* nane; *Gz., Wnrs. omit* ne.—414 *E.* ahten.—415 *J., B.[1] misread* gewealde.—421 *H.[2]* onælde.—423 *E., G.[1]* þam.—425 *T. n.: considerable gap after* mægðe (*so B.[1]*); *E.* mægðe feran *followed by a gap; Gz.:* fare *for* mægðe *or gap.*—426 *G.[1] n.:* end (*zuvor*) *for* and (?).—427 *T. gap of 2 hemistichs after* helle.— 428 *Gz.* wuldrcyning.—429 *T., E. gap after* 429.

430   Segdest ūs tō sōðe þætte seolfa God   65
     wolde helwarum hām gelīhtan.
     Ārās þā ānra gehwylc, and wið earm gesæt,
     hleonade wið handa; þēah hylle gryre
     egeslic þūhte, wæron ealle þæs
435   fægen in firnum þæt [Frēo]drihten   70
     wolde him tō helpe helle gesēcan.'
     Rǣhte þā mid handum tō Heofencyninge,
     bæd M̄eotod miltse þurh Marian hād:
     'Hwæt! þū fram mīre dohtor, Drihten, onwōce
440   in middangeard mannum tō helpe.   75
     Nū is gesēne þæt ðū eart sylfa God,
     ēce Ordfruma ealra gesceafta.'

[IX]

     Lēt þā ūp faran ēce Drihten—
     wuldre hæfde wītes clomma
445   fēondum oðfæsted, and hēo furðor scēaf   80
     in þæt neowle genip, nearwe gebēged,
     þǣr nū Sātānus swearte þingað,
     earm āglǣca, and þā atolan mid him,
     wītum wērige. Nalles wuldres lēoht

---

430 *E.* hætte, *misprint for* þætte; *E. n.* sægde (?); *G.*[1] segde.—
431[a] *G.*[1] *n.* helwarena (?); 431[b] *B.*[2] gelifan.—432 sæt *begins p.* 223;
J. earmge-rec *(this misreading was due to wrinkle in the parchment).*
—433 *B.*[1] hyllegryre.—435[a] *T. gap of 2 hemistichs after* firnum; *E.,*
H.[2] fægene.—435[b] *MS., J., T., W.* þæt heora drihten; *E.* freadrihten;
B.[1], *H.*[2], *Gz.* freodrihten; *G.*[1] feora drihten.—436 *G.*[1] ham *for* helle;
E. gap after 436.—437 *MS.* rihte; *C. cancels* i, *writes* æ *above; Edd.*
ræhte; *B.*[2] hand.—439 *J., T.,, B.*[1], *E., G.*[1], *W.* minre; *E.* dehter.—
441 *A second* god *written and canceled.*—442[a] 7 *erased before* ece;
J. 7 ece.—442[b] *J., T., B.*[1], *E.* gescafta.—443 *J., T., B.*[1], *E., W.*
upfaran.—444[a] *È. n.* wuldor (?); *B.*[2] wuldre hæftas; *G.*[1] werud to
wuldre; *W.* . . . wuldre.—444[b] *T. n.:* clomma *apparently error for*
clommas; *B.*[1], *E., G.*[1], *W.* clommas; *G.*[3] clomma; *S.*[2] *(p. 514), Gz.*
hæfde wites clom; *Hofer (Dat. u. Instrum., p. 22)* clom mā.—445
B.[2] on fæstede.—447 *E.* swearta.

450 habban mōton, ah in helle grund;   85
     nē hī edcerres æfre mōton wēnan.
     Seoððan him wæs Drihten wrāð geworden, sealde
         him wītes clom,
454 atol tō æhte and egsan gryre,
455 dim[n]e and deorcne dēaðes scuwan,   90
     hātne helle grund, insīðgryre.
         Þæt, lā! wæs fæger þæt se fēða cōm
     ūp tō earde, and se Eca mid him,
     Meotod mancynnes, in þā mǣran burh.
460 Hōfon hine mid him handum hālige   95
     wītigan ūp tō ēðle, Abrahames cynn.
     Hæfde þā Drihten seolf dēað oferwunnen,
     fēond geflēmed; þæt in fyrndagum
     wītegan sǣdon þæt hē *swā*, lā, wolde.
465 Þis wæs on ūhtan eall geworden,   100
     ǣr dægrēde, þæt se dyne becōm,
     hlūd of heofonum, þā hē helle duru
     forbræc and forbēgde; bān weornodon

---

450 *T., E. gap of one l. after* grund; *B.*[1] grund . . . ; *E.* grunde.—
451 *E.* moton æfre; *D., H.*[2] *omit* wenan; *Gz. (Metrik) omits* hi *and*
wenan.—452 *MS., Edd.* drihten god; *T. gap of a hemistich after* god;
Edd. print seoððan—clom *as 2 ll.; B.*[1] god * * (*W* . . . .) ; *E.* drihten
god dugeða aldor; *D.* wenan seoððan; *G.*[1] d. g. deofla cynne; *H.*[2]
domes (*or* dreames) wenan (*as* 452ª); *E.* clommas.—454 *MS., Edd.*
atole; *G.*[2] atolne (?).—455ª *MS., J., T.* dimme; *T. n.: apparently
error for* dimne; *B.*[1], *E., G.*[1], *W.* dimne.—455ᵇ *Trautmann in Wnrs.*
sceadwa *for* scuwan.—456ª *B.*[1] hellegrund.—456ᵇ *T., B.*[1] hinsið gryre;
E. hinsiðes; *G.*[1], *W.* hinsīðgryre.—457ª *G.*[1] þæt wæs la.—457ᵇ *T. n.:*
þæt *seems to be an error for* þa.—460ª *E., H.*[2], *Gz., Wnrs. omit* him;
E., G.[1] halige witigan /; *B.*[2] on handum.—463ª 4 *or more letters
erased after* feond; ge *of* geflemed *added in margin.*—464 *MS.* sawla;
T. gap of one l. after wolde; *B.*[1] wolde . . . ; *E. adds a line:* fram
helle grundum ham gelædan; *B.*[2] swa *for* sawla; *G.*[1], *W.* swa la;
Ziegler (Poetische Sprachgebr., p. 160) would add: fela þusenda
forð gelædan (*cf.* 402), *or* helle hæftas ham gelædan; *Gz.* wolde
swa.—467 *B.*[1] helleduru.—468 *T. n.: perhaps* bendas; *G.*[1] banan.

þā hīe swā lēohtne   lēoman gesāwon.

470   Gesæt þā mid þǣre fyrde Frumbearn Godes; 105
sǣde sōðcwidum: 'Snotre gāstas,
ic ēow þurh mīne mihte geworhte,
Ādām ǣrest and þæt æðele wīf.
(Þā hīe begēton on Godes willan

475   fēowertig bearna, þæt forð þonon   110
[on] middangeard menio onwōcon;
and wintra feola wunian mōston
eorlas on ēðle, oððæt eft gelamp

479   þæt hē āfyr[d]e fēond in firenum—   fāh is
ǣghwǣr.)

481   'Ic on neorxnawonge nīwe āsette   116
trēow mid telgum, þæt ðā tānas ūp
æpla bǣron; and git ǣton þā
beorhtan blǣda, swā inc se balewa hēt,

485   handþegen helle. Hæfdon forþon hātne grund, 120
þæs git ofer[h]ygdon Hǣlendes word:
ǣten þā egsan. Wæs se atola beforan,
sē inc bām forgeaf balewe geþōhtas.

'Þā mē gerēaw þæt mīn handgeweorc

476ᵃ *A later hand has added* e *to* middangeard; *T. n.: error for*
middangearde; *B*.¹ geond midd-; *E.* on middangearde; *G*.¹, *Klaeber*
(Later Genesis) on middangeard; *W.*, *Gz.* middangearde.—476ᵇ *MS.*,
J., *T.*, *G*.¹ onweocon; *the MS. has a dot under* e *of* onweocon (? *by*
scribe); *E.*, *W.* onwocon.—478 *T. gap of 3 hemistichs after* gelamp.
—479 *MS.*, *J.*, *T.* afyrhte eft; *B.* * * * þæt—eft /; *E. gap of a*
hemistich after eft; *E. n.* þæt hie afyrrode eft se feorh-sceaða; *B.*²
afirrde eft; *D.* afyrde est; *G*.¹ þæt þe (*G*.³ þæt he) afyrde freo-
drihtnes est; *W.* afyrde . . . est; *Klaeber (JEGP. 12. 257)* afyrde
foldbuendum.—480 *Edd.* feond—æghwær.—481 *Gz.*, *Wnrs.* -wong.—
483 æpla *begins p.* 224; *MS.* bæron 7 *blurred;* *G*.¹ æplas—þa/.—484
G.¹ þa beorhtan.—486 *MS.*, *J.*, *T.*, *W.* ofergymdon; *T. n.*, *Klaeber*
(Later Gen.) oferhygdon; *B*.¹, *E.*, *G*.¹, *Gz.* oferhyrdon.—488 inc
blurred.—489ᵃ *D.*, *G*.¹ gehreaw; *E.* hearde gereaw; *Gz.* hearde *or* æt
heortan gehreaw.—489ᵇ g *of* handgeweorc *either erased or blurred;*
T. gap of a hemistich after -weorc; *B*.¹ handweorc * *.

490 [þæs] carcernes clom ðrōwade.   125
Næs ðā monna gemet,   nē mægen engla,
nē wītegena weorc,   nē wera snytero,
þæt ēow mihte helpan,   nimðe Hǣlend God,
sē þæt wīte ǣr   tō wrece gesette.
495 Fērde tō foldan   þurh fǣmnan hād   130
ufan from ēðle,   and on eorþan gebād
tintregan fela   and tēonan micelne.
Mē seredon ymb   secgas monige
dæges and nihtes,   hū hēo mē dēaðes cwealm,
500 rīces [rǣd]boran,   hrefnan mihten.   135
Þā wæs þæs mǣles   mearc āgangen
þæt on worulde wæs   wintra gerīmes
þrēo and þrītig gēara   ǣr ic þrōwode.
Gemunde ic ðæs mænego   [on] þā[m] minnan hām
505 lange þæs ðe ic of hæftum   hām gelǣdde   140
ūp tō earde,   þæt hēo āgan [sceolon]
Drihtnes dōmas   and duguðe þrym;

490 *MS. om.* þæs; *T., B.*[1] *print* 490 *as one hemistich (omitting* þæs), *with gap of a hemistich thereafter; E.* þæs carcernes clommas; *G.*[1], *W. leave no gap; S.*[2] *(p. 514): a weak syllable to be supplied in* 490ᵃ *or a stressed syllable in* 490ᵇ *(i. e., before* ðrowade*); H.*[1] cwealm ðrowade; *Cs.* cealdan *or* cealdne *or* þises clom; *em. Gz.*—491 *E. n.* gemot (?).—492ᵃ *G.*[1] witgena word.—492ᵇ *J., E.* snytro.—494 *Gz.* sette.—497 *MS., J.* tintregan and fela; *T., B.*[1], *E., G.*[1], *W. as in text; S.*[2] *(p. 514)* tintregan fela ond fela teonan; *H.*[2] tintregan micelne and teona fela; *Gz. omits* and *(order as in MS.); Br.* tintregan and teonan micelne (??).—500ᵃ *MS., J., T., B.*[1], *E., G.*[1], *W.* rices horan; *D.* rice ræsboran (?); *S.*[2] *(p. 454), H.*[2], *Gz.* rædboran.—500ᵇ *E., Gz.* ræfnan; *D.* refnan; *G.*[1] arefnan; *H.*[2] refnan leten.—502 *Cs.* þæt ic.—503 þreo *blurred; Gz., Cs. omit* geara.—504ᵃ *G.*[1] þas; *G.*[2] þæs.—504ᵇ *MS.* 7 þa minan ham; *C.* minnan; *J., T., B.*[1], *G.*[1], *W.* and þa mīnan ham lange /; *T. n.:* lange *possibly error for* lædde; *E.* þa munan ham lange /; *D. understands* þæt *after MS.* þa; *G.*[1] *n.: perhaps* ham *should be canceled; H.*[2] þæt mæl lange; *Gz.* in þam minnan ham (*omits* lange).—505 *E.* hie ham; *H.*[2] heo of.—506 earde *blurred; E.* agan þær; *G.*[1] agan moton; *W.* agan . . .; *H.*[1], *Gz., Wnrs.* agan sculon.

wuniað in wynnum,   habbað wuldres blǣd
þūsendmǣlum.   Ic ēow þingade,
510 þā mē on bēame   beornas sticedon,   145
gārum on galg[an].   Hēow se giunga þǣr,
and ic eft ūp becōm,   ēce drēamas
tō hāligum Drihtne.   . . . . . .

[X]

Swā wuldres Weard   wordum sǣde,
515 Meotod moncynnes,   on morgen ǣr,   150
þæs þe Drihten God   of dēaðe ārās.
Nǣs nān þæs stronglic   stān gefæstnod,
þēah hē wǣre mid īrne   eall ymbfangen,
þæt mihte þām miclan   mægne wiðhabban,
520 ah hē ūt ēode,   engla Drihten,   155
on þǣm fæstenne.   And gefatiàn hēt
englas eallbeorhte   andleofan gingran;
and hūru secgan hēt   Sīmon Pētre
þæt hē mōste in Galilēam   God scēawian,
525 ēcne and trumne,   swā hē ǣr dyde.   160
Þā ic gongan gefregn   gingran ætsomne

508 *J., T., B.*¹ wuldrǣs; *E.* wunjað nu in.—511 *MS., Edd.* galgum;
C. gealgum.—512 *E.* becom to eðle minum /; *B.*¹ upbecom /; *H.*² ece
on dreamas (?).—513 *B.*¹, *E.* ece—drihtne /; *G.*¹ drihtne in heofonrice /; *W.* drihtne . . .; *Gz.* to. . . . haligum drihtne.—514 *Capital
omitted; s in margin.*—515 *MS., Edd.* ær on morgen; *em. H. (Eng.
Stud. 37. 205).*—516 *Scribe adds* þe *above line.*—517ᵃ *G.*¹ na; *G.*³ nan.—
517ᵇ *MS., J., T., B.*¹ satan; *G.*¹, *W.* stan.—518 *J.* þea.—520 *C. cancels
h of* ah, *adds* c *above; Edd. except J.* ac; *B.*¹ uteode.—521ᵃ on
*blurred; D., G.*¹, *W.* of *for* on.—521ᵇ *C. alters to* gefætian; *J., T.,
B.*¹, *G.*¹, *W.* gefætian; *D.* gefetian.—522 *T., B.*¹ -beorhte * * */; *MS.*
gingran winum (gingran *blurred*); *so J.; D.* and eowan (*or* æteowan)
gingran sinum; *G.*¹ ændleofan gingran sinum; *G.*² andleofan; *W.*
andleofan g. sinum; *H.*³, *Gz., Cs. omit* winum; *T.* and leofan gingran
winum . . . . . .; *B.*¹ and leofan g. winum georne /.—524 moste in
blurred.—525 *J.* trumme.—526 dyde þa ic go *much blurred; J.*
gefrægn.

ealle tō Galilēam; hæfdon gāstes blēd,
...... hāligne Godes Sunu
swā hēo gesēgon, hwǣr Sunu Meotodes
530 þā on upp [ge]stōd, ēce Drihten, 165
God in Galilēam. Tō ðæs gingran þider
ealle urnon, þǣr se Ēca wæs.
Fēollon on foldan, tō fōtum hnigon;
þanceden Þēodne þæt hit þus gelomp
535 þæt hī scēawodon Scyppend engla. 170
Þā sōna spræc Sīmon Pētrus:
'Eart þū þis, Drihten, dōme gewurðad?
Wē ðē gesāwon æt sumum cyrre:
þec gelegdon on lāðne bend
540 hǣþene mid hondum; him þæt gehrēowan mæg, 175
þonne hēo endestæf eft gescēawiað.'
Sume hīe ne mihton mōd oncnāwan
þæt wæs se Dēora —Didimus wæs hāten—
ǣr hē mid hondum Hǣlend genōm
545 sylfne be sīdan, þǣr hē his swāt forlēt 180
(fēollon tō foldan fulwihtes bæðe).
Fǣger wæs þæt ongin, þæt Frēodrihten

---

527 *J.* blæd.—528 *T., B.*¹, *W. gap of a hemistich before* haligne;
*G.*¹ ongeton haligne—sunu /.—530 *MS., J., T., B.*¹, *W.* þa gingran on
upp stod; gıngran *begins p.* 225; *G.*¹, *H.*¹, *Gz.* omit þa gingran; *H.*¹
cwic on upp stod, *or* on upp gestod *(Gz. accepts latter); Cs.* þa up
astod *or* þær on upp astod.—531 ðæs *blurred; J.* omits to.—533 *Edd.*
and tu fotum, *the* 7 *ın MS., ıf ıt was ever there, is now wholly
unrecognizable, what looks like the lateral stroke at the top of the
symbol* 7 *was probably produced by the smearing of the metrical
point.*—534 *J., G*¹ þancedon; *MS.* ꝥ hit *canceled after* þæt hit.—
537 *J. misreads* gewurðað; *T.* þus *for* þis.—538 *A smear in the MS.
after* sum *probably obscures* ū (um) , *Edd.* sumum; *W. misprints*
gasawon.—539 c *of* þec *canceled; Gz.* hu *or* hwær þec; *Br. places
cæsura after* on *and reads* laðe *or* laðan benda.—540 *MS., J., T., B.*¹
hæðenne; *em. G.*¹—541 *Gz., Wnrs.* sceawiað.—542ᵃ *B.*¹, *G.*¹, *W.* sume
hit.—542ᵇ *T., B.*¹, *H.*² mode; *T. gap of 2 ll. after* oncnawan; *G.*¹ soð
oncnawan.—546 *G.*¹, *W.* feallan; *G.*¹, *W., Gz. (Metrik)* bæð.

geþrōwode, Þēoden ūre:
hē on bēame āstāh and his blōd āgēat,

550 God on galgan, þurh his gāstes mægen.   185
Forþon men sceolon mæla gehwylce
secgan Drihtne þanc dǣdum and weorcum,
þæs ðe hē ūs of hæftum hām gelǣdde
ūp tō ēðle, þǣr wē āgan [sceolon]

555 Drihtnes dōmas [and duguðe þrym],   190
and wē in wynnum wunian mōton. Ūs is wuldres lēoht
torht ontȳned, þām ðe teala þenceð.

[XI]

[Þ]ā wæs on eorðan ēce Drihten
folgad folcum fēowertig daga,

560 gecȳðed mancynne, ǣr hē in þā mǣran gesceaft, 195
burhlēoda Fruma, bringan wolde
hāligne gāst tō heofonrīce.
Āstāh ūp on heofonum engla Scyppend,
weoroda Waldend. Þā cōm wolcna swēg,

565 hālig of heofonum. Mid wæs hond Godes, 200
onfēng Frēodrihten, and hine forð lǣdde

---

550 *C.* gealgan.—552 ne *of* drihtne *blurred; D., G.*[1], *W.* wordum.—
554 *G.*[1] agan moton; *W.* agan . . .; *H.*[1], *Gz.* agan sculon.—555 *T.,*
S.[2] *(12. 477) gap of a hemistich after* domas; *B.*[1], *G.*[1], *W., H.*[1] *as in*
text.—556 *T. prints as 3 hemistichs; B.*[1], *G.*[1], *W. as in text; S.*[2] *(12.*
477) gap of a hemistich after wynnum, wunian—leoht *as separate*
line; Gz. reads 556 thus: wunian in wynnum us is wuldres leoht /.—
557 *The remaining 5/8 of p. 225 after* þenceð *contains an unfinished*
ornamental design. Space is left at the beginning of p. 226 for a
capital.—559 *MS., J., T., B.*[1], *G.*[1], *W.* feowertig daga folgad folcum;
G.[1] *n.: beide vershälften zu vertauschen? Gz. transposes; Cs. omits*
folgad, *reads* folcum gecyðed /; *K.* folcum gecyðed, / mancynnes
folgad.—560 *MS., J., T., B.*[1], *W.* mancynnes; *G.*[1], *H.*[2], *Gz.* mancynne;
Cs. meotod mancynnes.—563 *Gz.* halig scyppend; *Br.* up astah.—564
G.[1] *n.* wuldres sweg (?).—565 *Br.* hond godes wæs mid.—566 *B.*
forðlædde.

tō þām hālgan hām heofna Ealdor.
Him ymbflugon engla þrēatas
þūsendmǣlum.
     Þā hit þus gelomp,
570 þā gȳt nergende Crīst . . . . . . ,   205
þæt hē þæs ymb [tē]ne niht twelf apostolas
mid his Gāstes gife, gingran geswīðde.
Hæfde þā gesette sāwla unrīm
God lifigende. Þā wæs Iūdas of,
575 sē ðe ǣr on tīfre torhtne gesalde   210
Drihten Hǣlend; him sēo dǣd ne geþēah
þæs hē bebohte Bearn Wealdendes
on seolfres sinc; him þæt swearte forgeald
earm ǣglǣca innon helle.   [eres;
580 Siteð nū on þā swīðran hond Sunu his Fæd- 215
dǣleð dōgra gehwǣm Drihten weoroda
help and hǣlo hæleþa bearnum
geond middangeard. Þæt is monegum cūð
þæt hē āna is ealra gescefta
585 Wyrhta and Waldend þurh his wuldres cræft. 220
Siteð him on heofnum hālig Encgel,
Waldend mid wītegum. Hafað wuldres Bearn
his seolfes seld swegl bet[o]lden.
   Laðað ūs þider tō lēohte þurh his lǣcedōm,
590 þǣr wē mōton seolfe sittan mid Drihtne, 225
uppe mid englum, habban þæt ilce lēoht,

---

568 *G.*[1], *W.* ymb flugon.—570[b] *D.* cyðan het; *G.*[1] mid niðum
wunode; *H.*[1] mid niððum wæs; *Gz. reads* 570: þa gyt mid niððum
wæs, nergende Crist.—571[a] *MS., J., T., B.*[1], *G.*[1], *W.* ymb ane niht;
Br., Wnrs. ymb tyn niht þæs.—571[b] *H.*[2] endleofan.—573 *One letter
erased after* ge.—574 *T., B.*[1] of . . ./.—575 *T. n. suggests* tibre *but
withdraws it in Corrigenda.*—579 *G.*[1], *W.* inn on.—580 *Gz. omits*
hond.—584 *J. corrects in Errata his misreading* gesceafta.—586 *D.* h.
engla waldend; *G.*[1], *Gz.* þengel *for* encgel; *W.* encgla.—588 *MS.*
swegl betalden, t *canceled and erased* (? *by C.*); *C. adds* he *above;
J., G.*[1], *D.* sweglbefalden; *T., B.*[1], *W.* sweglbehealden.—589[a] *MS.*
leaðað, e *erased; Edd.* laðað.—589[b] *G.*[1] *omits* his; *G.*[2] *restores.*

þǣr his hīred nū   hālig eardað,
wunað in wynnum,   þǣr is wuldres blēd
torht ontȳned.   Uton [teala] hycgan
595   þæt wē Hǣlende   hēran georne,   230
Crīste cwēman.   Þǣr is cūðre līf
þonne wē on eorðan   mǣgen ǣfre gestrēonan.

[XII]

Hafað nū geþingod tō ūs   Þēoden mǣra,
ælmihtig God . . . . . .
600   on dōmdæge   Drihten seolfa;   235
hāteð hēhenglas   hlūddre stefne
bēman blāwan   ofer burga geseotu,
geond [þā fēower]   foldan scēatas.
Þonne of þisse moldan   men onwecnað;
605   dēade of dūste ārīsað   þurh Drihtnes miht.   240
Þæt bið daga lengust,   and di[nn]a mǣst
hlūd gehēred,   þonne Hǣlend cymeð,
Waldend mid wolcnum   in þās woruld fǣreð.
Wile þonne gescea[r]ian   wlitige and unclǣne
610   on twā healfe,   tile and yfle.   245

___

592 h *of* his *added above line.*—594 *T. gap of a hemistich after*
ontyned; uton—hælende = *one hemistich; B.*[1] torht ontyned gif we
teala þencað; *D., G.*[1] uton teala; *W.* uton . . . hycgan.—595 *B.*[1]
uton hycgan—georne /.—596 *G.*[1] þæt *for* þær.—598 *Capital* H *distinctly resembles ornamental capitals of first portion of MS. Junius
XI.*—599 *T.* (n.) *thinks leaf certainly cut out after* god; *B.*[1]
god***; *G.*[1] *supplies for* 599[b]: oðre siðe; *W.* god . . . . . . /.—
600 *A repetition of* on *begins p.* 227.—601[a] *One letter erased before*
heh-; *C.* heah-.—601[b] *G.*[1], *W.* hludre.—602 *C.* byman.—603 *B.*[1]
sceatas***; *G.*[1] geond feower; *W.* geond . . .; *H.*[1], *Gz. as in
text; Wnrs. thinks this reading not long enough.*—604 *C., T., B.*[1],
G.[1], *W.* onwecnað.—606 *MS., J.* dimma; *T. n.: clearly error for*
dinna; *B.*[1] dynna; *G.*[1], *W.* dinna.—607 *C., T., B.*[1], *G.*[1] gehyred.—609
MS., J., T., G.[3], *W.* gesceawian; *T. n.: error for* gesceadan; *B.*[1],
Gz. gesceadan; *G.*[1] gescearian.—610 *B.*[1] ifle.

Him þā sōðfæstan on þā swīðran hond
mid rodera Weard reste gestīgað.
Þonne bēoð blīðe þā in burh mōton
. . . gongan in Godes rīce.

615 And hēo gesēnað mid his swīðran hond   250
Cynincg alwihta, cleopað ofer ealle:
'Gē sind wilcuman; gāð in wuldres lēoht
tō heofona rīce, þǣr habbað gē
ā tō aldre ēce reste.'

620 Þonne stondað þā forhtan, þā ðe firnedon; 255
622 bēoð beofigende hwonne him Bearn Godes
dēman wille þurh his dǣda spēd.
Wēnað þæt hēo mōten tō þǣre mǣran byrig
625 ūp tō englum swā ōðre dydon.
Ac him bið reordende   260
ēce Drihten ofer ealle gecwæð:
'Āstīgað nū, āwyrgde, in þæt wītehūs
ofostum miclum; nū ic ēow ne con.'

630 Sōna æfter þǣm wordum wērige gāstas,
helle hæftas, hwyrftum scrīþað   265

---

613 *C., T., B.*[1] þa þe.—614 *C. alters to* gangan; *T.* rice * * *; *B.*[1]
rice gumena bearn; *D.* þa in burhweallas / moton gongan; *G.*[1] glæd-
mode gongan; *G.*[3] gegnum gongan; *W.* . . . gongan.—618ᵃ *Gz.*
heofonrice.—618ᵇ *MS., J., T., B.*[1], *G.*[1], *W.* þær ge habbað; *H.*[2] þær
ge habban sculon; *Gz. as in text; Cs.* þær ge habbað nu.—619 *C.*
alters to rẹste.—620ᵃ *MS., J., T., B.*[1], *G.*[1], *W.* forworhtan; *Gz.*
(Metrik): stondað *should perhaps be omitted; Gz. (Beiträge)* forhtan
(?).—620ᵇ *G.*[1] on þa winstran hond /. *G.*[1] *then reads as* 621: þa þe
firnedon on foldan æfre.—622 *MS. at first* þonne; *scribe alters* þ *to*
w, *adds* h *above.*—626 ah *altered to* ac (? *by C.*); *J.* ah; *MS.*
reodende(?)+ 2 *erased letters; C. makes* e (? a, u) *into* i *by erasure,*
erases n, *adds* en *above, and* r *above* o, *i. e.,* reordiende; *J.* reodiende;
T., B.[1], *G.*[1], *W.* reordiende; *T. n. suggests* rodera waldend *for* 626ᵇ;
B.[1], *G.*[1] *accept; T., W. gap of a hemistich after* reordiende; *Cs.*
reordende and reðe word /.—627 *C., T., B.*[1], *G.*[1] gecwyð.—629 *Edd.*
except W. ofestum.—630 *MS.* æf̃t.—631 *B.*[1] hellehæftas.

þūsendmǣlum, and þider leaðað
in þæt sceaðena scræf, scūfað tō grunde
in þæt nearwe nīð.   And nō seoððan
635 þæt hīe ūp þonan ǣfre mōton,
ah þǣr geþolian sceolon [þ]earlic wīte,   270
clom and carcern, and þone caldan grund
dēopne ādrēogan and dēofles spellunge:
hū hīe him on edwīt oft āsettað,
640 swarte sūslbonan, stǣleð [fēondas]
fǣhðe and firne, þǣr ðe hīe [Frēo]drihten,   275
ēcne Anwaldan, oft forgēaton,
þone þe hīe him tō hihte habban sceoldon.
    Uton, lā! geþencan geond þās worulde
645 þæt wē Hǣlende hēran onginnen;
georne þurh Godes gife gemunan gāstes blēd: 280
hū ēadige þǣr uppe sittað
selfe mid swegle sunu Hǣlendes.
    Þǣr is geat gylden gimmum gefrǣtewod,

---

632 he (*or possibly* þe; *J., W. think* hi, *S.*[1] *thinks* þe) *erased before* þider; *MS.* leaðað; *C. erases first* a, *alters* e *to* ę *and first* ð *to* d; *J.* hi þider leaðað; *T., B.*[1], *G.*[1], *W.* lædað.—634 *G.*[2] nīð; *GK.* niðer (?).—636 *MS., Edd. except G.*[1] earmlic; *em. G.*[1]—638 *S.*[2] (*p. 514), Gz.* spel.—639[a] *Br.* on him edwit (*or* edwit on him).—639[b] et of asettað *almost hidden by wrinkle in parchment.*—640[b]-642 *MS., J.* stǣleð fǣhðe and in firne þǣr ðe hie drihten; *T.* swarte—fǣhðe = *one hemistich, then* and in firne . . . . .; *B.*[1] fǣhðe / in firne . . ., þæs—drihten / ; *D.* fǣhðe in firnum / þæs ðe hie—forgeaton / ; *G.*[1] þonne Satanus stǣleð / fǣhðe in firene þæs þe hie freodrihten / ; *W.* . . . . stǣleð / fǣhðe in firne—drihten / ecne—forgeaton / ; *H.*[1] þonne Satan stǣleð / fǣhðe in firene; *H.*[2] Satan stǣleð / ; *Cs.* synna stǣleð / fǣhðe and firene þæs ðe hie freadrihten / ; *K. (Anglia 27. 229-233)* fǣhðe and firne.—643 *MS.* þonne; *scribe erases first* n, *adds* þe *above* ne; *J.* ðonne, *omits* þe; *T., B.*[1], *G.*[1] þone hie; *W.* þone þe.—644 *Gz.* woruld.—645 *C.* hyran.—648 *C.* sylfe; *MS., G.*[1], *W.* mid swegle torht sunu; *T., B.*[1] swegeltorht; *G.*[1] *n.:* swegeltorhtne (?), 'oder sunu *Nom. Plur.?'* Sprachschatz swegle; *H.*[2], *Gz., Wnrs.* swegltorht; *H. (Eng. Stud. 51. 181) omits* seolfe *and reads* mid swegeltorhtne.—649 ne *erased after* gylden; *J.* gyldenne.

650 wynnum bewunden,   þǣm þe in wuldres lēoht
    gongan mōten   tō Godes rīce.   285
    And ymb þā weallas   wlitige scīnað
    engla gāstas   and ēadige sāwla,
    þā ðe heonon fērað. . . . . . .
655 Þǣr martiras   Meotode cwēmað,
    and herigað hēhfæder   hālgum stefnum   290
    Cyning in cestre.   Cweþað ealle þus:
    'Þū eart hæleða Helm   and Heofendēma,
    engla Ordfruma,   and eorðan tūdor
660 [ūp gelǣddest]   tō þissum ēadigan hām.'
    Swā wuldres Weard   wordum herigað   295
    þegnas ymb Þēoden.   Þǣr is þrym micel,
    sang æt selde.   Is sylf Cyning,
    ealra Aldor,   in ðǣre ēcan gesceft.
665   Þæt is se Drihten,   sē ðe dēað for ūs
    geþrōwode,   Þēoden engla.
    Swylce hē fæste   fēowertig daga,
    Metod mancynnes,   þurh his mildsa spēd.
    Þā gewearð þone weregan,   þe ǣr āworpen wæs   5
670 of heofonum,   þæt hē in helle gedēaf,
    þā costode   Cyning alwihta.
    Brōhte him tō bearme   brāde stānas,
    bæd him for hungre   hlāfas wyrcan—
    'gif þū swā micle   mihte hæbbe.'   10

653 sawla *begins p. 228*; *T. gap of a hemistich after* sawla.—654 *B.*[1]
ferað heofonrice to; *G.*[1] ferað to heofonrice; *W. as in text.*—658-9
MS., J. -deman, -fruman (? n *of* -fruman *erased*); *other Edd. as in
text; T. gap of 3 hemistichs after* tudor; *Gz. (Metrik)* tudr.—660
B.[1] * * * to—ham / *(so W.); G.*[1] *as in text.*—664 *MS., J.* aðor; *C.
adds* e, l *above and changes* ð *to* d (*i. e., reads* ealdor); *other Edd.*
aldor.—665 *Before* 665 *W. sets the title: Versuchung Christi.*—667
J. dæga.—670 *Scribe adds* he *above line; S.*[2] (*p. 514*) heah of h.;
Gz. of heofonrice.—671 *G.*[1], *W.* þæt he costode.

675 Þā him andswarode ēce Drihten:
'Wēndest þū, āwyrgda, þæt āwriten nǣre

. . .

nymþe mē ænne,

. . .

'ac geseted hafast, sigores Āgend,
lifigendum līht, lēan būtan ende, 15
680 on heofenrīce, hālige drēamas.'

. . .

680A   Þā hē mid hondum genōm [hæleða Scyppend],
atol þurh edwīt, and on esle āhōf,
herm bealowes gāst, and on beorh āstāh;
āsette on dūne Drihten Hǣlend:
'Lōca nū ful wīde ofer londbēwende: 20
685 ic þē geselle [on] þīnes seo[l]fe[s] d[ō]m
folc and foldan; fōh hider tō mē
burh and breotone bold tō gewealde,
rodora rīces, gif þū sēo riht Cyning
engla and monna, swā ðū ǣr myntest.' 25
690   Þā him andswarode ēce Drihten:
'Gewīt þū, āwyrgda, in þæt wītescræf,
Sātānus seolf; þē is sūsl weotod

676 *T., W. long gap after* nǣre; *G.*[1] *gap of more than one hemistich*
(*B.*[1] *had assumed gap of only one hemistich before* nymþe).—677 *B.*[1],
G.[1], *W. take* nymþe me ænne *as* 677[b].—678 *G.*[1] hafað; *Trautmann in*
Wnrs. ac þu.—680 *B.*[1], *G.*[1], *W.* on—genom *as one line;* *S.*[2], *Gz. divide*
as in text, but leave no gap after dreamas; *G.*[1] *n.* þa hine (?); *Gz.*
proposes for 680A[b] halig scyppend.—681 *C., W., Wnrs.* ehsle.—682
MS., J. her; *C., G.*[1], *W.* herm; *G.*[1] *n.* bǣr *for* herm (?); *T., B.*[1]
hermbealowes; *Gz.* blac bealowes; *MS.* s *of* bealowes *added later*
(? *by scribe*).—684 *C. erases* e, *cancels* w *of* -bewende, *writes* u
above e; *T., B.*[1], *G.*[1], *W.* -buende; *S.*[2] (*p. 515*), *Gz., Wnrs.* -buend.—
685[b] *MS., J., T.* þines seoferdum; *Manning in Suppl. to Lye's*
Dictionar., B.[1] seolfes dom; *G.*[1], *W. as in text.*—686[b] *B.*[1] feoll niðer.—
687[a] *J.* breoton; *B.*[1] beorhtne; *B.*[2] beorhte.—687[b] *C., Edd. except J.*
to *before* gewealde.—688 *G.*[1], *W., Wms.* þæt *for* gif.—689 e *of* ǣr
almost hidden in wrinkle.

geara tōgegnes, nalles Godes rīce.
Ah ic þē hāte þurh þā hēhstan miht   30
695 þæt ðū hellwarum hyht ne ābēode ;
ah þū him secgan miht   sorga mǣste :
þæt ðū gemēttes Meotod alwihta,
Cyning moncynnes.   Cer ðē on bæcling !
Wite þū ēac, āwyrgda,   hū wīd and sīd   35
700 hel heo[r]odrēorig, and mid hondum āmet :
grīp wið þæs grundes ;   gang þonne swā
oððæt þū þone ymbhwyrft   alne cunne ;
and ǣrest āmet   ufan tō grunde,
and hū sīd sēo   se swarta eðm.   40
705 Wāst þū þonne þē geornor   þæt þū wið God wunne,
seoððan þū þonne hafast   handum āmetene
hū hēh and dēop   hell inneweard sēo,
grim græfhūs.   Gong ricene tō,
ǣr twā seondon   tīda āgongene,   45
710 þæt ðū merced hūs   āmeten hæbbe.'
Þā þām wērga wearð   wrece getenge.

---

693 *C., Edd. except J.* gearo.—698 *C.* cyr.—699ᵇ *T. n.:* sy *or* seo
seems to be wanting; D.: add sie *or* seo; *Cs.:* sie *lost (Sievers, note
on Cs.: if* sie *lost, it must have come after* hu) ; *H. (Eng. Stud. 51.
181)* hu wid sie.—700ᵃ *MS., J., T., B.¹, G.¹, W.* helheoðo; *B.²* heahðo
or hel seo *for* helheoðo; *G.¹ n.:* hel heorodreorig? *(accepted by Gz.
and H., Eng. Stud. 51. 181); Cs.* hel heaðodreorig; *Trautmann,
Bonner Beitr. 2. 149,* hel deop sig.—704 *MS., J., T., W.* sid se swarta
eðm seo; *T. n.:* and wid *probably omitted after* sid; *B.¹, Wms.* sid
and wid; *G.¹ n.* swoleðm seo; *G.¹ (Nachträgl. Verbesserungen)*
sweðm; *cf. MHG.* swadem (?) ; *Cs. as in text; H. (Eng. Stud. 51.
181)* hu sid seo se swarta eðel.—705 *Gz. (Metrik)* þon.—706 *Gz.*
seoððan þu þon handum.—707 *S.² (p. 515), Gz.* inne.—708 *T. considerable gap after* to; *B.¹* to . . .; *S.² (p. 515), Gz., Wms.* grimme.
—709 *MS., J., W.* seond; *C., T., B.¹, G.¹, H.², Gz.* seondon; *Cs.*
seon.—710 *Cs.* þæt þu þæt merce.—711 *Another scribe begins p. 299
with* þa; *MS., J.* werga; *C., other Edd.* werigan; *C. alters first* e *of*
wrece *to* a, *cancels second* e, *writes* v *above; Edd. except J.* wracu.

Sātān seolua ran and on sūsle gefēol,
713   earm æglēce. Hwīlum mid folmum mæt
715   wēan and wītu. Hwīlum se wonna lēg   50
       læhte wið þes lāþan. Hwīlum hē licgan geseah
       hæftas in hylle. Hwīlum rēam āstāg,
       ðonne hē on þone atolan ēagum gesāwun.
       Hæfdon gewunnon Godes andsacan
720   . . .   55
       blāc bealowes gāst þæt hē on botme stōd.
       Þā him þūhte þæt þanon wǣre
       tō helle duru hund þūsenda
       mīla gemearcodes: swā hine se Mihtiga hēt
725   þæt þurh s[ī]nne cræft sūsle āmǣte;   60
       ðā hē gemunde, þā hē on grunde stōd.
       Lōcade lēas wiht geond þæt lāðe scræf,
       atol mid ēgum, oððæt egsan gryre
729–730 dēofla mænego þonne ūp āstāg;   64–5
       wordum in wītum ongunnon þā wērigan gāstas
       reordian and cweðan:
       'Lā! þus bēo nū on yfele, noldæs ǣr teala.'

FINIT LIBER II. AMEN.

712 *MS.* ra; *C., Edd.* ran.—713 *C. alters to* æglęce; *J., T., B.*[1]
æglæce; *G.*[1] æglæca in to helle; *W.* æglæca; *G.*[1] *reads as* 714: feond
in fyrlocan. Hwilum—mæt /; *H.*[2] earmum *for* folmum.—715 e *of*
leg *from* æ *by erasure; J.* læg.—716 *G.*[1] þæs.—717 *C., Edd.* hream;
C., T., B.[1], *G.*[1] astah.—718 *MS.* Ðonne; *T., B.*[1], *G.*[1], *W., Wms.* hie
for he.—719 *G.*[1] gryre gewunnon; *W., H.*[2], *Wms.* gewunnon; *H.*[2]:
hæfdon gewunnen = 719[a]; *then a gap of 2 hemistichs;* godes andsacan = 720[b].—720 *G.*[1] *proposes* þonne him se atola andweard stod;
W. n.: gap of one line.—721 s *of* bealowes *by another hand* (? *C.*) ;
J. bealowe.—723 *MS., J., T., B.*[1] *place end-pause after* mila; *B.*[1]
helleduru.—724 *B.*[1] mihtige.—725 *MS., Edd.* synne; *G.*[2] sinne; *G.*[1]
susl.—726 *G.*[1] gaste gemunde; *H.*[1] gemde þæt; *H.*[2] gemde.—729[b] *T.*,
B.[1], *W. leave vacant, as also* 730[b]; *for Grein's restoration of* 729-732,
see note on 731[b]-732; *H.*[1] dreogan (*for Grein's* adreogan).—730 *B.*[1]
upastag.—731 *J., T., B.*[1], *G.*[2] inwitum; *MS., J.* þa on þa; *T., B.*[1], *G.*[1],
W. omit on þa; *MS.* werigan /; *T., B.*[1], *G.*[1], *W.* gastas /.—732[b] *T.*,
B.[1], *W. leave vacant.*

STRUCTURAL OUTLINE

NOTES

1-20. Other passages in OE. poetry treating the theme of the Creation will be found in *Cædmon's Hymn; Gen. A* 97-234; *Beow.* 90-8; *Rid.* 41; *Chr.* 224-235; *Gu.* 21-4; *Gloria* 14-26. The similarities of *Sat.* with Genesis I are only very general.

1. Þæt wearð underne . . . þæt . . . þā: 'It was revealed . . . that . . . when.' The expression *underne* involves litotes.

2a. It is improbable that *hī (him)*, which the Corrector has inserted after *Meotod,* and which has not been recorded by other editors, was in the original. However, it cannot be a mere trial of the pen. I take it to be a superfluous addition of the Corrector, though, as far as sense is concerned, it could stand; cf. similar reflexive datives in 82 and 118.

As to who is meant by *Meotod* see the note on 9-10.

2b. So *Gen.* 950ᵃ.

3. Cf. Prov. 30. 4. (all Biblical references are to the Vulgate): 'Quis suscitavit omnes terminos terræ?' Ps. 103. 5: 'Qui fundasti terram super stabilitatem suam' (*Ps.* 103. 6: 'Hē gefæstnude foldan staðelas'); *Jul.* 499: *folde gefæstnad.*

4. gesette sunnan and mōnan. Cf. Gen. I. 16; also *Beow.* 94; *Ps.* 73. 16. 2.

4ᵃ=13ᵃ.

5. See Gen. I. 9.

5b-8. This passage taken as as whole has puzzled commentators more than any other in the poem. The metre rules out Thorpe's and Bouterwek's pointing of 5-6, as represented by the former's translation: 'the stream without, the sea-water and clouds.' Cosijn (*PBB.* 21. 21) suspects the phrase *strēam ūt on sǣ,* and suggests *strēamas and utsǣ,* without being satisfied with it himself. I see nothing suspicious in the MS. reading. *Ūt on sǣ* or *garsecg(e)* occurs in *Met.* 19. 19; 16. 12; and *Ps.* 96. 1. Indeed, 'the flood out on the sea' seems not without poetical fitness.

6a. The *e* inserted in *wolcn* is clearly by the Corrector. The *n* is syllabic.

6b. For similar phrases cf. 13, 14, 392, 585, and *Ph.* 394.

7. The MS. reading of line 7 is perfectly clear. Grein in his note on the form *ybmlyt,* by interpreting the accent intended to distinguish the *y* of *ymb-,* and the check after the letter *t,* which marks the cæsura, as crosses for ð's, which they never could have represented, constructs the unexampled *ȳþmȳð* (translated 'flutenmasse'). This reading he seems to have abandoned immediately. Lye *(Diction-arium)* considers *ymblyt* equivalent to *ymbwlīt* (for *ymbwlīteð*), which is unacceptable, even if we take *dēopne* as a modifier of *strēam*, and disregard phonology; for such a reading would lay absurd emphasis on Christ's powers of vision, in view of the clear expression of these powers in the very next lines. Grein, after 1857, and all other scholars save Holthausen and Bright, read *ymblyt*. *Clēne* also is clear in the MS. The *cl* has been usually mistaken for, or emended to, *d*. From the side of palæography, a reasonably normal OE. *d* would not be so likely to be misread *cl* as a modern *d*, but possibly it was thus misread here.

I shall not attempt to weigh separately each reading and interpretation which has been suggested for line 7, but merely give the three general views which appear fairly satisfactory. First, there is the reading of the MS. substantially as it stands. This we may translate: 'The Creator in his might wholly embraces the deep expanse (i. e., the ocean which surrounds the world) and all the earth.' This is the view at the basis of the present text, and is that held with slight variations by Thorpe, Bouterwek[1], Ettmüller, Wülker, and Kennedy. No good derivation has been proposed for *ymblyt*, but it has been assumed to be about equivalent to *ymbhwyrft* (cf. *Rid.* 41. 7). There is a verb, *ymblīðan*, 'surround,' represented by *emblīð* in Wulfstan, *Hom.* 146. 24, to which *ymblyt* might conceivably be related. The generic meaning of the verb suits the substantive perfectly. The normal WS. form of a verbal abstract, parallel to *ymblīðan*, would be *ymblīðe* or *ymblide* (cf. *scride,* etc., Sievers, *Gram.* 263. 1). In Northumbrian this might have been *ymblīð* or *ymblid* (*Gram.* 263, n. 5). The final *t* might be due either to scribal error, or to the fact that phonological confusion among the letters *ð, d,* and *t* was not uncommon in Old English (see *Gram.* 357, n. 2). The *y* for *i* would be another instance of a LWS. characteristic which occurs four times in the manuscript of *Christ and Satan* (see *Gram.* 22). But if any one feels suspicious of *ymblyt*, he may, with Holthausen, substitute *ymbhwyrft* in the text. For *clēne* as an adverb, cf. 18, and the other instances given in the Grein-Köhler *Sprachschatz*. The chief difficulty with this reading is that it involves the alliteration *ymb-* : *ymb-*. Thorpe sought to avoid this by changing the second *ymb-* to *ūp-*. A repetition, due to scribal oversight, of such a syllable as *ymb* is not uncommon; hence the emendation is legitimate. However, it may be said in defense of *ymb-* : *ymb-* that we have here merely an extension of the identical vocalic alliteration which, though avoided, is by no means wholly missing in OE. prosody. It may have been employed in this case

with the conscious purpose of emphasizing the wide inclusiveness of
the Creator's grasp. Prefixes (though, I believe, always atonic and
non-alliterating ones) are often repeated in OE. lines, as for example
in 468, *forbræc and forbēgde*.

The second interpretation accepts the substantive *ymblyt* (or
ymbhwyrft), but changes *clēne* to some word with initial *d*, which
alliterates with *dēopne*. As expanded D-verses are at least avoided in
the second hemistich of the OE. long line, words like *derne* and *dēre*
should be considered metrically suspicious, not to mention their questionable aptness. Therefore the acc. fem. *dene (Sprachschatz: vallis,
convallis, . . . abyssi? oceani?)*, as a parallel to *ymblyt*, is the most
acceptable word. *Dene* is sometimes used to describe the abyss of
chaos or hell.

Bright (*MLN.* 18. 129) has proposed a third, very ingenious
exegesis. He reads lines 5-8 thus:

> stānas and eorðan; strēam ūt on sǣ,
> wæter and wolcen, ðurh his wundra miht,
> dēopne ymblȳhte. Dene ymbhaldeð
> Metod on mihtum and alne middangeard.

Ymblȳhte is a completion of the 'predication begun in *gesette*'; *dēopne*
qualifies *strēam*. Bright thinks that the poet in this passage is reciting
'the initial acts of the creation, . . . in non-Biblical order, to be
sure, yet in essential agreement with the account in which the dis-
pelling of the darkness from the "face of the deep," upon which
moved the "Spirit of God," and the dividing of "the waters from the
waters" (cf. *wæter and wolcen*), are of importance coördinate with
the establishment of "the earth, the sun, and the moon." ' *Strēam*,
then, 'represents the undivided waters, as shown by the apposition of
wæter and wolcen.' It may be objected that, though *strēam* alone
might be, the very concrete phrase, *strēam ūt on sǣ*, does not seem at
all suited to the idea of 'the undivided waters,' which existed before
any land had appeared from which the *strēam* could be *ūt*, and hence
could not be equated with *wæter and wolcen*. The latter form an
independent component of the object of *gesette*, paralleling the
coördinated *sunnan and mōnan, stānas and eorðan*. The poet has
expressed himself very awkwardly if he intended to convey a conception somewhat similar to Milton's lines in the apostrophe to Light,
Paradise Lost 3. 8-11:

> Before the Sun,
> Before the Heavens thou wert, and at the voice
> Of God, as with a Mantle, didst invest
> The rising world of waters dark and deep.

9-10. Cf. Job 38. 16; also Job 28. 11 : 'Profunda quoque fluviorum scrutatus est.'

I have accepted the emendation *geofene,* proposed by Grein, for three reasons. First, it gives a more suitable meaning to the phrase of 10ᵃ : 'He can see through the ocean, the very bottom of the deep.' Secondly, the alliteration makes it especially appropriate. Thirdly, *in heofene* is to be suspected because in the *Sprachschatz,* for the phrase, 'in heaven' (usually in the sense of the abode of God and the blessed), there are but three cases of *on (in) heofone,* whereas *on heofonum* is very frequent; it occurs six times in *Sat.* alone. In prose also, when *heofon* is unmodified by adjective or article, it is, judging from the quotations in Bosworth-Toller, practically always in the plural after *on.* The three cases of the singular in the poetry are all in *Gen. B,* which, being a translation from the Old Saxon, may well reflect the usage of that language in this phrase. Heyne's glossary to the *Heliand* gives more than fifteen cases of *himil* in the dat. sing., none in the plural.

The reservation of the explicit subject of all the transitive verbs in the first ten lines, to wit, *Godes āgen Bearn,* until the tenth line is a stylistic blemish (even though the poet may have intended this late designation of the subject to furnish a climax to his period), in view of the fact that the actions previously recounted are more often assigned to the first person of the Trinity. The original source of the conception of Christ as creator is, of course, to be found in such passages as John 1. 3, Col. 1. 16, and Rom. 11. 36. In these verses, however, the central idea is that of Christ's being a mediating agency. Yet it was only a slight extension of this idea to say that Christ *created* the visible universe, as is continually done by the Fathers: e. g., Ambrose, *Hexaem.* 1. 5 (Migne, *Patr. Lat.* 14. 131), says, 'Egregie itaque Apostolus et hoc loco [i. e., Col. 1. 16] Filium dixit auctorem omnium.' See also *Chr.* 239-240; *Rid.* 7. 1-2.

11-13. Cf. Ecclus. 1. 2: 'Arenam maris, et pluviæ guttas, et dies sæculi quis dinumeravit?' General similarities to 11-13 may also be found in Isa. 40. 12; Job 38. 16; 36. 27; 28. 26; cf. *Harrowing* 116; *Ps.* 146. 4. For genitives in -*as* see Sievers-Cook, *Grammar of Old English,* 237, n. 1.

There is some question about the pointing of 9-17. The scribe, who has been followed by Thorpe and Bouterwek, begins a new sentence with *seolua,* 13. Ettmüller and Kennedy place a semicolon after *gehwelcne,* and a period after *miht.* This gives a greatly improved stylistic effect. Grein and Wülker have an impossible arrangement, beginning a new sentence with *daga,* and merely putting a comma after *miht.* I have followed Ettmüller, though not without considerable hesitation, because the first pointing would bring out a rather striking parallel between Ecclus. 1. 2 and the present passage, in the idea of Christ's numbering *both* the raindrops and the days.

15. Cf. *Gloria* 22-3; *Gu.* 22-1.

16a. *Dæles* is undoubtedly acc. plur. of *dæl,* not a late spelling of *dalas.* It means 'regions,' 'parts,' as in Napier's *Old English Glosses (Analecta Oxoniensia)* 1. 1443, where we read: 'climatis, i. partis, dæles' (our word exactly, both in meaning and inflection). *Dæles* is metrically and grammatically preferable to *dæles* (for *dalas*). *Eorðan (worulde) dæles (-as)* occurs in *Ps.* 138. 5; *Beow.* 1732. See Sievers, *Gram.* 237, n. 3, for the inflection.

16-17a. There is little doubt that the poet is referring to the triple creation of earth, heaven, and sea, which we meet with so often both in the Bible and in the other OE. poems. See *Ex.* 20. 11; *Ps.* 145. 6; *Acts* 4. 24; 14. 14; *Rev.* 14. 7; and especially *Chr.* 967:

> sæs mid hyra fiscum,
> eorþan mid hire beorgum, and ūpheofon
> torhtne mid his tunglum;

and *Gen.* 99: 'God . . . wolde þæt him eorðe and ūproder and sīd wæter geseted wurde.' For the collocation of *eorðan* and *ūpheofon* cf. *An.* 797-8: 'hwā . . . tēode eorðan eallgrēne and ūpheofon;' *Ps.* 101. 22: 'geworhtest eorþan frætwe and ūpheofen.' Graz is justified in calling the lines as they stand in the MS. metrically correct. But that reading leaves us with *holme,* which cannot be masc. acc., because Bülbring, *Altenglisches Elementarbuch* 440, denies to the combination *lm* the faculty of forming a syllable or developing an auxiliary vowel. This rules out Bright's description of *holme* as 'merely a phonetic spelling of *holm.*' *Sūsel* and the fem. nom. *sāwle (Soul's Address* 5), which he adduces as similar developments, do not seem perfectly analogous to *holme.* I do, however, accept Bright's reading of the text as the correct one. The scribe may have been misled into reading as he did the *ond ūpheofonond hēanne* which may well have stood in his copy, by his previous mistake in *in heofene,* 10.

On *hēanne* see Sievers, *Gram.* 222, n. 2; 295, n. 1. Although the *a* above the line looks like the scribe's hand, I suspect that Anglian *hēnne* was the original form.

18a. Neither 'pure intelligence' (Thorpe) nor 'den reinen Urgedanke' (Bouterwek) as renderings of *orðonc clēne* appears possible, because they imply 'gemination simplified' in a position in which it is not likely to occur. *Clēne* should be construed as an adverb. Literally the passage means, 'Who is there that understands art (or invention) perfectly save eternal God?' The absence of the article before a somewhat uncommon word is against considering *orðonc* to stand for 'the Creation' or 'that mighty work' (Kennedy). Grein's 'Kunstgeschick' is better.

Attention should be called to the LWS. Corrector's glossing of *nymðe* by *būton*. The occurrence of six cases of *nymðe* in a poem of 733 lines is favorable to Anglian, and against Kentish provenience. See Jordan, *Eigentümlichkeiten des Anglischen Wortschatzes,* pp. 62-3 and pp. 47-8. Even Tupper can bring little against this criterion of dialect (cf. *PMLA.* 26. 260 and *JEGP.* 11. 86).

19 ff. *Geþēode* is another crux. One may render the lines either: 'Joys he apportioned (or distributed), prosperity, and tongues (i. e., peoples) : first Adam and that noble race;' or, with Kock *(Jubilee Jaunts and Jottings): '*Joys gave he and prosperity, and made first Adam, etc.;' or, from Bright's reading: 'Joys he gave to old and young *(geogoðe):* Adam [was] first and that noble race, etc.' Kock retains *geþēode,* assigning it the sense of 'accomplish,' i. e., 'make.' In *Chr.* 377 the word means 'do,' 'perform,' but I nowhere find evidence for Kock's extension of this to 'make,' 'create.' Thorpe's slight emendation of *geþēode* to *getēode* would give a more satisfactory verb. Graz objected to pointing the text in this way, because a new independent clause would have to be begun in the middle of a hemistich; and such a period would be rather awkward, since the asyndeton would leave *duguðe* isolated. If one is inclined to accept *geogoðe,* Bright's interpretation is convincing. A very slight confirmation of his view is the scribe's capitalization of *Ādām,* which might indicate that he considered it the first word of a new sentence. (The scribes in this MS. never use capitals merely to indicate proper names.) Williams *(Short Extracts from Old English Poetry,* p. 81) takes *geþēode* as the pret. sing. of *geþēon (geþȳwan),* 'impress,' 'imprint,' 'mark.' He compares *Rid.* 41. 91, but there *geþēon* has its radical meaning of 'repress,' 'restrain.' *Leechdoms* 1. 354. 9 has *geþȳwan,* meaning to press into a certain shape. But, on the whole, as the angels would have to be included in the object, and as they were not likely to be thought of as molded into shape as man was molded from clay, this interpretation seems questionable. Since the MS. reading makes sense, and gives a fair transition to the fall of the angels, which is the real purpose of the lines, I let it stand. The use of *geþēode* for 'people' is similar to that of Lat. *lingua;* see Du Cange.

Cf. Deut. 32. 8: 'Quando *dividebat* Altissimus gentes.' For the collocation of *drēamas* and *dugoðe,* cf. *Chr.* 1409, and especially, 'sē þās foldan gescēop, duguðe and drēamas,' Grein-Wülker 2. 280. 10-1.

See *Sat.* 581 for the conception of God as a dispenser of gifts to men.

Bright intended by his interpretation to free the poet from the charge of heresy in 'placing the creation of man before that of the angels.' (Groschopp, p. 252, n. 2, accused his 'restaurator' of this.) Bright contends justly that the phrasing of line 20 does not imply chronological priority. It may be added that there was agreement among neither Jewish nor Christian writers in regard to the date of the creation of angels, an event of which we are not explicitly informed in the Biblical accounts. See R. H. Charles' notes on the *Book of Jubilees* 2. 2-4. *Jubilees* assigns this creation to the first day. Epiphanius, *Hær.* 65. 4, Augustine, *Civ. Dei* 11. 9, and the Fathers in general, accept this view, including the angels in the word *cœlum*, Gen. 1. 1, and citing Job 38. 7 as evidence that the angels were spectators of the later works of creation. According to Charles, 'Talmudic Judaism held that the angels were created on the second or the fifth day. . . . Philo, *Leg. Allegor.* 1. 2, represents [their creation] . . . as accomplished on the seventh day,' thus later than that of man. Ungemach (*Die Quellen der Fünf Ersten Chester Plays,* p. 20) interprets the first Towneley Play as placing the creation and fall of angels on the fifth day, just before man is formed, but, though this is possibly true, it is a pure assumption; for the text of the play does not specifically record their creation. There is some doubt whether our poet could have heard of any such tradition as that of Philo, but at any rate he is guilty of no special absurdity or heresy in the line.

20. On the orders of angels *(cyn)*, see note to 366. For the phrasing cf. 473; also *Gu.* 579: 'þāra giefena, þe God gescōp englum ǣrest and eorðwarum.'

The evolution of the conception of the Devil is most thoroughly treated in Gustav Roskoff's *Geschichte des Teufels.* More general and popular is Paul Carus' *History of the Devil and the Idea of Evil.* C. Abbetmeyer's *Old English Poetical Motives derived from the Doctrine of Sin* has very useful chapters on 'The Fall of the Angels' and 'Satan, the Fallen Archangel.' Grimm's *Deutsche Mythologie* contains material pertinent to devils and hell, as depicted in this poem (see chapters 25 and 32).

The following Biblical and apocryphal passages have been held to refer to the fall of the angels: Gen. 6. 2 ff.; Isa. 14. 12-5; Ezek. 28. 1-19; Enoch 6-10; the Slavonic *Book of the Secrets of Enoch* 29. 4; Luke 10. 18; 2 Pet. 2. 4; Jude 6; Rev. 12. 3-4, 7-9. The accounts in the following OE. poems should be compared: *Gen.* 12-77, 246 ff.; *Jul.* 418-428; *El.* 759-771, 939-952; *An.* 1185-94, 1376-85; *Gu.*

529-656 *passim; Minds of Men* 57-66; *Prayers* 4. 54-7; *Sal.* 449-474; also Rask's *Grammar of the Anglo-Saxon Tongue,* pp. 194-5, for Ælfric's treatment, and Wulfstan, *Hom.* 8. 12 ff.; 145. 22. The most interesting passages for our purpose in patristic literature are Gregory the Great's *Hom. in Evang.* 2. 34 (*Patr. Lat.* 76. 1249; for further references to Gregory, see Lau, *Gregor der Grosse,* pp. 362-4) and Aldhelm's *De Virg.* 2446-2904 (ed. Ehwald, pp. 452-471).

22. Ðūhte him on mōde. We find similar expressions of self-deception on the part of Lucifer and his followers in 55, 59, 84; *Gen. B* 268, 276; *Gu.* 635.

22b. Cf. *Gu.* 548: 'hit ne meahte swā,' for the omission of the substantive verb.

23b. swegles brytan. See *Chr.* 281. Compare especially *Sat.* 124-5 with lines 23-4. Ziegler (*Der Poetische Sprachgebrauch in der sog. Cædmonschen Dichtungen,* p. 22) notes that *swegl* as an expression for 'heaven' occurs six times in Part I of *Sat.,* but is not found in the other two parts.

24b. See 125, 175; *Gu.* 637 ff.; *Gen.* 28. One cannot decide whether the Corrector meant to change *wise* into *wiorse, worse,* or *wors,* but 125 shows that *wirse* was what the scribe intended.

25. Cf. 276, 345; *Gen.* 1556; *Ps.* 106. 35.

26a. ān æfter ōðrum. Schücking (*Untersuchungen zur Bedeutungslehre der Angelsächsischen Dichtersprache,* p. 26, n.) thinks this refers to *hām,* so that the phrase would amount to, 'took up a new (altogether different) home after an old one.' He compares *Prayers* 4. 30: *līf æfter ōþrum gesēo and gesēce.* Without challenging his interpretation of *æfter ōþrum* in *Prayer* 4, I believe that both grammar and the use of similar phrases elsewhere are against his view of *Sat.* 26. We should expect *ān* to agree in case with the word to which it refers. Besides, there is evidence that some form of *ān æfter ōðrum* was as much a stereotyped formula for denoting the succession of a series of many members in OE. as 'one after another' is in Mod. E. Cf. *Sal.* 385: *ān æfter ānum;* and especially Ælfric, *Hom.* 2. 32. 7: 'Hī urnon ān æfter ānum; . . . ælc æfter ōðrum cȳdde mē þæt wundorlice Godes tācn.' The poetical image in the present passage is much more vivid as usually interpreted.

26b. Cf. 73, 129, 419, 633, 727; *Gu.* 534; *Jul.* 684; and Milton's 'Hell's deep-vaulted Den,' *P. R.* 1. 116. The OE. descriptions of hell are treated most thoroughly in Becker's *Mediæval Visions of Heaven and Hell,* pp. 49-69. The whole thesis is of value for the general subject. For the origins, see R. H. Charles' *Critical History of the Doctrine of a Future Life.* The Teutonic features are discussed and rather overemphasized in Deering's *The Anglosaxon Poets on the*

Judgment Day, pp. 48-60, and Ferrell's *Teutonic Antiquities in the Anglo-Saxon Genesis,* pp. 21-5. Bede's picture of hell in *De Die Judicii* 90-111 (printed by Crawford in *Anglia* 48. 99-100 in connection with *Genesis B*) contains most of the features which combine to form the setting of *Sat.* 1-365.

27-28. Cf. *Gu.* 643:

> þæt gē wærnysse
> brynewylm hæbben, nales blētsunga.

This conception of surging flame or liquid fire, derived probably from the 'stagnum ignis' of Rev. 19. 20, appears again in 30, 39. Cf. Milton's 'tossing of these fiery waves,' *P. L.* 1. 184.

For the phrasing of this passage, see 42, 449, 693; *Soul's Address* 104; *Gu.* 588.

27b-28a. Cf. *Rood* 79-80.

See the other cases of weak adjectives unaccompanied by the definite article: 13, 35, 36, 168, 182, 215, 234, 327, 484, 598. This list is formed by correcting the lists of Brandl, E. Meyer, and Barnouw by one another, and omitting the cases of *seolfa,* which is a problem by itself. Barnouw (*Textkrit. Untersuch. nach dem Gebrauch des Bestimmten Artikels,* p. 108) explains the relatively large number of instances of this phenomenon in a late poem by calling them 'altertümliche floskeln, die dem dichter aus der älteren literatur geläufig waren.'

28b. swegles lēoht. So *Gu.* 457; *Ph.* 288; *Eadw.* 28.

29b. The correct reading is established by the parallel in *Gu.* 554-7:

> Nū þū in helle scealt
> dēope gedūfan, nales Dryhtnes lēoht
> habban in heofonum, hēahgetimbru,
> seld on swegle.

The scribe did not understand the neut. plur. *hēahgetimbra* (see Sievers, *Gram.* 237, n. 5; the ending in the original may have been the normal *u,* which is often mistaken for *a*); so he added a *d.* But *hēah* is not a proper member to form verbal compounds (*hēahþungen* being the only possible analogical formation in the *Sprachschatz*). Cf. also Holthausen's note, *Anglia* 44. 354.

Cf., in addition to *Gu.,* *Gen. B* 738-9 and *Chr.* 1182.

30. Cf. 670: 'þæt hē in helle gedēaf.'

Cosijn, *PBB.* 21. 22, thought 'die neueste Metrik' (meaning Graz's *Beiträge zur Textkritik der sog. Cädmon'schen Dichtungen*) went too far in calling the emendation *sceoldun* impossible. He adds: 'Dennoch ist die änderung *sceoldun* hier vorzuziehen, weil aus v. 27 hervorgeht, dass der sturz der engel hier nicht im praesens gedacht wird.' Though one may sympathize with Cosijn's dislike of the niceties of 'die neueste Metrik,' there can be no insurmountable objection to *sceolun*, considered as a historical present. (The existence of a historical present in OE. has, indeed, been questioned by some scholars.)

31=91. Cf. also 135 and *Gu.* 535: *niþer under næssas nēole grundas.* For the image which this phrase calls up, see Cook's note on *Jud.* 113. The whole passage, *Judith* 112-121, is full of ideas and turns of expression similar to those employed in the descriptions of hell in *Satan* and *Guthlac*.

32a. grēdige and gīfre. Cf. 192; *Gen. B* 793; *Seaf.* 62; *Soul's Address* 74.

32b. God āna wāt. So *Ph.* 355; *Fates of Men* 8.

33. The *ge* of *scyldige* looks to me like the scribe's hand. Frings' reference (*Zs. f. Deutsche Philologie* 45. 30) to Sievers (*Gram.* 214. 5) does not seem to support a wk. adj. *scyldī*, although it would allow us to accept *scyldī* as a strong form. Recent scholarly opinion is unfavorable to Wülker's statement *ad loc:* 'nach þæt auch die starke form stehen kann.' See Holthausen, *Anglia Bb.* 5. 232; Barnouw, *op. cit.*, p. 105. (On the other hand, cf. Carpenter, *Deklination in der Nordhumbrischen Evangelienübersetzung*, § 50.)

Cf. *Beow.* 106: *forscrifen hæfde.*

34 ff. See Abbetmeyer's discussion of the growth of the literary species which he calls 'plaints' of the fallen angels (*op. cit.*, pp. 17-9). Ungemach (*Die Quellen der Fünf Ersten Chester Plays*, p. 28) thinks these a special feature of the Old English epic poetry, which is based on the writings of the Anglo-Saxon theologians. There are short passages in the first plays of the York, Chester, and Towneley cycles of mysteries which remind one strongly of these laments in Part I of *Satan*. Avitus in *De Originali Peccato* (*Patr. Lat.* 59. 332; ed. Peiper, pp. 214-5), and Aldhelm in his riddle, *Lucifer* (ed. Ehwald, p. 135; cf. above, p. xxv, n. 33), put brief laments into the mouth of the fallen Lucifer. I quote the latter:

> O felix olim servata lege Tonantis!
> Heu! post hæc cecidi proterva mente superbus;
> Ultio quapropter funestum perculit hostem.

34a. See the note on 190-3.

The MS. form *cleopad* might be an error either for the pret. *cleopade* or for the pres. *cleopað* (on the possibility of present forms in *-d*, see Sievers, *Gram.* 357, n. 1, 2). The metre of the line makes the latter alternative much the more probable.

The present tense here would seem to be not merely an example of the historical present indicating an action taking place at a definite time in the past, that is, immediately after the fall of the angels, but rather, with *ðonne,* a means of introducing an action of indefinite date (or possibly even an action many times repeated), at any time between the fall and the New Testament period. The preterites used in the introductory phrases to all later laments, then, would simply signify the time of the speeches they introduce with reference to this first one. In other words, we should consider 1-33 as wholly preliminary, a sort of prologue giving the setting of the speeches to follow, but not recounting what is in any way a portion of the *central* action of the piece. This is one of the two possible ways of interpreting the apparently confused chronological relations of Part I, in which one is puzzled at first by the mention of men in both heaven and hell, immediately after we have been told of the expulsion of the evil angels from their heavenly home.

The second interpretation was proposed by Groschopp (*Anglia* 6. 261). He would consider lines 1-365 to have been made up, for the most part, by joining together the laments of the devils uttered before the Harrowing of Hell, or after the Judgment, or after their expulsion from heaven, which had previously formed portions of an extended poem on the life of Christ. Abbetmeyer also connects the laments with the Harrowing, but contends that they are to be dated after, not before, that event. The text of the poem, however, lays far too much emphasis upon the vivid recollection by Satan of his past glory, and the details of his revolt and first humiliating defeat, for it to be credible that these laments could have been uttered after the Harrowing or the Judgment, especially since absolutely no reference is made to these events as having recently occurred. We should expect the devil, after either the Harrowing or the Judgment, to have his mind occupied more with his recent disaster than with that which happened thousands of years before.

And yet it is more than probable that the part the devils play in the scene of the Descensus has influenced the poet's conception. But it is the story of the period which immediately preceded, rather than that of the period which followed, Christ's descent, which has exerted this influence. The speeches of the devils, terrified in anticipation of Christ's impending descent into hell, are an important part of the *Gospel of Nicodemus,* and may have colored somewhat this first section of *Christ and Satan.* Thus we may accept Abbetmeyer's statement (p. 13) that Satan's mention of the presence of men in heaven becomes 'clear if we assume that it is the descensus devil who is speaking, and embracing in one rueful look conditions past and present,' providing that we interpret the 'descensus devil' as the devil of the period just *before* the Descensus.

At any rate, a slight extension of Abbetmeyer's last clause brings us back to the first interpretation of the chronology given above. That is, we may say that, in our mundane sense, lines 1-365 have no chronology. The laments of the devils, and of Satan especially, take place in eternity, not in time. After the poet has set the stage by his short account of the fall of the apostates, he presents Satan as a character to whom past events and future prospects are as vivid as the impressions of the present; a character who can say, 'But now had I possession of all glory' (107), who can speak enviously of men as already enjoying the bliss of heaven (47), and who can characterize the date of his severer punishment in the future as 'not far off' (40)—all within sixty lines. (See Introduction, pp. xlv-xlvii and liv-lv, for a discussion of the relation of Parts I and II, a subject inextricably bound up with the question of the chronology of Part I.)

se alda. So *Fragment of Sermon on Ps. 28,* line 32. Cf. *El.* 207, *Pn.* 58: *se ealda fēond.* Cf. the *ealdfēond* of *Ph., Gu.,* etc. This recalls the 'serpens antiquus' of Rev. 12. 9, and the common epithet of Latin Christian literature, 'hostis antiquus.' See Rankin's 'Study of the Kennings in A.-S. Poetry,' pp. 54-9, for lists of Latin and OE. terms for hell and devils (*Jour. Eng. and Germ. Phil.,* Vol. 8). See also Klaeber, *Anglia* 35. 249-259, particularly 251, n. 4. Compare 34-5 with 160-2.

36a. eisegan. Thorpe, 'icy'! On the form of this derivative of *egsa,* see Sievers, *Gram.* 214. 2, and Bülbring, *Elementarbuch* 505, and especially cf. *eislicum* in Bouterwek's 'Ags. Glossen,' *Zs. f. D. A.* 9. 517 (bottom).

36b. Cf. this formula in *Wand.* 92; *Bl. Hom.* 99. 27, 31; Wulfstan, *Hom.* 263. 21-3.

37a. Williams (*Short Extracts from OE. Poetry,* p. 81) has a query concerning MS. *ðā þe:* 'Should be changed to *ðone ðe?'* It seems more probable that the scribe was misled by another common meaning of *þrym,* according to which the phrase *engla ðrym* would be equivalent to 'host of angels' (see *Chr.* 1064), and therefore changed the simple relative *þe* into the plural masc. *ðā þe* ('quos' in *Sprachschatz*) to agree with the collective idea of the phrase, as he interpreted it. I merely omit *þā.*

38-39b. Cf. the phrasing of 58, 103, 324, and 96, 100, 136-7.

The scribe first wrote *ðēostra,* but the *a* has been modified to *æ,* whether by the scribe or some later corrector one cannot be sure. Since it is very doubtful that the poet intended a weak form, I have accepted the emendation (yet see 598). Compare *ðēostræ hām* with *Jul.* 683; *Jud.* 121.

To speak in the same breath of the darkness, which is always an important feature of the descriptions of helle, and the fierceness and ubiquity of its flames was never, of course, thought to introduce any real paradox. One need not, with Becker (p. 60), see in this *swearte fȳr* (Ælfric, *Hom.* I. 132. 16) any reminiscence of Virgil's 'lux atra.' See the descriptions in Enoch 88. 1 and 90. 24 ff. The *locus classicus* on this subject is Gregory's *Moralia* 9. 66 (*Patr. Lat.* 75. 914-5). Milton's 'darkness visible' will at once come to mind (*P. L.* I. 61 ff.). Note, too, *Gen. B* 333: 'þæt wæs lēohtes lēas and wæs līges full.'

40a. Cf. 97, 322, 341, 421 (*fȳr, swȳðe, hāte, þearle onǣled*).

40b ff. This refers by anticipation to the severer punishment which is to come with the Harrowing of Hell (or possibly even the Last Judgment is the *ende*)—that is, if it refers to anything more than immediate torment, which, of course, the demons are already experiencing. I suspect some connection with the dialogue in the *Gospel of Nicodemus* between Satan and Inferus, in which the latter predicts that disaster will follow Christ's crucifixion. See also Isidore of Seville, *De Ordine Creaturarum* 8. 2 (*Patr. Lat.* 83. 931), where is mentioned the fear with which the devils await the time 'in quo durius judicabuntur.' Cf. *P. R.* I. 52-63. Satan has no trouble in comprehending in his thought the longest periods of time, and we should not expect him to adhere strictly, in the feverish activity of his mind, to earthly chronology. Hence Grein's emendation (accepted by Toller) is wholly unnecessary.

41b. sūsel þrōwian. Cf. 395; *Gen.* 75; *Dan.* 621.

42a. The MS. *wergum* has occasioned much discussion. Grein at first emended it to *wergung*, but later accepted Dietrich's *wergun*, fem., = 'maledictionem.' This Cosijn considers a Kentish form of *wergung*, and compares with *wergunge*, a variant in Spelman's *Ps.* 87. 19. He refers to the omission of *g* after *n* in the words listed by Zupitza in *Zs. f. D. A.* 21. 11, but in those cases the *g*'s are all medial, not final, which makes a great difference phonologically. Moreover, as Frings and Unwerth point out (*PBB.* 36. 559), the context would demand *wergunge*, which would disturb the metre. These scholars suggest that *wergum* is merely a phonetic spelling of *wergm*, a derivative of *āwærgan*, 'throttle.' Sperber (*PBB.* 37. 148-9) would read *wēan an* (*on*) *wergum*, 'leiden bei den verdammten.' Sievers, *ibid.*, p. 339, justly objects that *on* cannot have this meaning. He also disapproves of *wergm*, because (1) it would be a derivative of a verb itself a derivative; (2) a verbal abstract would signify an action, and not a condition, which the context requires; (3) *wergum* involves what he calls an unheard-of 'tonsprung,' one especially unusual for a hemistich with double alliteration. Sievers proposes *wærgu* or *wergu*, an abstract derived normally from *wērig*, and mean-

ing 'misery.' Kock (*Jubilee Jaunts and Jottings*, p. 72) is right in
considering either *wēan and wērgu* (cf. the parallelism of 319-320)
or *wēan on wērgum* (cf. *El.* 668) plausible. I accept *wērgu*. The
scribe may have thought the word should be in the instrumental, and
added *m*.

    42b. See Sievers, *Gram*. 198. 4. a, for the omission of *d* in *wulres*,
and cf. 85ᵇ.

    42b-43b. Cf. 508 and 593. *Wuldres blǣd* occurs in *Ph.* 662 and
An. 535.

    45a. song on swegle. So 143. Cf. *Ph.* 635: *singað on swegle.*

    46a. For *se Ēca* cf. 277, 373, 458, 532; *Gen.* 2368, 2897; *Met.* 11.
74; 20. 132.

    46-47. *Heleð*, of course, refers to the whole host of heavenly
spirits, but there can be no doubt that this host, in Satan's mind,
includes the souls of men, as well as angels. For other evidence that
he is throughout *thinking*, at least, of a time after the Fall of Man,
cf. 135, 145-9, 266-273, 334. The second and third passages, which are
explicit, make it certain that the poet did not intend to force a strained
meaning upon *heleð* and *men*, that is, by making *heleð*, 'heroes,' stand
here for the angel host alone, or *men* for 'devils' in 135. *Heleð* is
never used of angels without qualifying circumstances. In *An.* 362
the angels are disguised. In *El.* 73 the angel in Constantine's dream
is called *hæleða nāthwylc*, but he has been described as *on weres hāde*.
In *Gen. B* 285 the devil is thinking of his angels as warlike heroes.

    Moreover, the lines in *Sat.* are based upon the substitutional theory
of the relation in which men stand to the demons, a conception universally accepted in the Middle Ages. This theory is most completely
worked out by Gregory the Great. It can be traced in most of his
works, but see especially his exposition of the parable of the ten
drachmas (*Hom. in Evang.* 2. 34: *Patr. Lat.* 76. 1249. See also
Comm. in I Reg.: *Patr. Lat.* 79. 214, and my note on 366). Men
were created to fill the place of the order of angels which fell (see
Gen. A 86 ff.; *Gen. B* 364 ff.; Wulfstan, *Hom.*, p. 8). Hence naturally one of Satan's greatest torments is to see men standing round the
throne where he had formerly enjoyed bliss. The contrasts between
iū and *nū*, *nū* and the *and* of 48 are very sharp. *Gen. B* (364-8) is
more explicit:

                        Þæt mē is sorga mǣst,
þæt Ādām sceal, þe wæs of eorðan geworht,
mīnne stronglican stōl behealdan,
wesan him on wynne, and wē þis wīte þolien,
hearm on þisse helle.

Notes 59

Cf. Gregory, *Moralia* (*Patr. Lat.* 76. 663) : 'Valde, autem anhelat [diabolus] sæviens, quod cum ipsum ima cruciant, homo ad summa conscendat; quod in illa celsitudine subvecta caro permanet, a qua tantus ipse spiritus sine fine projectus jacet.' *Heliand* 1042-3 puts it thus :

> That uuas Sātānāse
> tulgo harm an is hugi, afonsta heban an-rīkies
> mannō cunnea.

See also *P. L.* 2. 830-5; cf. 677-680 of Bk. III, which are spoken ironically.

Compare *Sat.* 46-8 with 220-4 and 661-3.

Milton's lines (*P. L.* 1. 54-6) summarize thus the feelings of Satan which underlie 42ᵇ-50 :

> For now the thought
> Both of lost happiness and lasting pain
> Torments him.

47b-48a. Cf., in addition to 222 and 661, *Chr.* 429-430 and 917-8; for *wordum and wercum*, *Chr.* 1237; *Gu.* 553, 765.

48b. The *and* has adversative force: 'and at the same time,' 'while,' 'but.'

49. bīdan in bendum. Cf. *Sat.* 414: *beorneð on bendum; Chr.* 147; *Harrowing* 61, 88; *Gu.* 545: *in bendum bryne þrōwian. Christ and Satan* shows the same inconsistency in regard to the restriction of the devil's movements as do the Bible and Milton. The latter speaks of his dwelling 'in Adamantine Chains' (*P. L.* 1. 48) and lying 'chain'd on the burning Lake' (*ib.* 210) ; yet Heaven 'left him at large to his own dark designs' (*ib.* 212). As Roskoff points out (*op. cit.* 1. 206), the Second Epistle of Peter (2. 4) says that God delivered the angels who sinned to torment 'rudentibus inferni detractos in tartarum . . . in judicium reservari,' whereas in 1 Pet. 5. 8, 'diabolus tanquam leo rugiens circuit, quærens quem devoret.' Compare, then, 49ª, and the other passages in which bonds and prison are mentioned, with, e. g., 112-4, 145 ff. The poet of *Gen. B* seeks to avoid this paradox by having Satan carry out his designs through an envoy, whereas he says of himself (371-4) :

> ac licgað mē ymbe īrenbenda,
> rīdeð racentan sāl—ic eom rīces lēas—,
> habbað mē swā hearde helle clommas
> fæste befangen.

Jude 6 and Rev. 20. 1-2 also mention the binding of demons.

49b. Cf. *Gu.* 626: *tō þām betran hām.*

50a. for oferhygdum. So 69, 197, 228; *Jul.* 424; *Gu.* 606, 633; cf. *Gen.* 22; *Gen. B* 262; *Minds of Men* 58. Pride has been almost exclusively the fundamental cause assigned for the fall of the angels. (For other explanations see Roskoff 1. 231.) 'Omnis peccati initium est superbia,' says Ecclus. 10. 15. See also Gregory, *Moral.* 28. 8 (*Patr. Lat.* 76. 486-7), and the description of Antichrist in 2 Thess. 2. 4.

50b. Satan's utter hopelessness (cf. 115-6, 159[b]) is combined with an evident wistful longing, in striking contrast with the attitude of the theological devil of Gregory, according to whom Satan remains eternally impenitent. In fact, God has given him a mad insensibility, 'ut jam per duritiam se male egisse non sentiat' (*Moral.* 34. 21: *Patr. Lat.* 76. 741). Origen had held that the devil could better his condition. He even went so far as to regard the devil's conversion and salvation as ultimately certain. But Roskoff (1. 282) points out that such views were condemned as heresy in the sixth century by Justinian's Synod.

52a. It strikes one with surprise to read in Roskoff (1. 284) that black, a color which we assign to devils with hardly a thought, as arising from the eternal fitness of things, was probably first applied to the personal appearance of Satan in the fourth century. To be sure, devils had been called 'the powers of darkness' from the beginning, but with a moral rather than a sensuous connotation. In Rev. 12. 3, Satan is 'draco magnus, *rufus.*'

52b. *Begrorene,* in the sense of 'horridi,' 'formidolose obruiti,' 'horrore affecti,' etc., has been accepted as at least possible by Somner, Lye, Ettmüller, Grein, Bosworth-Toller, Sweet, Clark Hall, and others. The existence of an OE. *grēosan,* though this is the only example of it to be found, has been assumed by lexicographers of other languages and later English, e. g., Ten Dornkaat Koolman (*Wörterbuch der Ostfriesischen Sprache*), Mätzner (*Altenglische Sprachproben*), and *NED.* Dietrich was the first to doubt and emend the word. His reason, surely an insufficient one, was that, ordinarily in OE., devils are described as bound or chained in torment. Dietrich's emendation *begrōwene,* as Cosijn says, is unintelligible. Cosijn would prefer *sūsl begnornedon* to this. But Sievers, in a note, objects that *sūsl begnornedon* would give an expanded D-verse in the second hemistich. He would prefer, 'in case of need,' *behrorene* (cf. *Wand.* 77: *hrīme bihrorene*), which Holthausen had already definitely proposed as an emendation of Wülker's text.

The objections to the word seem to me quite unfounded, and in fact they have not been strongly urged. The series of phenomena which we have in *(for)lēosan, (for)luron : lyre (lore),* ME. *lure,* and in the development of other verbal stems of the second class of strong verbs, is paralleled exactly by *(be)grēosan, (be)gruron : gryre,* ME. *grure.* Moreover, the existence of a root **greu-, grū-* (extended in our word to **greus-, grus-*; see *NED.* under *grise*) is abundantly testified in the Germanic dialects, exclusive of the Gothic and Scandinavian. Translated 'horrified by,' or 'in terror at their torment,' the phrase is perfectly clear. Cf. Satan's fear in 76-7. The fact that the word is ἅπαξ λεγόμενον is no unique distinction in the OE. poetical vocabulary.

53-64. Compare the reproaches which his followers heap upon fallen Lucifer in the York, Towneley, and Chester Mysteries. All this is quite foreign to the conception of the poet of *Gen. B* and Milton.

54. Cf. 317: 'þæt hē heofencyninge hēran ne wolde'; see also 183, 364, 595, 645. *Scealdon* seems to be Anglian (Sievers, *Gram.* 423, n. 1).

55b-56a. Cf. 107, 118, and *Beow.* 1727.

56b. In *Gen. B* 283 Satan says: 'Ic mæg wesan God swā hē.' Cf. Milton's 'He trusted to have equall'd the Most High,' *P. L.* 1. 40.

57a. There is no need of substituting Wieners' *scyppend* for *scypend.* The latter presents merely an orthographic variation.

57b. I am indebted to Professor Menner for what is undoubtedly the correct reading of this line. It is a reading which harmonizes with all the facts presented by the MS. as it stands. The MS. reads: *nū earttū earm sceaða/* :: :::. The first two erased letters, which come at the beginning of a MS. line, clearly were *na.* By examining the rotograph, Menner was able to decipher the other three as *sum.* This word fits exactly both the width of the vacant space and the traces of the erased letters which are still visible. *Nū earttū sceaðana sum* suits the context, and is metrically unexceptionable. Paraphrase: 'Now art thou but one among the wretches fast bound in a fiery dungeon.'
Bright ('Jottings') has already suggested that 'paleographically a confusion of *eartū* and *earm* was possible.' What happened was this: the scribe copied *eartū* twice, reading it first correctly (and writing the more normal form *earttū*), but reading it the second time as *earm;* the Corrector did not recognize *sceaða/na,* divided as it was, and attempted to improve the corrupt and metrically faulty text by erasing *na sum.*

58a. **fȳrlocan.** Cf. *Chr.* 1621: *under līges locan (in līges locan, Jul.* 474).

58b. **feste gebunden.** So 104, 324; *Sal.* (277, 458) has *fæste gebindan.*

59-62. Cf. *Gu.* 635-7.

63a. So 430ᵃ.

63-64. The traditional interpretation of lines 63-4 (for which see
Ten Brink, *Hist. Early Eng. Lit.* I. 87; Groschopp, p. 252; Brooke,
Early Eng. Lit., p. 328) takes them literally as they stand: 'that thy
son was the creator of mankind.' Abbetmeyer points out (p. 14)
that no parallel has been adduced to explain this idea of Satan's
having one special son who could be singled out from the whole host
of 'children of the devil.'

The only other interpretation which has been suggested, that by
Abbetmeyer, is not very satisfactory. According to this view, these
lines are to be construed as a simple inversion, and paraphrased thus:
'that the Creator of mankind was thy son, i. e., thy subject.' The
difficulty here is that the equation of *sunu* with *þegn* rests upon a
rather involved deduction: in *Jul.* 321, 522, the devil is called the
fæder of his followers; elsewhere, *Jul.* 328, *An.* 43, and *Sal.* 117,
he is their *frēa,* and they are his *þegnas;* therefore *sunu* here means
þegn.

It seems possible that these lines contain a reference (anachronistic,
of course, in the context) to a common mediæval conception of the
Antichrist. Hilary (*Comment. in Mt. Cap. 27: Patr. Lat.* 9. 1056,
1073) twice uses the phrase 'Antichristus . . . diaboli filius' (cf. 2
Thess. 2. 3: 'filius perditionis'). Adso (ca. 954) is very circumstantial in his account of the birth of Antichrist (*Libellus de Antichristo:
Patr. Lat.* 101. 1291 ff.): 'Et sicut in matrem Domini nostri Jesu
Christi Spiritus sanctus venit, . . . ut de Spirito sancto conciperet,
et quod nasceretur, divinum esset et sanctum; ita quoque diabolus in
matrem Antichristi descendet, . . . ut diabolo per hominem cooperante
concipiat, et quod natum fuerit totum sit iniquum, totum malum,
totum perditum.' Adso then proceeds to draw a long parallel, or
rather contrast, between the career of Christ and that of Antichrist.
The actions of the latter he describes as directed by his father Satan.
This contrast is worked out in rather minute detail, and culminates
with Antichrist's exaltation of himself 'supra omne quod dicitur
Deus . . . ostendens se tanquam sit Deus' (2 Thess. 2. 4). Rupertus
Tuitensis, who practically reproduces Adso (*Patr. Lat.* 169. 1065),
adds a reference to Rev. 13, according to which the Dragon (= Satan)
gives his power, his throne, and great authority to the seven-headed
beast (= Antichrist). This process of drawing parallels between
Christ and Antichrist might very easily have been carried to such a
point that, as Christ was spoken of as the creator of the world, so
Satan might blasphemously say that his son Antichrist was *meotod
moncynnes.* That the conception of Antichrist as Satan's son was
known to the Anglo-Saxons is proved by passages in Wulfstan (*Hom.*
192 ff.). Note the following: 'Anticrīst þǣrinne [in his temple in

Jerusalem] hē gesit, and hine sylfne swā ūp āhefð þæt hē cwyð þæt
hē sȳ þæs ælmihtigan Godes sunu' (195. 6) ; 'ætēowiende hine, swylce
hē God sylf sȳ' (198. 3) ; 'and rihtlic bið þæt se Godes wiðersaca
Anticrīst fealle niðer intō helle tō ðām ealdan dēofle *his fæder*' (201.
19).

64a. Meotod mancynnes. So 459, 515, 668.

65b. fācnum wordum. So *Ps.* 136. 3.

66a. *Aldorðægn* occurs only in *Sat.; Beow.* 1308; *Jud.* 242; *Men.*
130.

66b. Bouterwek's *onreordadon* for the MS. *unreordadon* is impossible, because the *on,* being an inseparable prefix (cf. *onsecgan*) could
not take either ictus or alliteration, both of which it would have to
bear here. Grein *(Sprachschatz)* correctly construes *an* as an adverb,
and translates the phrase: 'redeten ihn an'; *a* and *u* are often confused in the MSS.

67a. Sievers *(PBB.* 10. 456) first objected to the MS. reading
cearum, because it would give a shortened C-verse with resolution of
the first arsis. He thinks *cearum* represents *ceargum,* and refers to
hungrum for *hungregum* in the Vercelli version of *Soul's Address*
116. Graz would emend by *Chr.* 1131 and *Gu.* 194 to *on cearum
cwīðdun,* whereas Kock *(Plain Points and Puzzles,* p. 24) retains
the MS. reading. He interprets *cwidum* as a parallel to *wordum,* 65,
and translates *on cearum,* 'in sorrow.'

The adjective *cear* must surely be given up as indefensible. The
modification (see *PBB.* 19. 457) of Sievers' *ceargum* to *cearium* (see
Sievers, *Gram.* 214. 5), accepted for the text, gives a form with six
parallel strokes in a row; the scribe might easily have left one out
and written *cearum,* as he wrote *wordun* for *wordum* in 48. The
phrase, 'in sorrowful words,' is even a more satisfactory parallel to
fācnum wordum than Kock's isolated *cwidum.* The well articulated
style of *Ps.* 144. 4, to which Kock refers,

Cnēorissa kynn cwidum symble
þīn weorc herigen wordum georne, etc.,

with *cwidum* and *wordum* ·in consecutive lines, each accompanied by
its adverb, is much more effective than the style of his arrangement
of *Sat.* 65-7. Compare with *on cearium cwidum, An.* 1108: *cearegan
reorde.*

67b. Cf. *Gu.* 720: 'hæfde se heorde . . . fēondas āfyrde;' also
Mk. 1. 34 (Lindisfarne) : 'Dīoblas hē āfyrde' (for 'cast out devils').

We have here the first specific mention of Christ's part in the
drama of the fall of the angels. Their revolt is likewise represented
as against Christ in *Jul.* 420, *Gu.* 570, and *Prayers* 4. 55 (see Abbet-

meyer, pp. 14, 15), but not so much is made of the fact as in *Sat.*, where the motive comes in several times. In the other OE. poems the rebellion is against God. Von Gajšek (*Milton und Caedmon,* pp. 37-42) notes the similarity between *Paradise Lost* and *Sat.* in Christ's position in heaven, and Satan's hatred of him (see especially *P. L.* 5. 600 ff.). She thinks that the war in heaven between Christ and Satan is derived ultimately from the Apocalypse, and that it has been transferred by both Milton and the poet of *Sat.* from the last days to the period before the creation of man.

68a. **drēamum bedēlde.** Cf. 344; *Beow.* 721, 1275; *Chr.* 1408-9. Kock's interpretation (*Jub. Jaunts,* p. 30) of *drēamum bedēlde* as coördinate with *hēo āfirde* gives a stylistic effect which is a great improvement over the usually assumed participial construction. Kock's view had, however, been anticipated in Kennedy's translation.

68b-69. Cf. 228^b-9; for the thought of the apostate angels surrendering, or leaving behind them, the bliss of heaven, see *Gen. B* 738-740; *El.* 946-8.

71b. The metre demands a long radical syllable in all three instances of *blāc* in *Sat.*: 71, 196, 721. One cannot be absolutely certain whether this implies that the word belongs in meaning to *blāc,* with the secondary sense of 'pale,' 'livid,' or, as the *NED.* would authorize us to believe, to *blac, blæc,* which is synonymous with *sweart.* As this latter adjective is applied to devils in *Sat.,* it would be only natural to translate *blāc* also as 'black.'

For the vowel of *hworfon* see Sievers, *Gram.* 388, n. 6.

72a. *Gen. B* 308-9 relates that 'hēo ealle forscēop Drihten tō dēoflum.' The same thought occurs in Wulfstan, *Hom.* 145. 23: 'Mǣre englas . . . wurdon gēo forsceapene tō atelicum dēoflum.' In *Sat.,* however, the participle is purely adjectival.

72b. Sievers' emendation (*PBB.* 10. 453) renders the hemistich a normal D-verse.

73a. This phrase in the singular is found in 448, 579, 713. It is applied to devils in *Gu.* 547 and *Ph.* 442. Schücking (*Bedeutungslehre,* p. 33) shows that *earm* by a gradual transition has come to mean 'bad,' 'wicked,' in a context such as the present one.

73b = 129^a.

74. We may paraphase: 'for the insolent deeds which they had perpetrated.' Cf. 429: *for onmǣdlan.*

76b. Graz shows that *forworht* is metrically impossible. It would have to be scanned ×‒, and, hence, the line would be without alliteration. Cf. 620 for another instance of this scribal error. Grein's emendation in his text is as satisfactory as the one he suggests in his note is wholly gratuitous. *Forht* really improves both metre and sense. *Agēn* is said in reference to *eisegan stefne*, 36, the first mention of Satan's fear. Compare 76ᵇ-80 with the introduction to Satan's speech in *Gen. B* 353-5.

77a. For gen. sing. *ðes*, see Sievers, *Gram.* 337, n. 4.

78a. A careful examination of the rotograph proves that Ettmüller's conjecture (see variants) was correct. OE. *þ* and *w* look very much alike. For *spearcade* the scribe wrote *swearcade*, which made no sense. Then, disregarding the alliteration, which could have guided him aright, he changed the *c* into a *t* by drawing a horizontal stroke through the top. But the little dot which forms the upper termination of the *c* is clearly visible above the cross of the *t*. Cf. 162-3: 'Word spearcum flēah āttre gelīcost, þonne hē ūt þorhdrāf.' As possible sources or analogues of this poetical image, I cite the following: Jer. 5. 14: 'Ecce ego do verba mea in ore tuo in ignem, et populum istud in ligna, et vorabit eos;' Ecclus. 48. 1: 'Et surrexit Elias propheta, quasi ignis, et verbum ipsius quasi facula ardebat;' 4 Esdras 13. 10: 'Quoniam emisit de ore suo sicut flatum ignis, et de labiis eius spiritus flammæ, et de lingua eius emittebat scintillas et tempestates;' Rev. 11. 5: 'Et si quis voluerit eis nocere, ignis exiet de ore eorum et devorabit inimicos eorum.'

80. Cf. 731: *wordum in wītum*.

80b. Bright would correct the metre of the MS. reading by prefixing *þā* or *þās* (Holthausen, *Anglia Bb.* 30. 2, adds *þæt* to the list) to *word*. Kock (*Jub. Jaunts*, p. 17) thinks *word* represents *word[e]*, which is 'often used pleonastically with verbs of saying.' Of course, a sort of graphic elision (see note on 96ᵇ) might have caused the omission of the *e*. *Worde* gives us an abnormal hemistich, $-\times\times-$, but since *word[e] indrāf* makes good sense, and, since, though metrically exceptional, it is not unparalleled, I accept it for the text. Besides, inasmuch as *indrīfan* occurs in this line only, it might be better to regard *in* as an adv., and scan the verse $-\times-\mid-$, which would approximate the metre of *Beow.* 2436ᵇ.

81a. iū in heofnum: so 151ᵃ.

81b. hālig ængel. So 586 (= Christ).

81-82. Gregory describes at length Lucifer's preëminence in heaven in *Hom. in Evang.* 34 (*Patr. Lat.* 76. 1250) and *Moral.* 32. 23 (*Patr. Lat.* 76. 664-5).

82a. Wülker notes that *Dryhten* is used for the dative. Cf. *Gen. B* 261: *Dēore wæs hē Drihtne ūrum; Gen. B* 339-340: *his Hearran lēof, Drihtne dȳre; Gen. A* 1247: *Drihtne dȳre*.

82b. Cf. *Chr.* 1637: *āgan drēam mid Gode*.

83b. swā some. Cf. *Gen.* 399; *Chr.* 940.

84-87. The same idea recurs in 173-5.

85b. Cf. Heb. 1. 3: 'splendor gloriæ.'

86b-87a. Cf. 253ᵇ-4ᵃ. The phrase *tō ǣhte* is peculiar to *Satan,* and occurs in 117, 254, 279, 454.

87b. There is no need to assume (i. e., accepting, for the moment, the MS. form *ðēos*) merely from this line that the gender of *hēap* may vary (see B.-T. and *Sprachschatz*). Sievers, *Gram.* 338, n. 4, records a masculine *þēos.* But in any case the *o* of *ðēos* has been erased, and the form was probably a slip. For nom. sing. masc. adjectives in *-e* in the weak declension, such as *earme,* see Sievers, *Gram.* 276, n. 5.

88. Cf. 92, 148, 178.

89a. I omit the Corrector's *ge.* Wülker remarks in a note that *wēne* here may represent *wēne ic,* and I so interpret it.

Lines 89-90 are very confused as they stand in the MS. I read and scan them thus:

$$\acute{-} \times \; | \times \; \acute{-} \; | \; \smile\!\times \; \| \times \times \times \; | \; \acute{-} \; \times \times \; | \; \acute{-} \; \times$$

Wēne þæt tācen sutol   þā ic āseald wes on wærgðu.

This is an expanded long line ('schwellvers'). The rhythm of the first hemistich is the same as that of *Dan.* 446 (Kaluza's Type 64, *Eng. Stud.* 21. 373). I scan *tācen* as a monosyllable in accordance with the customary practise of the poet (see Richter, *Chronologische Studien zur Ags. Lit.,* p. 34). The second hemistich is perfectly normal for the second member of a *schwellvers.* 89-91 may be translated as follows: 'I think that a clear sign (i. e., of our fate) when I was given over to punishment, down beneath the ground in the yawning abyss.' This reading is proposed with no pretensions that it restores the original text, but as giving a satisfactory line with a minimum of change from the MS. I merely cancel *of,* and alter the position of MS. 7 *(ond) wærgðu,* which may be considered a natural misreading of *on wærgðu.* See textual footnote on 105 for an instance of the same mistake. Previous attempts at reconstruction have been either too elaborate, or metrically faulty, or have left the phrase *and wærgðu* in a hemistich by itself, without explaining its import or construction.

The way in which *tācen sutol* is employed here reminds one a little of *Beow.* 833-4.

92b. Forms of the verb *ferian* with *æ* for radical vowel (see variants) are to be found. The original reading might have been *gefærde.* To the Corrector is almost certainly to be assigned the erasure of the *a,* although it is always barely possible in such cases that the scribe himself did the normalizing.

93b. Cf. *An.* 1681: *tīr ēadigra.*

94a. Ziegler (*Der Poetische Sprachgebrauch in den sogen. Cædmonschen Dichtungen*, p. 28) thinks that *wloncra wīnsele* is derived from a common epithet descriptive of Valhalla, and that it means 'der tapferen bewirtungssaal.'

94b. Cf. *Rood* 133.

95a. Cf. 167; *engla þrēatas* occurs in 424 and 568.

95b. There is real need this time of the subject, *wē*, with which the Corrector supplies *mōten*.

96b-97a. Cf. 100. *Fȳr* for *fȳre* seems to be an instance of graphic elision; cf. *word indrāf*, 80. I call it 'graphic,' because, although we do not know how far elision was carried out in OE. enunciation, it would be very natural for a scribe carrying a phrase in his head, without being conscious of its meaning, to omit the weak inflectional *e* from his MS. But whether this be considered a case of elision or not, there are plenty of instances recorded of uninflected datives and instrumentals. The meaning is unmistakable, and the metre correct; hence *fȳr* has been allowed to stand.

97b. fāh wið God. So *Beow.* 811; *An.* 1188.

98a. helle duru. Cf. 380, 467, 723. Graz's objections to the metre are not damaging. (Holthausen accepts these objections in *Eng. Stud.* 37. 205.)

98-99. Becker (p. 62) thinks 'the fire-breathing dragons which guard the entrance to hell . . . are certainly a reminiscence of the Cerberus myth or its concomitants, with perhaps an admixture of the Germanic dragons.' But it is probable that the source is a more immediate one, i. e., Jewish or Christian apocryphal writings; for example, we read in the Slavonic *Book of the Secrets of Enoch* 42. 1 of 'key-holders and guards of the gates of hell standing, like great serpents, and their faces like extinguished lamps, and their eyes of fire.'

99a. reðre. The omission of the *h* in this and the other four instances (208b, 456b, 489a, 717) is merely graphic, and nothing can be argued from it as to an early date (see Groschopp, pp. 266-7; Sievers, *Gram.* 217, n. 2 and n. 3; Bülbring, *Elementarbuch* 480, n.). There are exactly five cases of the same phenomenon in the MS. of the *Phœnix*, which no one considers an early poem.

100. Cf. the phrasing of 137.

101a. See Shipley, *Genitive Case in A.-S. Poetry*, p. 48, for the construction.

101-102. Cf. the similar idea in 130-1. These lines remind one of the terror of men before the Judgment in Rev. 6. 16: 'Et dicunt montibus et petris: Cadite super nos, et abscondite nos a facie sedentis super thronum.'

102a. Cf. 180, 446. Mist and fumes are common features of hell. Gregory speaks of its 'aer caliginosus' (*Moral.* 13. 48).

103b-104a. *Ex.* 536 says that in hell 'þær bið fȳr and wyrm.' *Sal.* 468 mentions *wyrmgeardas*, which expresses the same idea as the phrase *wyrmas gewunade*. Cf. also *Jud.* 119, *wyrmsele*. The participle *gewunad* is used similarly in *Ps.* 139. 3; prose *Life of Gu.* 142. 23.

103b. *Wītes clom* is found in 157, 444, and 453, and nowhere else in the poetry. For the possibility of a masc. *þis*, see Sievers, *Gram.* 338, n. 4.

105a. dimme and deorce. Cf. 455; *Ps.* 108. 8. The damned are called *þære deorcan scole* in *Chr.* 1523.

105b. *Lȳhteð* has been written (almost certainly by the Corrector) over the erasure of a word that cannot be deciphered. An *e* can be discerned after *dæg* and what looks like another *e* under the *h*. The last letter was *d*. I suspect that the line originally read *nis hēr dægerēd*, a faulty hemistich. This form of *dægrēd* is found in prose. The Corrector's reading is satisfactory, and recalls *Dan.* 158, and especially *Dom.* 19-20: 'þær næfre dæg scīneð lēohte of lyfte.'

106a. Cf. *æfter sceades scīman, Sal.* 116. *Scīma* seems to be one of those twilight words which may mean either light or dark.

107a-110. The Corrector's *ic* may be dispensed with, as well as Thorpe's emendation of *nū* to *iū*. Satan's memory of his lost happiness is so vivid that he can say (literally) : '*But now* had I possession of all glory; whereas I was forced to abide whatever God wills to condemn me to, his enemy on hell's floor.' Retention of the MS. reading removes the occasion for Sievers' note in *PBB.* 10. 195, in which he argues that the alliteration of *iū* (*gēo*) with *ealles* points to Kentish origin. Frings (p. 232) accepts *iū*, but splits the sentence in two by a period after *wuldres*. This, of course, causes *iū* to lose its emphasis, and hence its alliteration. But then, there is no necessity of accepting *iū*. Grein's *rendering*,

> Einst hatte ich Gewalt über all die Glorie,
> eh ich in dieser heillosen Heimat harren musste,
> was mir Gott der Herr nun geben wolle, etc.,

is no more forceful than can be made from the MS. as it stands.

If Thorpe's translation of 110ᵃ, 'on his glittering floor,' were to be accepted, the phrase would have to apply to the position of God, which it surely does not. Neither 'glittering' nor 'variegated' seems a suitable epithet for the floor of hell. *Fāgum* fits into the context best as a modifier of *mē*.

Bosworth-Toller has other instances of dat. *flōra*.

108. Cf. 327ᵃ, *atolan ēðles.*

109. Cf. the phrasing of 622-3.

110b. On this 'predicative infinitive with a verb of motion,' see Callaway's *Infin. in A.-S.*, pp. 89-91, 291. Cf. *Dan.* 698; *Gen.* 852, 2759; *Jud.* 12.

111a. Following Hofer (*Dat. und Instrum. bei Cædmon*, p. 32) I construe *menego* as an instance of the instrumental of accompaniment. Cf. 729, *dēofla mænego.*

111b. Cf. *þone dimman hām, 337.*

112. Graz's transposition of *flyge* and *flyhte* both avoids anacrusis in the second hemistich and greatly improves the rhythm of the first. Such a mistake as misplacing these similar words would be very natural.

112-113. See the notes on 262ᵇ-5 for an explanation of these lines. I take *earda* here to mean not the devils' 'solum nativum' or 'patria' *(Sprachschatz),* but rather the 'lands' of earth, where the fiends will carry out the baleful designs against men which are mentioned in 147-9 and elsewhere.

114a. For *ðes* see Sievers, *Gram.* 337, n. 3, 4.

114b. For *ord onstaldon* see *Beow.* 2407 (*se ðæs orleges ōr onstealde)* and *Rid.* 4. 59.

115-117. Cf. the phrasing of 277-9. *Sat.* 525 and *Gen.* 1840 have *swā hē ǣr dyde.*

116-117. Ferrell (*Teuton. Antiquities in the A.-S. Genesis,* p. 13) thinks the conception of heaven as a hereditary home *(ēðel)* Teutonic (but cf. Lat. 'patria'). He then says most aptly that because of the universal Teutonic attachment to home it would be considered the greatest of punishments to deprive the devils of this heavenly home, theirs by inheritance, as it were. Such a feeling must have prompted the poet to put this despairing cry into the mouth of Satan.

119a. Cosijn thinks *wuldres and wīta* equivalent to 'über himmel und hölle.'

119b. Waldendes Sunu. Cf. 396; *Chr.* 635.

120a. Cf. *Gu.* 425, *hēan and earm.* It seems necessary here to avail ourselves of the Corrector's *sceal.*

120-122. Cf. the curse of Adam, *Gen. A* 927-930; also *An.* 676-7:

> Hwæt! gē syndon earme ofer ealle menn,
> wadað wīdlāstas.

Abbetmeyer (p. 15) lists the poetical passages in which the devils are called exiles, or the penalty of banishment from heaven mentioned. He thinks there may be some connection between these conceptions and Gen. 4. 11-2, where Cain is condemned to be 'vagus et profugus super terram.'

121b. Cf. *Gu.* 116 and *An.* 1618: *wuldre bescyrede.*

122a. duguðum bedēled. So *Gen. A* 930; *Chr.* 563. Compare 121^b-2^a with 343^b-4^a.

123a. uppe mid englum. So 142, 293, 330, 391, 591; *Chr.* 387; *Ph.* 629; *Hymn* 5, etc.

126a. Cf. *wērige gāstas,* 630, 731.

126-127. Cf. *Jul.* 494-6: *Ic āsecgan ne mæg . . . eal þā earfeþu.*

127b = *Ps.* 148. 12 (2^b). Cf. 526: *ætsomne ealle.*

128a. Cf. 479-480: *fēond in firenum fāh is æghwǣr.*

128b-129. These lines are parallel to 78 and 162; that is, they refer to the emission of fire which accompanied Satan's words. Compare the similar use of *stondan* to depict vividly the streaming of light and flame in *Beow.* 726, 1570, 2769.

129b. Cf. *Gu.* 640: *ād inǣled āttre geblonden.*

131b. Cf. 157: *gewundod mid wommum.* The figure of sin's causing wounds, seems, according to Cook (note on *Rood* 14^a), to be peculiarly Cynewulfian. It certainly appears in no poem of the Cædmonian group.

132. Cf. 335. It was for long assumed that the inclusion in OE. poetry of extreme cold among the torments of hell, alongside of the usual *ignis gehennæ*, was due to a reminiscence of the old Teutonic Niflheim, the cold and misty abode of the dead (see e. g., Ferrell, p. 24). This notion was first moderately opposed by Becker (pp. 11, 54-9). Cook (note on *Chr.* 1546, q. v. for some references not repeated here) thinks the ultimate source of the combination of these two modes of torment is Job 24. 19: 'Ad nimium calorem transeat ab aquis nivium' (see Bede on Luke 13. 28). Enoch 14. 13 describes the outer court of God's palace thus: 'And I entered into that house, and it was hot as fire and cold as ice: there were no delights of life therein.' In the *Book of the Secrets of Enoch* (Version A, 10. 2) hell is described as a place of 'cruel darkness and unillumined gloom, and there is no light there, but murky fire constantly flameth aloft, . . . and everywhere there is frost and ice, thirst and shivering.' Ephraem Syrus mentions both 'frigidus tartarus' and 'ignis inextinguibilis.' Bede's famous picture of purgatory in the vision of Dryhthelm (*Hist. Eccles.* 5. 12), according to which the souls leaped back and forth from one place 'flammis ferventibus nimium terribile' to another 'furenti grandine ac frigore nivium omnia perflante atque verrente non minus intolerabile,' need not be quoted in full. Milton's lines (*P. L.* 2. 587-603) on this alternating torment will come to mind at once. In OE. poetry it is mentioned in *Gen. A* 43: 'geondfolen fȳre and fǣrcyle'; *Chr.* 1547: 'æleð hȳ mid þȳ ealdan līge ond mid þȳ egsan forste'; and *Gen. B* 313-6 (cf. Adam's speech, 806-812).

Sal. 467 calls hell *wælcealde wīc wintre beþeahte.* I give three passages from the homilists: *Bl. Hom.,* p. 61: 'þǣr hē hæfþ weallendene lēg, and hwīlum cyle þone grimmestan;' the eighth Vercelli hom., fol. 60ᵇ: 'þǣr is unmǣte cyle and unāhefendlic hǣto gemēted;' Ælfric, *Hom.* I. 132, has the phrases, *on ðām micclum bryne, on swiðlicum cyle.* Cf. also Ælfric, *Hom.* I. 530, 532; Wulfstan, *Hom.* 138. 27 ff.

It is therefore wholly unnecessary to see in the OE. passages any direct influence of old pagan ideas, but we may at least say that the torment of extreme cold had rather a stronger hold upon the imagination of the northern race of Englishmen than upon that of more southerly peoples.

134. Cf. *Gu.* 400: 'Bonan gnornedon, mǣndon murnende.'

135b-136a. As they stand in the MS., these lines would have to mean either, 'naked men fight over serpents' (Kennedy's 'strive with serpents' is impossible, because the object of *ymb* when used with verbs like *winnan* is always the subject of dispute, never one of the antagonists; cf. *Beow.* 506-7: *sē þe wið Brecan wunne, on sīdne sǣ ymb sund flite;* also *Bl. Hom.* 99. 10: *ūs is myccle māre nēdþearf þæt wē winnon ymb ūre sāule þearfe*); or, 'naked men fight around serpents (or dragons)'; or, 'serpents fight round about ('rings um') naked men' (Bouterwek). The latter is certainly the only interpretation which is tolerable. But better than all is it to follow Thorpe's suggestion that *winnan* is an error for *windan,* a very simple mistake, and especially natural because *winnan* and *ymb* occur so often together. Grein retains *winnað* in his text, but bases his translation on *windað:* 'bald um nackte Männer winden sich hier Würmer.'

Compare the picture in *Apoc. of Peter,* verse 10: 'And I saw the murderers . . . cast into a certain narrow place full of evil reptiles, and being smitten by those beasts;' also that in the homily in MS. Hatton 116 (printed by Förster in *Festschrift für Lorenz Morsbach,* pp. 128-137), 135. 19: 'ac ā þā dracan and þā wyrmas þāra ārlēasra manna sāwla slītað.' Cf. *Jud.* 115: 'wyrmum bewunden'; *Minds of Men* 56: 'wyrmum beþrungen'; Wulfstan, *Hom.* 139. 10: 'hī wælgrimme wyrmas slītað.'

136b. Cf. *windsele,* 320, 386.

137a. Cf. *Gu.* 1291-4: 'blissum gefylled . . . eal innanweard.'

137b. Though an adv. *(fægere)* is once used with *fyllan,* it seems better to construe *atole* here as a substantive. We have a clear case of the substantive in 395. This use of *atol* is peculiar to *Sat.,* if Cook's *atolearfoða* is to be accepted for *Chr.* 1265.

138b-139a. Cf. *Gu.* 191: *ne mōtun hī on eorþan eardes brūcan; Gu.* 353: *fægran botles brūceð;* and *Dom.* 90: *brūcan þæs boldes.*

139-140. Cf. 170. This use of *gesceaft,* modified by *beorhtan,* *mǣran,* or *ēcan,* specifically for the heavenly creation, i. e., heaven, is found in 560, 664; *Gen.* 93; *Gu.* 749; *El.* 1088; *Ph.* 660.

141a. The Corrector has changed the *a* of *wyrsa* to *æ.* Sievers, *Gram.* 276, n. 5, records a weak neuter substantive in *-a;* and the same inflection may have here crept into the weak adjective (unless *wyrsa* is a mere blunder).

141b. **wuldres lēoht.** So 253, 449, 556, 617, 650.

141-145. An OE. variation upon the theme of 'sorrow's crown of sorrow.'

143-145. Kennedy: 'where blessed souls are lapped in music by the Son of God'! As far as sense is concerned, it is possible to retain the *ēadigne* of the MS., construing it, after Ettmüller, as a modifier of *sunu* (*bearn* being neut.), and to translate with Grein: 'wo den Sohn des Schöpfers den seligen die Kinder selber haben all mit Sang umfangen.' Graz objects to scanning *habbaðˇ* as anacrusis, as in

$$\times \times | \; \acute{-} \; \grave{-} \; \times | \; \acute{-}$$

habbaðˇ ēadigne bearn. Whether his objection is valid or not, it must be admitted that the retention of *ēadigne* renders the progress of thought broken, and the rhythm unbearably jerky. The passage can be greatly improved if we read *ēadige bearn* and interpret these 'blessed children' to be the same as the *æðele heleðˇ* of 45-6, that is, the host of good angels and of the men who have been admitted to the joys of heaven. Against these Satan's envy has already *(loc. cit.)* burst forth. This interpretation of the company of *ēadige bearn* as composed of men in part, or even exclusively, gives especial point to the lines immediately following. Satan's state of mind is clearly revealed also by 266-7:

> Nē mōt hē þām sāwlum þe ðˇ ǣr sēcaðˇ ūp
> ēadige of eorþan ǣfre gerīnan.

He sees men enjoying the bliss that was his, and more of them, too, mounting up to enter into it; yet he cannot harm or hinder the righteous, though he dearly longs to seize them, but must content himself with those 'þe hē tō āgan nyle.' The redeemed are continually called *ēadige. Seolfa* is here nom. plur. masc.; cf. *Ps. Cott.* 108. Translate: 'where [God's] happy children have surrounded the Son of the Creator with their songs.' The situation is the same as that portrayed in 46-8, 220-4, and 661-3.

146a. Grein's *þāra ǣfæstra* suits the context well, but, as neither *ǣ* nor *ǣfæst* occurs elsewhere in *Sat.,* and as the latter is a relatively rare word, and found almost exclusively in the older poems, it is better to follow up Barnouw's suggestion (*Textkritische Untersuchungen,* p. 104) and insert 356[b] as 146[a], to fill the gap. Translate:

'Nor can I harm any of the souls who ascend from the earth, but rather only those whom He will not have.'

147. tō āgan. It is difficult to see why a simple uninflected infinitive as object of *tō* should have inspired so many emendations. Cf. Sievers, *Gram.* 363, n. 3. Sievers is right in asking whether one could find another so precise expression as 'nicht zu eigen wollen,' and his alternative suggestion (see textual footnote) that *tō* may be anticipated from the next line is unnecessary. Cosijn's *tō āgen* is impossible.

148. Cf. 92. *þā* here is emphatic.

149a. *Jul.* 114 employs *bringan tō bolde* for 'to marry' (cf. Lat. *domum ducere*).

150-152. This recalls *P. L.* 1. 83-6:

> If thou beest he; but O how fall'n! how chang'd
> From him, who in the happy Realms of Light
> Cloth'd with transcendent brightness didst outshine
> Myriads though bright.

Thorpe renders the anacoluthon satisfactorily: 'unlike to what we were when we, etc.'

152b. Grein's reading, *wuldres swēg* (cf. 237), both fills out the hemistich and supplies an object to *brōhton* which suits the context (see 155ᵇ-6ᵃ).

153. The phrase *bringan tō bearme,* 'proffer,' 'give,' is found in lines 153, 357, and 672, but nowhere else in OE. *Beow.* 2404 has *him tō bearme cwōm,* while in Lk. 6. 38 (Lindisfarne) 'Hīa sellaδ on bearm iūer' merely translates the Lat.: 'dabunt in sinum vestrum.' Cf. also *Beow.* 1144: *on bearm dyde; Beow.* 2194: *on . . . bearm ālegde.* The lap or bosom was figuratively represented as the seat of possession in several languages. Thus in Ps. 78. 12 the Lord is adjured to pay back the injuries which Israel's neighbors have done him seven times 'in sinu eorum.' Cf. Ps. 89. 51; Prov. 17. 23; Isa. 65. 6, 7; Jer. 32. 18; and see also Livy 21. 18. 10, and Horace, *Sat.* 2. 3. 172. Among the Hebrews and Romans this manner of speaking was derived from the custom of carrying articles in the loose folds of the upper garment. Heyne (Glossary to the *Heliand*) says: 'Das legen oder setzen in den schoss war das symbol der eigentumsübertragung.' He interprets *Heliand* 1104 (*ef thu . . . bedōs te mīnum barma*) thus: 'wenn du . . . mich als lehnsherr anerkennst.'

Kock (*Jub. Jaunts,* p. 69) says that *tō bearme bringan* requires a dative. In 672 we have *brōhte him tō bearme,* but in 357 no indirect object can be discovered, and we should have to emend 357 to *bringaδ* [*him*] *tō bearme,* if this requirement were absolute. It is probable that the phrase had become so stereotyped that it could mean 'offer,' 'proffer,' 'bring,' and that the indirect object was optional. Hence, it is not necessary to construe *bearn* as dat. (= Christ); it may be nom. plur.: 'We, the Saviour's (or better, the Lord's) children.' Kock's interpretation of 153 is, however, equally satisfactory. *Bearn* might be a Northern uninflected dative.

154-156. At first blush, Bouterwek's emendation, *lēoðu,* seems to give these lines the most suitable meaning: 'where, surrounding Him, we all raised our songs, sang hymns of praise to the Lord.' However, *lēoðu,* notwithstanding that it involves only a slight change in the MS. reading, is objectionable, for it would have to be considered an abnormal LWS. plural form. And, although it is a trifle awkward, we may retain the MS. *leomu* without giving it such a fantastic interpretation as that of Kock (*Jub. Jaunts,* p. 69). He would translate: 'lifted our wings,' a phrase which might have delighted the later Middle Ages, but one which distorts the meaning of *leomu.* So far as I can discover, *lim* is never applied to wings alone, although, in one or two cases relating to birds, wings are to be included under the term. Numerous examples, however, could be adduced to show that *lim* was commonly used in OE., as its equivalent was in other languages (cf. Gregory, *Hom. in Evang.* 21: *Patr. Lat.* 76. 1172: 'Si ergo membra nostri Redemptoris sumus'), to denote beings who were subordinate to one head. Its use is even painfully specific at times: *Prayers* 4. 51-2: 'ne læt þū mec næfre dēofol se þēah, þīn lim lǣdan on lāðne sīð;' cf. also *Bl. Hom.,* p. 33: 'Unrihtwīse syndon dēofles leomo.' Moreover, 'we lifted our songs' is a natural and common expression (cf. *Ex.* 276, 574; *Dan.* 543; *Jul.* 693; *El.* 889), whereas 'we raised (or lifted) our wings' gives a ludicrous picture if we take it as a single movement, or is very feeble if it is intended to represent 'flew' or 'circled in flight.' But, æsthetic judgments aside, the parallels for both *leomu* = 'members,' 'servants,' and *hebban* plus some word for 'song' or 'praise' show what was certainly the intended meaning.

For *Lēofne* = Christ, cf. *Ph.* 561.

156b. Cf. 186: *iūdǣdum fāh.* Compare 156[b]-7[a] with *Rood* 13: 'and ic synnum fāh, forwunded mid wommum.'

159a. So 281[a]. Cf. *An.* 1186: 'bǣles cwealm hātne in helle.'

159b. *Jud.* 121: *hyhtwynna lēas.*

160. The prosodists agree that the first hemistich is faulty in the MS., being a shortened C-verse with resolution of the first arsis. Moreover, the attempts of early scholars to explain the MS. reading are unsatisfactory. Bouterwek's *herede,* pret. of *herigan,* 'praise,' 'celebrate,' Dietrich's *harede*, 'clamavit,' and the same scholar's interpretation of *firna* as equivalent to *se firna*, 'der verbrecherische,' are all more than doubtful, even were the metre correct. Rieger's happy solution of the difficulty has been accepted by all later scholars save Wülker. The identical phrase, *fyrena hyrde* (used of Grendel), occurs in *Beow.* 750; in *Gu.* 522 the devils are called *synna hyrdas*.

Cosijn remarks: 'mit seinem *cwidum* am rande beweist der "corrector" seine nichtswürdigkeit'; and in general we may agree with him.

161. Cf. 579. The devil is called *atol ǣglǣca* in *El.* 901; *An.* 1312.

162. wītum wērig. Cf. 343, 428, 449. The phrase is not found elsewhere in the poetry.

162b-163a. Ziegler (*Der Poetische Sprachgebrauch in den sogen. Cædmonschen Dichtungen,* p. 166) says: 'Nicht wort und eitergift sind hier verglichen, sondern funken und eitergift, die beide durchmengt das wort in gleicher weise verderblich, giftig, machen.' This seems confirmed by 78-9 and 128-9.

164 ff. Wülker (*Gesch. der Engl. Litt.* I. 62) considers such speeches as this incompatible with Satan's character. He was probably thinking of the Satan of *Paradise Lost* and *Genesis B;* but this is unfair, because the whole of our poem, as well as other mediæval documents, shows that the conception of a disillusioned elegiac Satan grew up alongside that of a grandiose and inflexible epic Satan.

168. *Ealles—drēames* = 182. Cf. also 330.

169. Cf. 437: *rǣhte þā mid handum.*

171-172. Cf. the similar thought in 327-8.

172b. bēman stefne. So 238. Cf. *Dan.* 179; *Ph.* 497; *Chr.* 1062.

173-174. Cf. 187 and 256-7; also 201. Graz notes that the normal metre demands some short word before *Sunu* to complete the line; cf. 143, 529.

176. Holthausen's emendation, *habban mōste,* certainly improves the alliteration. Yet as personal pronouns do sometimes, even though very rarely, alliterate (cf. Rieger, *Zs. f. D. Phil.* 7. 30, and *Chr.* 1313), it is safer to leave the line unchanged. Bright's suggestion that we read *þone þe,* construed as referring back to *Sunu Meotodes* in 173, and interpret *Drihten—gelamp* as a larger parenthesis, within which *mē þǣr wyrse gelamp* forms a smaller parenthesis, as he says, would gain for us a 'well-wrought stylistic period and [he adds with reference to 643] the clear expression of a thought to which the poet, in his well-marked manner, returns for a second application.' The similarity to 643 is indeed close. Yet Bright's pointing seems to give a period that is rather over-wrought than well-wrought, for the involved

parentheses completely break the continuity. Besides, Bright's feeling
that the connection between 176 and 175[b] is obscure does not seem
justified. Translated 'worse befell me in that [enterprise] than I
might have had in expectation [i. e., had I remained faithful],' the
passage is clear enough.

179. Cf. Met. 15. 9: *ne mæg ic þeah gehycgan hwȳ him,* etc.
The alliteration of such a line as 179 may well inspire doubts of
its purity. Grein's *þæm = þeam* from OHG. *doum,* 'vapor,' was a
mere guess. Bouterwek's rendering of *in ðæm,* 'während dessen,'
does not give a good meaning. If we must resort to emendation,
Graz's *in þæt hām* is most satisfactory, in spite of the repetition of
hām in consecutive lines. As far as the meaning is concerned, however, the line can be made intelligible as it stands, if we construe
hām in 178 as the antecedent of *ðæm,* and paraphrase: 'Nor can I
understand how I came to be there (i. e., in the home I just mentioned).' We can infer from Satan's admission in 181-3 that he is
referring here not to the method by which he was thrust into hell,
but to his own folly in ever allowing such an event to take place.

180b. Bouterwek's clever emendation, *nīðsynnum* for *mid synnum,*
provides the needed alliteration with a minimum of textual alteration.
His word is not found elsewhere, but *nīð* is used to form compounds
perfectly analogous to it.

181a. Grein's emendation, *wuldre* for *worulde,* is very plausible.
The same emendation was proposed by Klaeber for *Ph.* 386, where,
indeed, it is practically indispensable to the context. Here we can
retain *worulde,* interpreted as the whole universe aside from hell.
The poet may intend to imply that hell is to be thought of as outside
the limits of the real universe of God. This *woruld* would then be
the same as that which Satan is said to have believed he possessed
(see 59).
Cf. the phrases in 669: *āworpen wæs of heofonum; Sal.* 462:
āweorp hine ðā of ðām wuldre; also *Gen. B* 300, 304, 342; *El.* 761.

181b. The ꝥ added by the Corrector at the right hand margin is
wholly unnecessary.

182b. Gen. sing. *drēamas* occurs also in *Dan.* 30, 115.

183. Cf. 317.

184a. Meotode cwēman. Cf. 305, 596, 655; *Gu.* 277; *Jul.* 252;
Creed 58.

184b-185. Kock's interpretation (*Jub. Jaunts,* p. 70) of *þæt
morðer* as parallel to *wēan and wītu and wrace* gives a satisfactory
meaning, and involves only a slight change in the text.

185. Cf. the series in 336; also *wēan and wītu,* 715. *Wēan and
wītu* is found only in *Sat.*

188a. weoroda Waldend. So 253, 564.

189b. *Sīdas* is probably a mere slip. The *d* might theoretically have derived from a very old MS., but it would be the only instance in *Sat.* of this orthographic phenomenon (see Sievers, *Gram.* 199, n. 1). The frequent collocation of *sīd* and *wīd* probably caused the scribe to write *sīdas* for *sīðas.* For *sīðas wīde* cf. *Gen.* 905; *Beow.* 877.

190-193. Groschopp (p. 252) thinks these lines chronologically inconsistent, because from earlier passages we know that Satan has already been in hell. Abbetmeyer (p. 11) considers them omitted after 33 by scribal oversight, and later inserted at this point. But it is not necessary to draw such conclusions. Both of these scholars have failed to notice the relation of lines 190-3 to those which follow. They are introductory to the first of the poet's long didactic passages, and give in a very proper place a summary of the fate of the fallen angels as a foil to set off both the description of the joys of heaven and the exhortations in which we are urged to strive to enter into these joys. The lines begin a new section, and do not refer to the words just preceding. *Þā* in 190 is purely resumptive; it does not signify any definite time. We may paraphrase: 'God's foe, then, went to hell when he was humbled; so did his followers . . . when God drove them into that dwelling which is called Hell. Wherefore every man must be mindful, etc.'

Cf. *Jud.* 112: *gǣst ellor hwearf, under neowelne nǣs and ðǣr genyðerad wæs; Gu.* 569: *sē ēow gehȳnde and in hæft bidrāf; Gen. B* 746: *ūs on helle bedrāf.*

190a. So 400[a].

191a. Godes andsaca. See 269, 280, 340, 719; *Gen. B* 442; *Ex.* 502.

192b. For the existence of acc. plur. *hē,* see Sievers, *Gram.* 334, n. 3.

194-195. Cf. 283-5 and *Wonders of Creat.* 98. The tone of the exhortations in *Sat.* may well be compared with *Chr.* 429-439.

195a. ābelige. It is not necessary to assume with the dictionaries a special weak infinitive *ābeligan* for this form (or *ābæligan* for the *ābælige* which first stood in the text; on the stem-vowel of *ābælige* see Luick, *Hist. Gram. d. Engl. Spr.* 188. 1; 366. 1). Sievers, *Gram.* 213, n., says: 'For (palatal) *g* after *r, l* the digraph *ig* is not infrequently employed when the combination is preceded by *y, e,* or *i,* especially in later texts.' He cites the WS. third sing. *æbyligð* for *æbylgð.* Hence, *ābelige* may be merely a graphic variant of *ābelge.*

195b. So 577[b].

198b. Cf. 581: *Drihten weoroda.*

199a. There is no support to be found for an adj. *ūp,* which previous editors have accepted (see p. 137). The scribe evidently miscopied *uppe* as MS. *ūpne* because of the immediately following *ēcne.* For *ēcne gefēan* see *Gu.* 1052, 1159, 1345; *Chr.* 159, 743; *Men.* 173.

200a. On the form of *gecȳdde* see Sievers, *Gram.* 405. 2.

200b. The *mægencræft* of the MS. looks very much like a conflate reading, unless we are to take it as an addition made by the scribe subconsciously. *Mægen* may have been in the scribe's copy a gloss intended to indicate that *cræft* is to be interpreted as 'power,' not 'skill' or 'cunning,' whereas the scribe took the two together as the compound substantive *mægencræft.* At any rate, the compound is metrically impossible.

Compare 200 with *Gloria* 16, 53.

203-204. The pointing of these lines has been very puzzling, and the meaning also is somewhat confused. The first attempts to set things to rights consisted in prefixing to *cēosan* some word which would alliterate with *eard.* If lines 203 and 204 are considered by themselves, this is legitimate. But when one notices that we have a *schwellvers* in both 202 and 205, one cannot help suspecting that that which intervenes was also originally a *schwellvers.* Schmitz (*Die Sechstakter in der Ae. Dichtung,* p. 9) says that 203-4 cannot be united into an expanded long line. This is true—as the lines stand in the MS. Graz and Kaluza merely printed them continuously as one *schwellvers,* but the result is a metrical monstrosity. Yet a very little emendation of the most inoffensive sort gives us a normal expanded line. The two phrases *in wuldre* are separated by exactly one MS. line. This is what happened: in the scribe's copy, *in wuldre* (the second of the two in our MS.) stood just after *ēcne,* but in the line below it. The scribe simply wrote straight along *ēcne in wuldre,* and, as he probably interpreted *ēcne* as a modifier of *Drihten,* the phrase as he wrote it suited the context perfectly. He then copied the following line correctly, with *in wuldre* in its proper place.

The only change necessary, aside from omitting this obvious dittograph, is the substitution of *l* for the *r* of *alra,* since *mid* never takes the genitive. *Ēcne,* of course, modifies *eard.* We may scan the line:

$$\acute{-} \times \times | \acute{-} \times \times | \acute{-} \times || \times \times \times | \acute{-} \quad \times | \quad \acute{-} \times$$
ēcne mid alla gescefta cēosan ūs eard in wuldre;

and translate: 'Let us, with all creatures, choose an eternal dwellingplace in glory with the King of all kings, who is called Christ.'

203. Cf. *Gen.* 1927: 'Him þā eard gecēas.'

205. ealra cyninga Cyninge. Cf. *Chr.* 136, 215; *An.* 978, etc.

The phrase derives from the scriptural *Rex regum*, Rev. 17. 14, and elsewhere. There is no valid reason for emending to *cyning*.

206. Cf. *Gu.* 770: *berað in brēostum beorhtne gelēafan; Father's Instruction* 44: *þurh blīðne geþōht.* Cf. also *Harrowing* 96-7.

207b. This common phrase, *sōð and riht,* recalls the *vera et justa* of Rev. 16. 7. Cf. also *Gen.* 21; *Gu.* 782; *Chr.* 700; *Beow.* 1700; *Ps.* 111. 6; *Pater Noster* 3. 75.

210-213. The translators, with the exception of Kennedy, have misinterpreted this passage. The word *wlite* is the chief cause of the trouble. It was thought to refer to *land;* whereas there is a shift in the thought to a different subject after *gesēceð,* and hence *wlite* must refer to the subject of *wunað.* Grein's translation will illustrate the older view: 'Das bedarf der einst, wer hier auf Erden wohnet . . . dass ihm in Wonneglanz erscheine, wenn er aufsucht wieder das andere Leben, ein weit angenehmer Land als diese Erde sei.' The distortion in the rendering of *behōfað* which this interpretation necessitates is final proof that it is unsound. *Behōfian* has, in addition to the meaning 'need,' that of 'must,' 'needs must,' but the necessity involved is never that of external circumstances; rather it springs from some personal need or from moral obligation. It cannot at all be equated with *necesse est.* Lines 210-2 are a continuation of the exhortation, and it is only in the words, *þonne hē ōðer līf eft gesēceð* (which are parallel to 208-9), that the transition to the actual description of heaven appears. We may either interpret *wlite,* with Kennedy and Kock (*Jub. Jaunts,* p. 70), to mean 'in beauty' (cf. *El.* 1318), or take it concretely as 'countenance.' According to Eccl. 8. 1, 'Sapientia hominis lucet in vultu eius,' and the shining of the countenance of righteous beings, both human and divine, is to be found throughout the Bible. The parallel in *Chr.* 1077 is close: 'Ðonne bēoð bealde þā þe beorhtne wlite Meotude bringað.' Both in *Sat.* and *Chr.* the more general sense probably suits the context better. *Him* is dat. of reference. (If *wlite* is interpreted as 'countenance,' *him* will practically signify possession.)

The passage may be paraphrased thus: 'He who has dwelt here amid earth's joys must needs shine in beauty when he seeks that other life.' Compare the references to the beauty of the good man's soul after it leaves its earthly dwelling, in *Gu.* 1277-8; *Chr.* 1058-9; *Soul's Address* 139-141. Exhortations to be mindful of our soul's beauty similar to that in 210-2 are found in *Chr.* 848, 1057, 1581. The passage which most clearly illustrates the meaning of these lines, however, is that from *Bl. Hom.* 95. 19, cited by Cosijn in connection with *Chr.* 1073: 'Mid gōdum dǣdum ond hālgum wē sceolan bēon gefrætwode, gif wē þonne willaþ bēon on þā swīþran healfe Drihtnes.'

The phrase *sē—wynnum* is merely a general periphrasis for 'every man,' and is not intended to be interpreted literally. It is equivalent to 'those who have passed through this earthly life.' For *weorulde wynnum* cf. *Gu.* 76; *Wife's Complaint* 46; see also Schücking's *Bedeutungslehre*, p. 103.

212. This euphemism is also found in *Gen.* 1627; *Prayers* 4. 30.

213a. Both metre and sense demand the compar. *fǣg[e]re* instead of *fǣgre*. The scribe made a similar mistake in 389, and still other instances are found in *Ph.* 330, *El.* 242, and *Gu.* 353. It may be that the scribe's copy had *fǣgere* (see Sievers, *Gram.* 231. 4), and that he, not noticing the metrical demands of the hemistich, mistook the form for the positive, and syncopated it. I read *fǣg[e]re*, since it preserves as nearly as possible the MS. form, but the penultimate syllable must be given a secondary accent in reading. The Corrector's attempts at restoration in 213-4 show that he was not collating a copy purer than our text, if indeed he had any other copy at all.

Fǣg[e]re land takes up the topic suggested by *ōðer līf*, to which it is so closely connected that it seems almost an appositive; yet we must construe it as the subject of *is*, 214. Sievers' notion (*PBB.* 10. 449) that *fǣg[e]re* here has a short radical vowel is certainly wrong, based as it is upon the Corrector's false reading of the line.

213-214. This charming little picture of the heavenly home, together with that in 359-365, reminds one slightly of the Augustinian hymn beginning, 'Ad perennis vitæ fontem' (Mone, *Lateinische Hymnen des Mittelalters* 1. 422). I quote 16-8:

> Virent prata, vernant sata, rivi mellis influunt,
> Pigmentorum spirat odor, liquor et aromatum,
> Pendent poma floridorum non lapsura nemorum.

Cf. Bede's vision of Dryhthelm (*Hist. Eccl.* 5. 12): 'Ecce ibi campus erat latissimus ac lætissimus, tantaque flagrantia vernantium flosculorum plenus, etc.' Both the Apocalypse of Peter (5) and that of Paul speak of the trees, flowers, and fruits of heaven. See also the much more extended passage in *Ph.* 589-631.

214. wlitig and wynsum. Cf. *Ph.* 203, 318; *Wonders of Creation* 63; *Rid.* 84. 19; *Eadg. B* 3; *Heliand* 1393.

215. Kock (*Jub. Jaunts*, p. 70) would emend to *brād[r]e lond*, in order to obtain what by his interpretation would form a third parallel, to be grouped with *hyhtlicra hām* and *Crīste gecwēmra*. But the adjective in the latter of these two phrases is much more effective if construed, not as a comparative modifying *hām*, but as a genitive plural used substantively. The important idea to bring out is not that the home itself is more pleasing to Christ, but that those who have attained unto it are so. Hence the poet continues: 'Let *us* turn thither where He sits, . . . and [where] companies of angels and the blessed stand about the throne.' *Cwēman* is used to signify the well-pleasing service of persons, rather than the pleasure afforded by an impersonal object. When, as happens in a few instances, *gecwēme* is applied to things, it expresses the idea of use or service, not gratification.

The phrase *hyhtlicra hām* might be syntactically parallel with *Crīste gecwēmra,* and signify 'the home of the happy.' However, since we have the same phrase in the gen. sing. in 138, with the adj. in the comparative, and since *hyhtlic hām* seems to be a well-known expression for heaven (cf. *Dom.* 24; *An.* 104), it is preferable to construe *hyhtlicra* here as a true adjective in the comparative, rather than as a substantive in the gen. plur. As to *brāde lond,* Barnouw points out (p. 108) two parallels to this use of the weak adj. minus the article, in the *brāde rīce* of *Beow.* 2207 and *Ex.* 556.

For *Crīste gecwēmra,* cf. 596; *Gu.* 277; *Jul.* 259; *El.* 1049 (used of persons in every case).

217b. The Corrector's emendation, *uton ācerran,* is altogether unnecessary. He did not understand *uta* (for *utan*—see Brown, *Lang. of Rushw. 1,* 2. 43), and, as it stood at the end of the line, he thought the *a* belonged to the *cerran* of the next line. So he drew a dash after *a* and before *cerran,* to indicate that the two were to be joined, and then added *on* above *ut.* He corrects *uta* again in 252.

218a. *Sit* is the only case of this sort of contraction in *Sat.* Sievers, *PBB.* 10. 474, remarks that *siteð* would also be metrically correct.

218b. sigora Waldend. So *Gen.* 126; *Ex.* 16; *El.* 731.

219a. Drihten Hǣlend. So 576, 683.

219b. dēoran hām. So 257; *Gu.* 40, 843.

221b. Cf. *ēadigra gedryht, El.* 1289; *Chr.* 1664. Carpenter (*Deklination der . . . Lindisfarner Hs.,* p. 16) records one instance of a gen. plur. in *-re.* Cf. also *hǣþenre* in 268.

223b-224a. Cf. *wlite scīne,* 211.

224b. If any one is disposed to question the metre of this hemistich, it will be found a normal C-verse if *Wuldor-* is read as a monosyllable.

225-280. There is an evident confusion in the MS. as to the speaker or speakers who utter 230-279. Within the passage there is no indication, aside from the change in number which the personal pronouns and verbs present, that more than one person (or group of persons) speaks. From 230 to 246 the first person plural only is used. Then in 247-255 the first person singular appears. Lines 256-267 shift back to the plural, while in the section from 268 to 279 the first singular is employed except in 270-2 and 277-9. Yet there is not the slightest stage-direction which would hint at a change in the speaker. This might be explained in three ways. First, the original poet himself might have become confused in the management of his dialogue. Secondly, the hypothesis suggested by Abbetmeyer that 1-365 represent an arrangement of 'plaints,' made with a view to dramatic recitation in connection with the Church, might be applied here: the necessary stage-directions were simply left out by the man who composed this reading version. The third explanation, on the basis of which I have emended the text, seems to me the most generally satisfactory. Some scribe, either he of our MS. or the writer of an earlier copy, seeing in the lines between 230 and 246 so many verbs and pronouns in the first person plural, concluded that the verbs in 225-9, which introduce the speech, and which were then in the singular, ought to be changed to the plural, because he thought that the speech itself belonged to the whole troop of devils. By the time he finished the whole section with 279, he was completely possessed by this notion of a group-plaint, and altered 280 accordingly. But when one keeps the whole speech in mind, it is evident that this speech would be perfectly consistent and in character if it had been given by Satan alone. If we compare each of the earlier laments in turn, we see that this practise of speaking for considerable periods, now in the first person singular, now in the plural, is a general one with Satan. The present lament, if we disregard the form of the introduction and conclusion as they stand in the MS., presents nothing that would lead one to suspect any difference between it and the others which Satan utters.

With this interpretation in view, it is possible to divide 225-7, as they have come down to us, into two lines which are satisfactory in both metre and import. In the MS. they stand thus: *þā gēt ic furðor gefregen fēonda ondetan wæs him eall ful strang wom and wītu.* We have only to read *fēond,* and take *wæs—Wuldorcyning* as a line with an expanded first hemistich, which may be scanned:

$\times \times \times \times - | - \times | - \times.$ *Ondetan* is used absolutely.

226a. Cf. 322: *wæs þæt eall full strong.*
226b-228. Cf. 68-9. For *ānforlǣten,* see *Anglia* 27. 270.
230a. So 441[a].
232. The objections to the metre of 232[a] are not serious (Graz, *Eng. Stud.* 21. 17; Sievers, *PBB.* 12. 467). It can be scanned as an expanded E-verse; cf. *Gnom. Cott.* 3. *Dōmlēase* may be another

instance of the archaic weak adjective unaccompanied by the article, or an adverb, or an adjective in the nom. plur. Thorpe, Kennedy, and Bosworth-Toller translate: 'wage a hapless (powerless) war.' This interpretation attempts to take *drēogan gewinn* in the sense which it has in *Beow.* 798 and *Gu.* 86. It is possible to abandon the usual meaning of *drēogan gewinn* (Graz would even cancel *gewinn*), and either follow Bouterwek's 'erdulden, machtlos, Mühsal,' or render the line: 'Dishonored we must suffer tribulation, through the might of the Lord.' But, on the whole, the most satisfactory rendering is: 'We must wage (or endure) an inglorious struggle, because of the might of the Lord.'

232b. Cf. *þurh Drihtnes miht*, 605.

233a. The Corrector's <u>in</u> *wuldres wlite* improves the sense. Cf. *Ph.* 609; *Pr.* 16.

235a. Cf. 663: *sang æt selde. Sceoldon* in 236^b is auxiliary (Grein: 'hätten . . . dürfen').

236a. *þūsendmǣlum*, which is found elsewhere only once each in *Ex., Jud., An.*, occurs four times in *Sat.*: 236, 509, 569, 632. Cf. especially *An.* 872: *þegnas ymb þēoden þūsendmǣlum.*

236b. In want of a better word, we may accept the Corrector's *wǣron* to fill out the line.

237a. Cf. 508, 556, 593.

238a. *Byrhtword* is a striking formation. One would hardly expect *word* to become the second member of such an adjective compound. Grein's very doubtful *rōfword* (*Rhymed Poem* 16) is the only possible parallel. The phrase *beorhtan reorde*, however, is found in *Chr.* 510; *Ph.* 128; cf. *An.* 96. Rankin (*JEGP.* 8. 421, n. 92) suggests that *byrhtword* may mean 'famous.'

239a. Cf. 659; *An.* 146; *Fates of Ap.* 28.

239b. Cf. *An.* 871: *ūtan ymbe Æðelne.*

240a. Cf. *Gen. A* 237 and *Gen. B* 741-2.

241a. So 261, 410, 443, 530, 558, 627, 675, 690.

243a. Cf. 581: *dōgra gehwǣm.*

243b. Cf. *Jul.* 725, and *se Dēora*, 543.

244b. God seolfa. So 260, 350, 430, 441.

245-246. It is evident that the poet has here allowed the mood which held sway over him when he was writing the exhortations to control him again for a moment. He forgets for the time being that it is Satan who is supposed to be describing heaven, and lets slip three lines which are not dramatically consistent with the rest of the speech, in that they imply that men were already mounting up to heaven to receive the reward of their faith, before the fall of the angels had taken place.

Cf. Ps. 53. 6: 'Dominus susceptor est animæ meæ,' which is rendered in Spelman's *Psalms:* 'Drihten andfeng is sāwle mīnre.' Cf. also Ps. 61. 3, and the vivid picture in 1 Thess. 4. 16.

Since, according to *NED., eall* in OE. never has a distributive sense, the relation between *eallum* and the verbs *becōm* and *gelēfde* is anacoluthic.

247. When we remember that Satan utters the whole lament, Grein's *mē* 'for clearness' (Wülker) is not needed.

248a. So *Rood* 40.

250b. So *Ex.* 6; cf. *Heliand* 1458, 2701, 4529; *lāre longsume, Gu.* 766; *Chr.* 44.

251. For *mīre,* see Sievers, *Gram.* 188, n. 5, and cf. 439.

253b-254a. Cf. 86ᵇ-7ᵃ.

254b-255. It might be possible to conceive these lines as the conclusion of Lucifer's speech to his followers, in which case they would have to mean that God's supreme position rested on mere empty boasting. Thus Kennedy (following Thorpe and Bouterwek) translates: 'For this is empty boasting which we have borne so long.' With this interpretation the transitions in lines 254-8 are smooth and straightforward. Grein's paraphrase of *drugon īdel gylp,* 'eitel prahlen . . . begiengen,' does not accurately render the sense, unless he really intended the quotation-marks, which in the *Dichtungen* are printed after this sentence, to come at the end of the preceding one. If such an error in punctuation has occurred, Grein's rendering would agree with the interpretation here proposed. I have nowhere found Lucifer presented as accusing God point-blank of boasting, but rather as himself vaunting that he would equal God. Of course, this very attitude of Lucifer implied that he thought God overrated himself. Still, he is usually too much occupied in exalting himself to make such a flat accusation against God. Hence, although the first interpretation is quite possible, it is better to take these lines as a parenthesis, in which Satan admits the futility of such speeches as he has just reported. I interpret the phrase *īdel gylp drugon* as exactly parallel to the *anmēdlan þe hīe ǣr drugon* of 74, and translate literally: 'This is mere empty boasting that we formerly perpetrated all that while.' This is only an aside, and in 256 Lucifer resumes his narrative. Some confirmation of this view lies in the fact that *īdel gylp* is a phrase which is very frequently used to describe the cause of Lucifer's fall. Thus Christ in *Bl. Hom.,* p. 31, says in repulsing the tempter: 'Gemyne þē sylfne hū mycel yfel þē gelamp for þīnre gītsunga and oforhȳdo, and for þīnum īdlan gilpe.' Cf. also *Gu.* 633-4.

257. Cf. 173, 187.

258a. Cf. 657, *Cyning in cestre.*

258b. Cf. *Beow.* 2923; *Chr.* 185; *Gu.* 507, 791; *Met.* 9. 5; *Gnom. Ex.* 199.

259. Thorpe: 'that our exile-steps must seek the grim abyss.' The possibility of such a misconstruction as this led Grein and Wülker to insert *wē*. But since the omission of the pronominal subject of verbs is a characteristic feature of the style of *Sat.*, and since there is no real uncertainty involved, the original text can be left unaltered. Cf. *Heliand* 3603: *uunnun uuracsīthōs.*

260a. grimme grundas. Cf. *Chr.* 1527; *Gen. B* 407.

260A. Grein's and Wülker's pointing of 260-1 as two expanded lines is impossible. Though 260A lacks alliteration in the MS., there is nothing to lead us to suspect a gap. Cosijn's emendation of *āna Cyning* to *on riht Cyning* (cf. *Rid.* 41. 3) and Graz's *hē is riht Cyning* are both possible. But one is loth to surrender the idea of the uniqueness of God which *āna* conveys. On the basis of 584 and 688 I suggest, *hē is āna [riht] Cyning:* 'He alone is true King.'

262a. Bouterwek's suggestion, *swīð*, has much in its favor. *Ic* for *ð* is no great error for a scribe to make. We have another possible instance in *Sat.* itself (see 322). The phrase *Meotod mihtum swīð* was a common formula. Cf. *Chr.* 716; *An.* 1209, 1513; *Gifts of Men* 4. Yet there is no real necessity for changing the text either here or in 322. *Swilc* in the sense of 'so great' is not common, to be sure; but it appears to have this meaning in *Gu.* 1101, and it is not a great step from *talis* to *tantus*. We do not have to assume absolute identity in all the cases of an OE. alliterative formula.

262b-264a. Cf. the lines quoted by Ungemach (p. 26) from the Chester Plays:

> Sum in þe air, sum in the lift,
> þar þai drei ful hard[e] schrift.

The ultimate source of the conception is the Pauline phrase, 'princeps potestatis aeris huius' (Eph. 2. 2). Gregory in *Moral.* 2. 47 (*Patr. Lat.* 75. 66) expands this: 'Et scimus quod immundi spiritus qui e cœlo æthereo lapsi sunt, in hoc cœli terræque medio vagantur.' See also Isidore of Seville, *De Ord. Creaturarum* 6. 7; 8. 1 (*Patr. Lat.* 83. 927, 931). As Abbetmeyer points out (p. 32), the same conception underlies *Gu.* 176-196. Cf. also *Sat.* 112-3.

264b-265. Cf. *P. L.* 4. 20-3:

> The Hell within him, for within him Hell
> He brings, and round about him, nor from Hell
> One step, no more than from himself can fly
> By change of place.

The parallelism of 264-5 with the passage in Bede to which Todd refers Milton's lines is still closer: 'Ubicunque, vel in aere volitant, vel in terris aut sub terris vagantur, suarum secum ferunt tormenta flammarum.'

266-269. Cf. 145-9.

268. The MS. reads *hǣþenre sceal*. Grein was surely on the right track in his suggestion (withdrawn in the *Sprachschatz*) that *sceal* here means 'throng,' and is connected with *scolu, scalu*. The scribe's copy read *sceale*. This he thought a mistake for *sceal*, which in his mind should govern the infinitive which immediately follows. Kluge (*Zs. f. Vgl. Spr.* 26. 101, n.) gives a list of words which exhibit this *o : a* variation in their radical vowels, among them *rodor : rador (Elene)* and *scolu : scalu*. *Scalu* is found in the compound *handscale, Beow.* 1317. For gen. plur. *hǣþenre*, see the note on *ēadigre*, 221.

The meaning of *hǣþenre sceale* is especially fitting here. Since the blessed have just been described in the plural, the collective *sceale* is at least *slightly* more acceptable than the generalized individual, *scealc* (Bouterwek's reading; Thorpe's *hǣþene scealcas* involves a more elaborate alteration). Moreover, *scolu* is often used with some substantive adjective in the gen. plur. in contexts similar to the present one. Cf. *womfulra (scyldigra) scolu, Chr.* 1535, 1608; *Gu.* 175; *ārlēasra sceolu, El.* 835; and also *sēo wērge sceolu, El.* 762; *þǣre deorcan scole, Chr.* 1523.

Compare with this passage the part played by the devils in the Judgment scene, 630-4.

274. The line has been corrupted in the MS., possibly because of the double meaning of *geþolian*. With the genitive, *þolian* means 'lack,' 'be deprived of' (cf. *Gen. B* 633) ; with the accusative, 'suffer,' 'endure.' The genitives *bitres* and *ðæs* clearly are out of place, and may be due to an overflow of the influence of *geþolian* into a line which is really parenthetical. Moreover, *beala* as dat. sing. of the *wo*-declension would be a very unusual form. Grein's hemistich is unsatisfactory both in metre and sense, yet his collocation of *biter* and *bryne* is suggestive. Cf. *Az.* 57: *se bittra bryne;* and *An.* 616: *biterne bryne.* The line, *in ðǣm bitran bryne beala gnornian,* scans perfectly, and is grammatically correct. *Beala* as acc. plur. arouses no suspicions (see Sievers, *Gram.* 237, n. 5). The only difficulty with the new reading is that there are no cases recorded of *gnornian* with an object, although, of course, *begnornian* is used transitively. However, the more common *murnan*, which is usually intransitive, takes an object in at least one case (*Fates of Men* 20; possibly also in *Sal.* 483). This may countenance a similar interpretation of *gnornian*.

276. *Hām staðelian* here and in 345 is a periphrasis for *wunian*.

277-279. Cf. 116. *Heofona rīce* is found in 618.

281-282. Cf. for the wrath of God, 429, 452; *Gen. A* 54; *Gen. B* 299. *Hǣlend God:* so 493. *Gen. B* 621 has *womcwidas.*

283a. Cf. 194. *Mæg* is here adhortative. Cf. *Dom.* 3; *Deor* 31.

283b. *Sē ðe his* = 'whose.' Cf. *An.* 460: *gif his ellen dēag.*

287a. Cf. *geara tōgēgnes,* 693; *Dom.* 91: *gearwað tōgēanes.*

287b. Schücking points out (*Bedeutungslehre,* p. 10) that *grēne* here has more the meaning of 'schön,' 'mühelos gangbar,' than that of the sensuous 'green.' Cf. the phrase in *Chr.* 1673: *wegas þē sindon wēþe.* This curious use of *grēne* meets us again in line 339 of the *Poema Morale* (Morris's *OE. Homilies,* pp. 173 ff.) : 'Go we þene narewe wei and þene wei grene.'

288a. So 625.

288b. Barnouw (p. 106) notes that *se ælmihtiga God* is found only here. Graz for metrical reasons would cancel *God.* If *God* is retained, we must consider the line a *schwellvers* with only the second half expanded. Since this is a possible scansion, I let the word stand, but it surely has the appearance of either a conflation or a subconscious addition by the scribe.

289. Cf. 310, 359.

290. Cf. 246, 303, and *Wald. B* 29: *gif ðā earnunga ǣr geðenceð.*

291. Cf. *Wald. B* 27: *sē ðe him tō ðām Hālgan helpe gelīfeð;* and see the similar construction in *Beow.* 1272. Cf. also *An.* 1566: *ūs þone Hālgan helpe biddan.* For the scribe's correction, *gelēfeð,* which very likely was in the original, see Sievers, *Gram.* 360. 1, n. 2.

292a. Cf. *An.* 459.

293. Compare the phrasing of *Chr.* 661: *uppe mid englum ēce staþelas.*

293b = 354[b].

295b-296. Cf. the same picture in 307-9, 652-3.

297a. Grein's *wīdeferð* (spelled thus in *Ex.* 51) restores the alliteration, and is sufficiently like *æfre forð* in meaning for us to assume that the latter is a scribal blunder. Cf. *Chr.* 163[a]: *wunast wīdeferh.*

298a. For this collocation cf. *Pn.* 49: *of ceastrum and of cynestōlum.*

298-300. Dietrich wrote concerning the MS. reading of line 300: '*Lūcan* braucht durch *onlūcan* (erschliessen) wohl nur erläutert, nicht ersetzt zu werden.' It is true that post-classical *recludo* means 'close,' as well as 'open,' but there is no evidence that a similar paradoxical development occurred in OE. (i. e., that *lūcan* ever came to mean 'open'). Kock's conjecture that the *on,* which was appended by the scribe to *lifigend* (as is proved by the fact that a point marking the

end of the line stands after *on*), really belongs to *lūcan* enables us
both to rectify the meaning and to obviate Graz's objection to the
metre of the MS. reading of 299[b] on the ground that it was an
expanded D-verse in the second hemistich. Dietrich's interpretation
of *locen* as signifying 'the Lord's holy place,' i. e., 'the Scripture,' is
far-fetched.

Kock renders 299: 'Let us extol those having lived on earth.' But
this does not fit the context well. It is preferable, with Grein and
Kennedy, to consider that *dēman* has the same object as *cȳþan,* namely,
þæt, which we may take as referring to the attainment of the bliss of
heaven by the righteous. This interpretation fits in well with the
hortatory tone of the context. The poet has just said: 'The Lord
points out to us an abiding home, bright city-walls; there the blessed
souls freed from all sorrow shine resplendent, where they shall for
ever inhabit a royal seat and city.' He then breaks out: 'Let us
make this known! While we live on earth, let us extol it! Let us
unlock the mystery, let us be spiritually discerning! For if we do
this while on earth, and are allowed to go thither, thousands of angels
will come to meet us.' Thus the object of *dēman* is not the *gesǣlige
sāwle,* who form merely one feature of the picture of heaven, but the
whole scheme of the soul's salvation and reward, which the poet has
summed up in the phrase *locen Waldendes. Dēman* is used in exactly
the same way in the common phrase, *dēman Dryhtnes ǣ.* Cf. especially *Fates of Ap.* 10. In the sense of 'extol,' it takes an impersonal
object in all the cases listed in the *Sprachschatz* except in the debat-
able lines, *Gen.* 17 and 1718. At any rate, the parallelism is drawn
much closer in the above rendering than in Kock's.

Kock notes that *lifigend* is here a plural substantive, meaning
'dwellers.' We may construe it as nom., and interpret *ǣrror lifigend*
as a general parallel to such phrases as that in 210[b]-1[a], the *on eorðan
ǣr* of 303, and the *ǣror on his līfdagum* of *Met.* 26. 87.

onlūcan . . . locen. See the comparison of Christ to a key in
Chr. 19 ff. (based upon the Antiphon, *O Clavis David*).

301b-302a. Compare the angels' meeting with Christ as he ascends
in *Chr.* 545-6.

303. Cf. 290.

306a. Cf. the figure of quenching sin in *Alm.* 5-9.

306-309. The correct pointing of these lines is established by the
fact that 307-9[a] are a close paraphrase of Mt. 13. 43: 'Tunc justi
fulgebunt sicut sol in regno Patris eorum.' Such a quotation at least
renders doubtful, if it does not finally disprove, Groschopp's dictum
(p. 262) that *Sat.* was written by some one who was not familiar

with the Bible at first hand. Ælfric (*Hom.* I. 218) translates the verse literally.

308a. Cf. *Soul's Address* 139: *þīn gāst . . . fǣgere gefrætewod.*

309a. Grimm (*Deutsche Myth.* 2. 583) takes *sceldbyrig* to be a reminiscence of the old pagan Valhalla, which was covered with golden shields. He refers to the *Edda,* which speaks of Valhöll as 'skiöldum þökt, lagt gyltum skiöldum, sva sem spanþak.' Rankin (*JEGP.* 9. 53, n. 7) disagrees: 'It is more likely that the author had in mind the idea of heaven as a sheltering city.'

309b. Holthausen's transference of *hēo,* which in the MS. follows *þǣr,* to 310ᵃ normalizes the metre of the latter hemistich. Cf. 359.

312-315. Graz's explanation of the MS. reading (see variants) is very satisfactory. He suspects that 314 immediately follows 312, and that the intervening phrase, *āwa tō aldre,* which is repeated in different form in the two hemistichs of 315, *ā tō worulde, ā būton ende,* was copied down too soon. The two phrases, *āwa tō aldre* and *ā tō worulde,* are about the length of one MS. line apart, so that anticipation would be quite easy, especially as the sense of *wunian mōton* joins very smoothly to *āwa tō aldre.* When the scribe discovered that he had copied this last phrase already, he filled up the vacant space with the similar *ā tō worulde* to eke out the line.

314a. drēama drēam. Cf. especially *Chr.* 1637; also *Chr.* 580; *Ph.* 658; *Gu.* 652ᵇ-3ᵃ.

315a. āwa tō aldre. So *Beow.* 955; *Gu.* 758; *Chr.* 479, 1646; *Ex.* 424; *Jud.* 120.

315b. ā būtan ende. Cf. 379, 679; *El.* 801, 893; *Prayers* 3. 59. Rieger (*Zs. f. D. Phil.* 7. 18) notes that this is an impossible second hemistich, in that it has two alliterating syllables, and emends by *Jud.* 120 to *būtan ende forð.* But one should not be too scrupulous in the case of such a tag as 315.

316. *Ēalā hwæt:* 'O how wicked it was for the accursed one to determine that he would not obey heaven's King.' For *ēalā hwæt,* cf. *Bl. Hom.* 33. 28.

317. Cf. 183; *El.* 367.

318a. Cf. *Fæder frōfre Gǣst, Jul.* 724; *Chr.* 728; *El.* 1105; and *frōfra Fæder, Gloria* 8. These expressions recall St. Paul's 'Pater misericordiarum et Deus totius consolationis,' 2 Cor. 1. 3.

318-322. Kock's note on this passage (*Jub. Jaunts,* p. 71) is very illuminating. Holthausen had previously divided the reading of the older editors, *wēacwānedon,* into *wēa cwānedon. Wēa* is, of course, a northern equivalent for *wēan.* (Hence we do not need actually to emend, with Kock.) Kock interprets *mān and morður* as parallel in meaning to *wēa*, i. e., as 'pain and distress.' He points out that both words (that is, when used independently of each other) mean, according to the context, either 'crime' (the normal signification) or 'punishment,' 'torment.' One is at first loth to give up here the radical meaning of the words, because of the frequency with which the alliterative phrase *mān and morður* occurs as a designation of iniquity. See *Met.* 9. 7; Wulfstan, *Hom.* 188. 14; Verc. hom. 21 (folio 116ᵃ). But a passage in Verc. hom. 2 (Förster, p. 93) removes all scruples: 'Þær þonne mid dīoflum drohtigan, in morþre and on māne, in sūsle and on sāre, on wēan and on wyrmum.' Cf. also Wulfstan, *Hom.* 187. 18.

Kock regards *hrēopan—morður* as a parenthesis, and *wæs—onǣled* as a second predicate of *flōr*. Accepting Grein's *ðǣre*, he translates: 'The floor . . . was to the many there ignited thus: this all was very hard.' Kock admits, however, that Grein's interpretation of *wæs—onǣled* as impersonal may be right. (*Gu.* 639-640 presents a somewhat similar construction, though the verb is not impersonal.) There is not much to choose between the two views. The phrasing of lines 39ᵇ-40ᵃ, *flōr is on welme, āttre onǣled,* adds some slight confirmation to that of Kock. At any rate the two clauses, *hrēopan—morður* and *wæs—onǣled,* evidently stand in the relation of an effect to its cause.

Thorpe's suggestion that the first *ðǣr* of the MS. is an error for *sēo* offers a third possibility. His reading gives a very smooth text, and is paralleled in thought by 420-1.

319b. The *hrēowan* of the MS. is impossible both in grammar and syntax. *Hrēowan* is always used impersonally with the dat. The letters þ and w are so nearly alike in OE. script as to be in some cases indistinguishable. This explains the scribe's mistake.

320. Cf. 386: *wīde geond windsele wordum mǣndon;* also 136. The scribe's *winsele* here and in 386 might be retained. The poet may have intended by this word to describe hell as the meeting-hall of the infernal *comitatus,* the devil and his thanes.

322a. On *swylce,* see the note on 262ᵃ.

322b. Cf. 226.

323b-324a. 'Who first came thither at the head of his troop.'

324b-325a. Cf. *Chr.* 1539: *lēge gebundne.*

327a. Cf. 108.

327b. *ūp þanon.* So 635ᵃ.

328. Cf. 171-2.

329-330a. Cf. *Chr.* 390: *habbaþ folgoþa cyst mid Cyninge.*

331-332. On the basis of *El.* 1289, where souls are described as being *in þām āde,* it may be suggested that the scribe left out *ād* after *gryndes,* because of its somewhat similar appearance to *ah.* This would be especially easy if *gryndes* happened to end a line in his copy. *Ad* or *wælm* suits the context as well as, if not better than, Grein's *bealu*. *Grynde* is not found elsewhere, but *æfgrynde*, 'abyss,' is cited in the Supplement to Bosworth-Toller. *Ah* is here practically equivalent to *and*, as in *Beow.* 1448. Thorpe's *ne* before *mōten* is necessary to the meaning. Cf. *nabbað . . . nymþe* in 335.

Kock's *nymþe grundas an / wunian mōten:* 'and only could reside in the abyss' (see *Jub. Jaunts*, p. 73), presents a very unusual adverbial construction with *wunian*, i. e., acc. + prep. or adv.

333. On *wōm* see Schücking, *Bedeutungslehre*, p. 94. Cf. *An.* 1554: *þǣr wæs wōp wera wīde gehȳred*.

334. The reading of the MS. is metrically suspicious. Holthausen corrects it by emending to *gristbitung* and *gnornung*. It is probable that these nouns should be singular, as two such plurals would sound forced. Cosijn's emendation, *gristbitungc and gnornungc*, is very acceptable, because it is evident that the scribe might easily have thought the final *c*'s (indicating palatalization as in *þingc*, Wulfstan, *Hom.* 305. 7) should be *e*'s. Cosijn is altogether wrong, however, in giving the impression that this orthographical phenomenon would point to Kentish influence, or that it is meant to signify hardening of final *ng*. It occurs in other dialects as a sign of palatalization. Compare this line with the Biblical 'fletus et stridor dentium' (e. g., Mt. 8. 12). Cf. also 339. Grein translates *mecga* by 'Teufel,' but, for evidence that the poet intends us to take the word literally, see the note on 46-7.

335-337. Groschopp (p. 257), on the evidence of *wē*, 335, considers these lines to have been abstracted from one of the laments and introduced here in the wrong place. It is more likely that *wē* is a mere slip of the scribe for nom. plur. *hē*, which we have met before. Otherwise, unless we accept Groschopp's view, we should have to interpret 335-7 as a brief lament of the *mecgas*, thrown in without an introductory phrase.

If it is the scribe who is guilty of *wē*, his doze must have lasted through 335ᵇ, which in the MS. lacks alliteration. Cosijn's *hāt and cyle* restores the line with the least possible change. Cf. *hāt and ceald*, 132.

337b. Cf. 111ᵇ.

338b-339a. This might mean: 'he who in hell was within twelve miles'; but it is better to consider *æt* equivalent to *tō*, and to translate: 'he who was within twelve miles of hell.'

339b-340a. Cf. Assmann's *Ags. Homilien und Heiligenleben* 168. 128: 'þār bið ēagana wōp and tōða gehēaw.'

341. For an explanation of this preterite form (for *hwurfon*) see

Sievers, *Gram.* 72, n., and Bülbring, *Elementarbuch* 268, 280, n. *Weor* for *wur* is very rare.

342. Cf. *Gen. B* 375: *hēr is fȳr micel ufan and neoðone;* and *Gen. B* 353: *hāt wæs him ūtan.* The line reminds one of Milton's "Twixt upper, nether, and surrounding Fires' (*P. L.* 1. 346).

343b-344a. Cf. 121ᵇ-2ᵃ. *Gu.* 116 and *An.* 1618 have *wuldre bescyrede.* 344ᵃ = 68ᵃ.

344b. hēofon. See Sievers, *Gram.* 384, n. 2.

345. See the note on 276. One might be tempted to connect *hām staðelodon* in this case with Isa. 14. 13, 'super astra Dei exaltabo solium meum,' which is the ultimate source of 372-3; but the phrase does not correspond closely to the verse in Isaiah, and it is better to interpret it as in 276. We may paraphrase: 'They lamented the deep plot, contrived while they were yet in heaven, by which they meant to rob the Saviour of his celestial kingdom.'

Cf. *Jul.* 431 (*þurh dēop gehygd*) for *dēop gehygd* employed in a different sense.

346b. Cf. *nergende Crīst,* 570.

347a. Cf. 688; *Gu.* 654, 764.

347b. Cf. 260Aᵇ, 688ᵇ.

349-351. 'Nam quis promat summæ pacis quanta sit lætitia' (Augustinian Hymn, 'Ad perennis vitæ fontem,' l. 7). Compare this impassioned mode of utterance also with *Chr.* 219-223 and *Dom.* 30.

The alliteration *swā : swā* is striking indeed, and has provoked several commentators to emend, but the intense emotion of the poet may account for the rhythm of the line. In modern English 'so' is often enunciated with extreme emphasis.

352. The alliteration of the line as it stands in the MS., *sunnu: scīneð,* is incorrect. Holthausen's *scīma* for *sunnu* rectifies this, and since it contains several consecutive vertical strokes, may very well have been misread *sunnu* (which is an error for *sunna,* as Groschopp pointed out). This is a natural mistake, because *swegles lēoma* would normally be associated with the physical sun (see *Ph.* 103). Grein's *hū scīr sunnu þǣr* is also perfectly possible, notwithstanding Graz's objection that it is metrically too long. It is simply a D2-verse with anacrusis. *Hū scīr Sunu þǣr,* which Cosijn proposed with diffidence, presents a much more doubtful scansion. Cosijn's own objection to his reading, viz., that, if *Sunu* (= Christ) were accepted, *Meotodes mihte* would be out of harmony with the context, is not a serious one. That Christ should shine in heaven 'by the power of God' is intelligible enough.

The scribe has, I think, failed to follow the poet in 351-5. This becomes evident when we examine his treatment of 355ᵇ. *For God* arouses suspicion at once. *For* with the acc. never means 'before' in a local sense, when no motion is expressed. Holthausen's *for seolfan Gode* is unacceptable, because it contains an unnatural construction in the weak dative of *seolf* unaccompanied by the article, a construction which is never used, so far as I can discover. Holthausen was on the right track when he previously suggested the omission of *for*. There is an erasure within this hemistich as it appears in the MS., which, if rightly interpreted, shows us what happened. The scribe copied correctly *se* before *seolfa;* but because of his misunderstanding of the passage as a whole, and because he had to fit the hemistich into the context as he conceived it, he added *for* after *seolfa* and erased *se.*

Now what was the original misconception which led the scribe to write such a line as 355^b? He thought that *swegles lēoman* meant the physical sun, whereas it really refers to God as the light of the Holy City. Although the earlier visions (e. g., *Apoc. Petr.* 5) sometimes include the sun among the features of heaven, it was a theological commonplace that heaven had no need of material sources of light. This view is based upon Rev. 21. 23, 24 (which derives in turn from Isa. 60. 19-20) : 'Et civitas non eget sole, neque luna, ut luceant in ea : nam claritas Dei illuminabit eam : et lucerna eius est Agnus. Et ambulabunt gentes in lumine eius;' also Rev. 22. 5: 'Dominus Deus illuminabit illos.' Cf. the Augustinian hymn, l. 20: 'Agnus est felicis urbis lumen inocciduum.' There is plenty of evidence that the Anglo-Saxons were acquainted with the idea. Rev. 22. 5 inspired this sentence from the Vercelli homilies (Förster, p. 113) : 'Ne þearf man næfre nē sunnan nē mōnan nē næniges eorðlices līohtes, forðan þær is se ælmihtiga Dryhten scīnendra and līohtra þonne ealle ōðre līoht.' Cf. the homily in MS. Hatton 116 (Förster, p. 136) : 'On þēre ceastre sunne ne līhteð nē mōna; ac Godes beorhtnesse hī onlīhteð. And sēo beorhtnes wes þæt sōþe Lamb, þæt wes se ælmihtiga Drihten.' Of the poetical passages, *Ph.* 587-8 is most similar to that in *Sat.:*

> þær sēo sōþfæste   Sunne līhteð
> wlitig ofer weoredum   in wuldres byrig.

Cf. also *Chr.* 106, where Christ is called *sōðfæsta sunnan lēoma; Chr.* 1651-2; and *Chr.* 696-7 :

> Hē is se sōðfæsta sunnan lēoma,
> englum ond eorðwarum æþele scīma.

Thus we see that there was every possibility that a poet who frequently shows acquaintance with orthodox views, even on minute points, might introduce such a feature into his picture of heaven. Yet it is just such a feature as a scribe of more limited knowledge might have failed to encounter. In the original the sentence is climactic. The poet even suspends the definite statement that the heavenly light he has been describing is God himself, over a parenthesis of a line and a half (354-5ᵇ).

Se seolfa God is paralleled by *se sylfa Cyning, Chr.* 1209, and by *se seolfa Sunu Waldendes, Sat.* 396.

There are two other possible ways of treating the passage. One would be to consider *sunnu* a mistake for *Sunu* (= Christ), and to emend 352ᵃ to *hū þǣr scīr Sunu.* In this case, *seolfa God* or *se seolfa God* would be a sort of remote echo of the *Deum de Deo* of the Creed. The second would be to abandon the notion that anything more than the material sun is meant in these lines, and hence to accept Grein's *hū scīr sunnu* [better *sunna,* for transcriptional reasons] *þǣr,* to omit *se* in 355ᵇ, to construe *seolfa* as nom. plur. (see 145) referring to *englas* and *sanctas,* and to add the dat. ending to *God.* Lines 354-5 could then be literally translated: 'There angels have eternal bliss and saints sing: that is, themselves before God (i. e., in the very presence of God).'

353. þæt mǣre cynn. Cf. *Ps.* 104. 11.

356-357a. 'The blessed then shall be they who come from the earth, who bring, etc.' E. Meyer (p. 103) rightly construes *bringað tō bearme* as an asyndetic relative clause parallel to *þe of eorðan cumað.*

For *bringan tō bearme* see the note on 153.

356-363. Cf. *Ex.* 543-7. Compare 356 with 613-4.

357-358. Bouterwek translates correctly: '(Sie) bringen zum Schosse (Gottes?) Blüten des Wohlgeruchs, wonnige Würze; das sind Worte Gottes.' Ziegler (p. 165) explains the somewhat obscure imagery of this passage thus: 'Die verwandlung der hingeschiedenen seelen in blumen war nebst der in vögel zum fluge gen himmel der naiven anschauung des altertums verwachsen. Ein vergleich der worte Gottes mit dem geruche der blüten, der wonnesamen würze, lag daher sehr nahe; die seelenblumen duften in befolgung Gottes willens, sie geniessen seinen segen und geben ihn wieder. . . . Wie dem Phönix aus dem neste blütengeruch anhaftet, so spenden die seligen vor Gott den duft ihres irdischen frommen lebens als himmlischen lohn.' Ziegler's assumption that the poet implies that the souls 'þe of eorðan cumað' are themselves 'seelenblumen' is very doubtful. But his suggestion that lines 357-8 are connected with the *Phœnix* is enlightening. I give below the pertinent sections:

> þǣr þā ēadgan bēoð
> æfter wræchwīle weorcum befongen,
> āgnum dǣdum; þæt þā æþelan sind
> wyrta wynsume mid þām se wilda fugel
> his sylfes nest biseteð ūtan. (526-530)

Swā nū æfter dēaðe þurh Dryhtnes miht
somod sīþiaþ sāwla mid līce,
fægre gefrætwed, fugle gelīcast,
in ēadwela[n] æþelum stencum.   (583-6)

      þær hī Dryhtne tō giefe
worda and weorca wynsumne stenc
in þā mǣr[an] gesceaft Meotude bringað,
in þæt lēohte līf.   (658-661)

Cf. also *Ph.* 465 ff.

It is not the idea of the fragrance which good lives present to God that proves the connection with the *Phœnix,* for we have this conception in 2 Cor. 2. 14: '[Deus] odorem notitiæ suæ manifestat per nos in omni loco;' cf. also Eph. 5. 2; Phil. 4. 18; and Rev. 5. 8: 'Phialas aureas plenas odoramentorum, quæ sunt orationes sanctorum.' It appears also in the sweetness of Guthlac's breath when his death was near (*Gu.* 1246 ff.). The proof would seem to lie in the fact that the fragrance mentioned in *Sat.* is described as that of flowers and plants, which, of course, recalls the herbs and spices of the pyre which the Phœnix builds for itself.

The designation of that which the 'pleasant herbs' signify as *word Godes* is illustrated by the passage from the Greek *Physiologus* which Cook cites in connection with *Ph.* 659: 'The Phœnix resembles our Saviour, who came from heaven with his two wings full of fragrance, that is, *of virtuous celestial words, in order that we with holy prayers may extend our hands, and send up spiritual fragrance by means of our good lives.*' The idea in *Sat.* seems to be that we bring with us to heaven the teachings of God which we have carried out and embodied in our lives—that we thus reflect them, as it were.

Compare also with lines 357-8 *Ph.* 542-3: 'Sāwla sōðfæste . . . stīgað tō wuldre wlitige gewyrtad mid hyra weldǣdum;' and *Bl. Hom.* 75. 14: 'Gif wē ōþre men teala lǣraþ, and hīe be ūrum lārum rihtlice for Gode libbaþ, þonne bringe wē Drihtne swētne stenc on ūrum dǣdum and lārum.'

For *stences,* see Sievers, *Gram.* 237, n. 3.

358a. So *Ph.* 194, 529.

359. See 289, 310.

360. Cf. 615.

361. For the ending of *lǣdað,* see Sievers, *Gram.* 358, n. 2. Compare 361-2 with 589-590.

362. Cf. 619. *Dom.* 29 has *ā tō ealdre.*

364. Cf. 183.

365a. See for other instances of this phrase in a similar context *Chr.* 1080; *Ph.* 516; *An.* 885; *Beow.* 186; *Pater Noster* 3. 17.

365. Dietrich remarks concerning 365 that the poet must be charged with an alliteration poor beyond compare, in *þām : þæt,* 'unless perchance it should be that *wyrcan* has been omitted before *mōt.'* It will be noticed that in every one of the other cases of *wel is þām,* the phrase occurs in a line of which *w* is the alliterating letter. Dietrich's *wyrcan* suits the context far better than Holthausen's *fōn,* even though we may grant the latter's contention that the alliteration Dietrich objected to is not unparalleled. There is no good reason for accepting Graz's notion that this line is a prosaic addition of the good scribe, who, inspired by the preceding picture of the bliss of heaven, writes, 'wohl dem der das kann!' Dietrich's emendation is perfectly satisfactory, and stands on as firm a footing as any other which is made *metri gratia.*

366a. encgelcyn. This line must mean that Lucifer by himself constituted an order of angels, unless we are to consider *encgelcyn* an error for *encgelcyning,* which is improbable; no one has suggested *encgelcyning,* but Kennedy translates by 'angel prince.' Such a conception as that first mentioned is not really so strange as it sounds. Jewish writers had developed the system of the orders of angels before Gregory the Great gave it its definitive Christian form. They set the number at ten. Cf. the *Book of the Secrets of Enoch* 29. 3: 'And from the fire I created the orders of the incorporeal ten troops of angels.' Gregory interprets the nine stones of Ezek. 28. 13 as the nine orders of angels (*Moral.* 32. 23: *Patr. Lat.* 76. 664-5, *et al.*). Satan was created preëminent and preferred before all these orders (*ibid.;* cf. also *Hom. in Evang.* 34: *Patr. Lat.* 76. 1250). In the thirty-fourth of the homilies on the Gospels, Gregory applies the parable of the ten drachmas to his angelology: 'Decem vero drachmas habuit mulier, quia novem sunt ordines angelorum. Sed ut compleretur electorum numerus, homo decimus est creatus.' Thus we see that Gregory did not explicitly teach that there were ten orders of *angels.* The sequence of events was this: Lucifer was put over the nine orders. He rebelled and drew half of the heavenly host after him. Man was created to repair the loss, and the elect (who will equal in number the faithful angels) will form the tenth order. As Ungemach (p. 24) remarks, doubts about the arithmetical relations of Gregory's system would be removed by the assumption of a tenth choir of angels, led by Lucifer. Yet the true interpretation seems to be that Lucifer, as Abbetmeyer puts it (p. 13), 'grew into the tenth choir when he had gathered about himself the host of his loyal adherents from the ranks of the other choirs.' Hence, it is not unnatural that Lucifer should be called 'that angel-order' by a sort of synecdoche.

See Bouterwek's discussion of angels in Cædmon, pp. CXLI-CXLVIII. The ten orders are mentioned in *Gen. B* 246-250; *Sal.* 454; Ælfric, *Hom.* I. 342 (See also Rask's *Grammar,* p. 194.)

The translation of *encgelcyn* by some such phrase as 'offspring' or 'progeny of angels' would be insipid. It is possible that Ettmüller's interpretation of *cyn* here as signifying 'one of a genus' may be correct, but it would be an instance of a rare idiom.

Cf. the reference to the order that fell in 20: *þæt æðele cyn, engla ordfruman, þæt þe æft forwarð.*

366b. Kühn's argument (p. 12) that the use of *ǣr genemned* proves 366-664 to be an independent poem, on the ground that there is no *encgelcyn* mentioned in 1-365, is fallacious. In the first place, *þæt æðele cyn, engla ordfruman,* 20-1, is surely a definite enough mention of an order of angels; and, secondly, *ǣr genemned* may not only mean 'afore-mentioned,' but may be merely a parallel of *hāten,* and mean literally 'was named of old.' (A similar pleonasm occurs in the use of *hāten* and *nemned* in *Met.* 10. 46-7.) By this interpretation, *ǣr* and *on gēardagum* would form still another parallel.

367a. According to Roskoff (I. 267), Eusebius (*Demonstr. Ev.* 4. 9: Migne, *Patr. Gr.* 22. 271) was the first to name the chief apostate 'Lucifer'; Eusebius quotes in full the *locus classicus,* Isa. 14. 12 ff. Cf. also Verc. hom. 19 (folio 106[b]).

368b. So 614, 651, 693; *Gen.* 88.

369a. Cosijn interprets *in wuldre* as 'in cælo.' It might mean equally well 'in his glory,' 'in his beauty.' Cf. *ðurh wuldor,* 59.

369b. Cf. *Gen.* 911, 932: *wrōhte onstealdest.*

370. Bright commends Toller's translation: 'that he would give way to pride.' Grein renders: 'dass er Hochmutgedanken haben wollte.' One is almost tempted to interpret the line metonymically, i. e., by letting *oferhȳda* stand for the pomp and state which Satan in his lofty thoughts hoped to possess. Cf. Thorpe's translation of *oferhȳda:* 'preëminences.'

371a. The hemistich in the MS. is a syllable short. Groschopp (p. 261) points out that 'Satan' is not used in 1-365. Compare 371 with 447 and 316.

372-373. Cf. *Gen. A* 32-4 and *Gen. B* 272-6. The source of these passages is Isa. 14. 13-4.

374a. Cf. the OE. *Gospel of Nicodemus* (*PMLA.* 13. 507. 25): *ordfruma ealra yfela;* and *El.* 771: *ealre synne fruma.*

376b. The MS. is clearly at fault here, but it can give us more assistance toward a correct reading than it has been allowed to do.

It may be recalled that this MS. shows a tendency to omit initial *h*'s. (Or, more properly speaking, the scribes' copy must have shown such a tendency, because instances of the phenomenon are found in the work of all three scribes.) A case in point is *insīðgryre*, 456. In 456, however, no accent marks the syllable *in*, whereas in 376 there is one to indicate some special emphasis on the syllable. But the scribe, even though he copied the accent, thought the repetition of the syllable *in* in the reading of his copy (i. e., *in inðo*) was a mere dittography. Ettmüller suggested *in tō hēnðo*, but without reference to the MS. Moreover, the sort of anacrusis which his emendation involves arouses suspicion in a second hemistich, whereas a single unemphatic syllable like *in* is often found as anacrusis elsewhere. [*H*]*inðo* (see 399) is a word continually used to denote the degradation of the devils, and it fits in naturally here between *helle* and *Nergendes nīð*, to the latter of which it stands in parallel relation.

Holthausen adduces the collocation of *hete* and *nīð* in *Gen. B* 768 and *Dan.* 619-620 in support of his emendation.

377b. and nō seoððan þæt. Cf. 634.

378. Another corrupt line. There is no authority for a verb *and-* or *onwlītan,* and the existence of an analogical *onsēon* is not above suspicion. *Andwlitan* had better be taken as the substantive, and the omission of some infinitive assumed. Holthausen's *sēon* suits the context. We may compare the thought of 170. Bright's *andwlītan mōsten,* besides retaining the doubtful verb, is metrically abnormal, since expanded E-verses do not seem to have been used in the second hemistich.

379b. Here begins the narration of the Harrowing of Hell, of which the ultimate source is the apocryphal *Gospel of Nicodemus.* It is not necessary to assume with Groschopp (p. 255) and Balg (*Der Dichter Cædmon und seine Werke,* p. 37) that there is a gap at this point. The transition seems a little abrupt, but 366-379, which are a *résumé* of the career of Satan, prepare in a general way for the introduction of the new theme. The treatment of this theme does not pretend to narrative completeness, emphasis being laid rather upon the personal relations involved. Since several circumstances are left unexplained, the story appears to us fragmentary, if we try to discover every event related in the *Gospel of Nicodemus* reproduced in the same order in *Sat.* But we must remember that the story of the Harrowing was common property in the Middle Ages, and that many things which seem to us disconnected rest on presuppositions which any one then would have understood perfectly. The poet has omitted all the speeches given in *Nicodemus,* in which the patriarchs repeated in hell the prophecies of the Descent which they had spoken while on earth, as well as the dialogue between Satan and Inferus. He greatly reduces the *dramatis personæ,* so that Eve, the Saviour, and the group of fiends, stand out clearly.

No full list of references on the growth of the story of the Harrowing of Hell need be given here. For our purpose the best general studies will be found in J. Monnier's *La Descente aux Enfers: Étude de Pensée Religieuse d'Art et de Littérature;* J. Turmel's *La Descente du Christ aux Enfers;* Wülker's *Das Evangelium Nicodemi in der Abendländischen Literatur;* and W. H. Hulme's *Middle English Harrowing of Hell and Gospel of Nicodemus* (pp. lx ff.). The other OE. poems to be compared are: *Gu.* 1076-7; *Chr.* 140 ff., 558 ff., 730 ff., 1160 ff.; *El.* 181 ff., 902 ff.; *Credo* 30-2; and the whole of the poem called the *Harrowing of Hell.* References to Biblical and patristic sources will be found in the Introduction, p. xxxiii, n. 44.

379b-380a. Cf. *Nicodemus,* Version B, 2. 1 (all references in these notes, unless otherwise specified, are to Version B of the *Descensus Christi ad Inferos,* edited by Tischendorf in *Evangelia Apocrypha*): 'Et audita est vox Filii Patris altissimi tanquam vox tonitrui magni.' Cf. 393^b-4^a. Compare 379^b with 406^b.

380b-381a. Cf. Ps. 106. 16: 'Quia contrivit portas æreas; et vectes ferreos confregit;' in *Nicod.* 8, at the voice of Christ, 'Portæ mortis et seræ comminutæ, et vectes ferrei confracti sunt et ceciderunt in terram.' Cf. Aldhelm, *De Laudibus Virginum* 454-7 (ed. Ehwald, p. 372):

> Sed tamen optatam senserunt sæcla salutem,
> Dum Deus ad herebi vagas descenderit umbras,
> Ferrea vectiferæ fracturus limina valvæ;
> Ærea portarum quassavit claustra tetrarum.

Cf. also 468.

381b-382. Into these short but vivid lines is compressed the long section of *Nicodemus* in which the patriarchs and John the Baptist tell of their joy at the fulfilment of their prophecies.

384. Either of the lines proposed by Ettmüller and Grein (see variants) may be employed to fill up the gap, but we cannot be absolutely sure that what has been lost did not refer to Satan alone, who had just been 'named' in 366-7. Still it is probable that *nemdon* here simply means 'mentioned.'

385b. Cf. *egsan āfyrhte, Chr.* 1020.

385 ff. All accounts of the Descent emphasize the terror of the fiends at Christ's approach. This goes back to the anxious dialogue in *Nicodemus* (chapter 4) between Satan and Inferus, the keeper of hell.

386a. Cf. 136, 320.

388a. In the normal versions of the story, Christ comes to Hades unaccompanied, or at most with only the converted thief. Yet one of the earliest circumstantial accounts, that by Epiphanius in the *Homilia II in Sabbato Magno* (*Patr. Gr.* 43. 459), mentions a troop of angels who accompany Christ, and assist him in the occupation of hell. (See also the note on 403.)

Cf. *þēoden engla*, 666.

389-391. Cf. the diction of *Chr.* 931: 'fore Dryhtne fǣreð wælmfȳra mǣst.' The ultimate source of the lines in *Sat.* is *Nicod.* 2: 'Subito illuxit nobis lux magna;' Version A has: 'Subito factus est, aureus solis calor (*var.* color) purpureaque regalis lux illustrans super nos.' The phrasing of the lines in *Sat.*, with the definite reference by the devils to their former condition, is peculiar to this account of the Descent, and seems to be a direct reminiscence of 1-365.

For *fǣgere,* see the note on 213ᵃ.

390b. So 718ᵇ.

392. Grein refers to *Jul.* 211 for another instance of *wītu,* conceived as the torments which the demons inflict upon the souls under their power. Brooke's translation, 'So will now our pains be deeper,' misses the point entirely (*Hist. Early Eng. Lit.*, p. 329), as does Cosijn, when he interprets *ūre wītu* as 'unsre hölle.' Adam says to Satan in *Nicod.* 20. 1: 'Dominus ecce venit, qui omnia figmenta tua nunc destruet.' Satan is also represented as especially downcast at losing, as one OE. version puts it (*Mod. Phil.* 1. 606), 'eall þæt wē hider habbeð gestrȳnd, [and] fīf þūsend and fīf hund wintre on pīne and on synbǣnde gebrōht hæfden.' Cf. *Bl. Hom.* 85. 15: 'Nis nō þæt ān þæt hē him ūre wītu [ne?] ondrǣde, ac hē wile ēac ōþre of ūrum bendum ālēsan.'

392b = 585ᵇ.

393b-394a. Cf. 379ᵇ-380ᵃ, 406.

394b. The damned are called *drēorge* in *Chr.* 1545.

395a. So *Beow.* 602. The phrase reminds one of 40-1.

395b. Cf. *sūsel þrōwian,* 41.

397a = 520ᵇ.

397b. Graz confirms Grein's emendation, *wile ūp heonan,* by 424. The hemistich, though uncommon, may be allowed to stand.

398b-399. Cf. *Beow.* 283: 'ā syþðan earfoðþrage, þrēanȳd þolað;' and *An.* 1379-80: 'þǣr ðū syððan ā, sūsle gebunden, in wrǣc wunne.' *Syððan ā* occurs in *An.* 1193, and *ā syððan* in *Beow.* 2920.

399a. The line has no alliteration in the MS. reading. *Yrreweorc* is, moreover, not elsewhere found. Graz's *hereweorces* (cf. *El.* 656, and *heaðoweorc, Beow.* 2892) neatly restores the line. It is just possible that the omission of an *h* in the scribe's copy is responsible for his mistake. It would be quite natural for him to change *ereweorces* to *yrreweorces*. (In *Bl. Hom.* 89. 12, *et al.*, *yrre* is spelled *erre*.) Christ's descent to hell came to be quite generally considered as a sort of military expedition, as well as a mission of deliverance, so that the meaning of *hereweorc* suits the context. For *hēnðo*, cf. *Gen. B* 776; *Chr.* 591.

400a = 190ᵃ.

400b = 582ᵇ. Christ now enters hell. All that precedes has been merely preparatory to the actual entry.

402a. Cf. 421ᵃ.

402b-403a. Cf. 566ᵇ: *hine forð lǣdde;* 553ᵇ-4ᵃ: *hām gelǣdde ūp tō ēðle;* 461ᵃ: *ūp tō ēðle.*

403b. Cf. 564: *þā cōm wolcna swēg.*

This mention of the angels' song of rejoicing is somewhat similar to that in the Greek *Anaphora Pilati* (Version B 8; I quote from the translation in the *Ante-Nicene Fathers* 8. 463) : 'And on the first of the week, about the third hour of the night, . . . majestic men of indescribable splendor of dress and of glory appeared in the air, and an innumerable multitude of angels crying out and saying: Glory in the highest; . . . come up out of Hades, ye who have been kept in slavery in the underground regions of Hades.'

404a. Cf. *Harrowing* 9: *on dægrēd;* and 17: 'þǣr cwōm on ūhtan ān engla þrēat.'

404b. Cf. 600: *Drihten seolfa.*

405a. Cf. *Gu.* 775: *fēond oferfeohtað;* also *Sat.* 462-3.

405b-406. We may paraphrase: 'The struggle began at dawn, when that terror came upon them.' For the chronology involved in this statement, see the note on 512ᵇ.

407a = 443ᵃ.

407b = 653ᵇ. The speech of Eve evidently interrupts the progress of the company to heaven. This reminds one of the order of events in the A-version of the *Descensus* (24. 2-3).

408a. Cf. *Abrahames cynn,* 461.

408b. The Corrector has set things to rights here by changing what was almost certainly *æfre* to *efe,* and by adding *o* to *hē* in 409ᵇ (the *o* might possibly be by the scribe). The scribe evidently thought, at least at first, that Adam made the following speech, in spite of the fact that Adam is mentioned by name in 411.

The thought of 408ᵇ-9 is related to the passage in *Bl. Hom.* 89. 5, where we are told that, after Christ had already freed some of the imprisoned souls, 'Ēua þā gȳt on bendum and owōpe þurhwunode.' The B-version of the *Descensus* in *Nicodemus* describes in separate sentences the joy and thanksgiving with which Christ is greeted singly by Adam and Eve. In the Blickling Paschal homily this is expanded, so that a separate confession, supplication, deliverance, and thanksgiving are assigned to each member of the original pair. The OE. passages rest on some such Latin source as the dialogue found in the *Book of Cerne* (*The Prayer Book of Aedeluald,* ed. Kuypers, pp. 196-7). First, we are told: 'Adam autem et Eua adhuc non sunt desoluti de vinculis;' and after Adam's prayer and release: 'Adhuc Eua persistit in fletu.'

And in 408b is adversative.

410. With the accounts of the fall of man which follow in 410-421 and 471-488 should be compared *Jul.* 494-505; *Chr.* 1380-1419; *Gu.* 791-850, 953-969; *Ph.* 393-423; and the unique narrative in *Gen. B* (491 ff.).

411a. This curious dual construction is found, though without *twā,* in *Gen. B* 387 (*unc Ādāme*); *Wids.* 103. Old Norse also employs it (see Grimm, *Deutsche Grammatik* 4. 294). The sense is: 'We two, Adam and I.'

411b. Bouterwek (p. CCXXXIV) classes *eaples* among the words in which *e* replaces *a,* that is, he construes it as acc. plur. It may also be gen. sing. after *þigdon.* See Shipley, *Gen. Case in A.-S. Poetry,* p. 58.

412. It came to be universally accepted that the serpent of Gen. 3 was Satan (or his tool or emissary) in disguise; hence, the *nǣddre* is called *se atola* in 413. *þurh nǣddran nīð* does not mean 'through the serpent's guile' (Kennedy), but 'because of the serpent's enmity.' Cf. *Ph.* 400: 'þǣr him nīþ gescōd, ealdfēondes æfest;' and *Ph.* 413: *þurh nǣdran nīþ.*

412b. Cf. Gen. 901b; *Minds of Men* 63: *swā hit ryht ne wæs.*

413a. Cf. 487.

414a. Cf. 49.

415a. hāligne hām. Cf. 567; *Gu.* 120; *Chr.* 1675; *An.* 1683.

417-418a. Cf. *Gen. B* 891: 'blǣde nāme on trēowes telgum.' Cf. 484a: *beorhtan blǣda.*

418b-421. The orthodox view (represented in *Nicodemus*) was that the souls of the righteous who died before the new dispensation would be held, until the Redeemer should come, *in claustris inferni,* not in order that they might be punished, but because of primal guilt. (See Gregory, *Moral.* 4. 29: *Patr. Lat.* 75. 666.) Their place of confinement came to be identified with the 'bosom of Abraham' (Lk. 16. 23), which Augustine describes as 'locis quidem a tormentis impiorum remotissimis, sed apud inferos' (*Civ. Dei* 20. 15). However, though this was the accepted view, opinion regarding the con-

dition of the patriarchs was not unified or always consistent. Thus
the Pseudo-Augustinian *Sermo CLX* (*Patr. Lat.* 39. 2060-1), after
having stated that they lived 'in tranquilitatis sinu,' says that after
the Descent their *torments* were transferred to their tormentors.
Even the Jewish apocryphal writings show this confusion. In the
Apocalypse of Moses (37. 5), God issues the following command in
regard to Adam's soul: 'Lift him up into paradise unto the third
Heaven, leave him there until that fearful day of my reckoning;'
whereas in the *Vita Adæ et Evæ* (48. 2), God says to Michael: 'Let
him be in thy charge till the day of Judgment in punishment, till the
last years.'

The Anglo-Saxons also held both opinions. Curiously, even a
version of *Nicodemus* (see *Mod. Phil.* I. 606, quoted above in the note
on 392) expresses the more rigorous view. Verc. hom. 19 (folio
107ᵃ) is very close to our poem. After recounting Adam's fall, the
homilist says: 'Ac hit him wearð biterlice forgolden on hyra lífe.
Ādām . . . syððan tō helle fōr, and þær grimme wītu þolode fíf
þūsend wintra and eahta and twēontig wintra.' (Cf. also *Heliand*
3604-5: 'Sie guldun is im mid fiuru lōn an theru hētun helliu.')
Cynewulf, on the other hand, writes (*Chr.* 146-7): 'Nu hīe sōfte
þæs bidon in bendum hwonne Bearn Godes cwōme to cearigum;'
which seems to imply not actual torment, but merely imprisonment.
Ælfric (*Hom.* I. 94; 2. 80) follows Gregory.

418b. Cf. 578: *him þæt swearte forgeald.*

419. Cf. 72ᵇ-3; *Chr.* 31-2.

421b. Holthausen's *onǣlde* is unnecessary, the participle being in
the predicative position. *Onǣled* is also uninflected in 341, where it
is to be construed as modifying the plural *andsacan,* not the singular
helle.

422-425. Such prayers for deliverance, while not found in *Nicodemus,* form an important part of the story of the Descent in many
versions, e. g., that by Epiphanius (*Patr. Gr.* 43. 454) and the seventh
Blickling homily.

424a = 568ᵇ; *Gen.* 13ᵇ; *Wonders of Creation* 92ᵇ. Cf. also 95ᵃ,
167ᵃ.

425a. *Gān* understood. Note the unusual alliteration of 425.

426. Since *ymb* in a temporal sense elsewhere means either 'about'
or 'after,' Grein-Köhler (*Sprachschatz*) suggest that *and* is here
written for *end,* 'before.' It is more probable that *and* is a simple con-
nective, used with the following phrase in just the same manner as
in *Men.* 11, 19, 83, 215. Since *ymb* originally was indefinite, not
signifying whether the time indicated is before or after, it is only
natural that it should be used for the former, as well as the latter.

The formula cannot be taken literally, referring as it does to the period of Christ's entombment. This can with some truth be reckoned as three days, but three nights is impossible. However, as the Anglo-Saxons measured time by nights, the phrase means no more than the usually alloted 'three days.' Cf. *El.* 483-6.

There are three possible candidates to be considered in deciding who is meant by the *þegen Hælendes* (who is also the person addressed in 430). The problem has puzzled some investigators so much that they assume a gap after 379, in which it would all be explained (cf. Groschopp, p. 255). Hippolytus (*De Christo et Antichristo* 45) had introduced John the Baptist as a precursor of Christ in hell, as well as in this world. In *Nicodemus* this conception is considerably expanded. It appears also in the OE. *Harrowing of Hell*. Dietrich and Wülker (in the *Bibliothek*), therefore, accept John as the *þegen*. But, as Holthausen points out (*Anglia Bb.* 5. 233), according to Mt. 14. 6-13, Mk. 6. 21-9, John had been dead a long time, and could hardly be said to have come to hell 'three days ago.' Now in the B-version of the *Descensus* in *Nicodemus* (chap. 23), the converted thief immediately precedes Christ, and announces his imminent approach. (In the A-version, the thief meets the patriarchs in the paradise to which they are led after the Harrowing.) Hence the converted thief is accepted by Hammerich (*Älteste Christl. Epik der Angelsachsen*, p. 67), Groschopp, Ebert (*Allgem. Gesch. d. Lit. d. Mittelalters* 3. 256), and Wülker (*Gesch. der Eng. Litt.* 1. 62). But, aside from the fact that the thief did not go to hell as soon as he died, but to paradise, the bonds, torments, and wrath mentioned in 427-9 would altogether misrepresent the relation to Christ in which he stood. (The same objection would hold good in the case of John the Baptist.)

Grein, in his translation, and Holthausen (*loc. cit.*) solved the problem by proposing Judas, who would be called, as were the disciples generally, Christ's *þegen*. (Judas is mentioned again in 574-9.) The *Heliand* (5429-36) contains a passage which shows that Judas' arrival in hell was conceived as premonitory of Christ's coming thither:

> Thuo uuarth thes thie uurêtho giuuaro uuamskathôno mêst,
> Satanâs selbo, thuo thiu sêola quam
> Iûdases an grund grimmaro helliun.
> Thuo uuissa hie te uuâron, that that uuas Uualdand Crist,
> Barn Drohtines, that thâr gibundan stuod;
> uuissa thuo te uuâron, that hie uuelda thesa werold alla
> mid his henginnia hellia githuinges,
> liudi, alosîan an lioht Godes.

On a very small point one must disagree with Holthausen. He says that Judas' suicide took place on the night of Thursday-Friday, and that *for that reason* it could be said that he *ymb þrēo niht cōm*. But the passage in Matthew (27. 3-10) which Holthausen cites, immediately follows a verse (v. 1) according to which the leaders of the Jews, *when morning was come,* took counsel against Jesus to put him to death; so it is probable that Judas destroyed himself on Friday morning, and the explanation of 426ª offered above is still pertinent.

428a. Cf. 162, 343, 449.

428b-429. Cf. 281-2, 452-3; also *for ðām anmēdlan,* 74.

430a. Cf. 63. Eve here turns to Judas, and addresses him directly.

431. Cf. 436.

432b. So *Beow.* 749.

433b. Schücking (*Bedeutungslehre,* p. 48) considers *hylle gryre* a compound in which *gryre* is merely an intensive.

435b. Holthausen's emendation restores the alliteration, and really suits the context quite as well as the MS. reading. Cf. 430-1. *Frēodrihten* is a loftier term than the more intimate *heora Drihten.* What delights and amazes the *hellwaran* is that 'God himself, the noble Lord,' is going to visit hell to save them. Cf. also *Frēodrihten,* 547. Of course, metrically, *þæt heora Frēodrihten* is also satisfactory.

437. Cf. 169.

438a. Cf. *Jud.* 84-5.

438b-440. The adjuration of Christ in the name of her daughter Mary, which Eve utters, is founded upon the doctrine expressed in *Chr.* 96-9:

> in Dāuīdes dȳrre mǣgan
> . . . is Ēuan scyld eal forpynded,
> wærgð[o] āworpen, ond gewuldrad is
> se hēanra hād.

See also Ælfric, *Hom.* 2. 22. Förster (*Archiv.* 116. 306) has indicated that this prayer is found also in the Blickling Paschal homily and the OE. *Martyrology.* I quote the similar passages. 'Ic þē hālsige nū, Drihten, for þīnre þēowene, Sancta Marian; . . . þū wāst þæt þū of mīnre dehter, Drihten, onwōce. . . . Āra mē nū, mīn Drihten, for hire wuldres weorþmyndum' (*Bl. Hom.* 89. 17). 'Þǣr Ēua hine hālsode for Sancta Marian mǣgsibbe þæt hē hire miltsade. Hēo cwæð tō him: "Gemyne, mīn Drihten, þæt sēo wæs bān of mīnum bānum and flǣsc of mīnum flǣsce: help mīn forðon"' (*Martyrology,* EETS. Or. Ser. 116, p. 50). Mary is also invoked in *Harrowing* 84 ff.

Compare the phrasing of 439ᵇ-440 with 475-6.

Note the Anglian dat. *dohtor,* for WS., Kent. *dehter.*

440b. So *Rood* 102ᵇ.

441a. So 230ᵃ.

442. Cf. *Gu.* 610: *ēcne Onwealdan ealra gesceafta.*

443a. So 407ᵃ. The poet again postpones telling of the ascension of the host to heaven, as he had done at 408, this time to recount the actual 'harrowing.'

444. On the ending of *clomma,* see Sievers, *Gram.* 237, n. 3, and cf. *clomme (Sprachschatz).* It is not necessary to assume a gap here (see variants). *Wuldre* is in the instrumental case, and is used similarly to *mid wuldre, Ps.* 79. 3. Thorpe renders the line: 'He in glory had bonds of torment on the fiends fastened.' We may translate *wuldre* better by 'gloriously.' Holthausen rightly rejects Hofer's metrically impossible *clom mā (Dat. u. Instrum. in den Cædm. beigelegten Dicht.,* p. 22).

Cf. *wītes clom,* 103, 452.

Abbetmeyer (p. 12) regards 444-456 as 'a variant of the monologues contained in 75-189.'

444-446. Cf. *Nicod.* 24: 'Et ecce dominus Iesus Christús veniens in claritate excelsi luminis mansuetus, . . . catenam suis deportans manibus Satan cum collo ligavit, et iterum a tergo ei religans manus resupinum eum elisit in tartarum, pedemque suum sanctum ei posuit in gutture.' 'In claritate excelsi luminis' recalls *wuldre,* while *furðor* seems to represent 'in tartarum'; Tartarus was the lower portion of hell.

With 445ᵇ-6 compare 633-4 and *El.* 941:

> þ[ec] se mihtiga Cyning
> in nēolnesse nyðer bescūfeð,
> synwyrcende, in sūsla grund,
> dōmes lēasne.

For *in þæt neowle genip,* cf. 102, 180.

447. *þingian* in OE. never seems to have the meaning 'to rule,' by which Bouterwek and Kennedy translate it. Nor is it used elsewhere in an absolute sense. Compare this line with 371.

449b-450. Cf. 28, 42. Translate: 'Never may they have the light of heaven, but only the abyss of hell (literally, *in* hell).' Compare 450ᵇ with 456ᵃ, 485ᵇ. The construction of these lines tempts one to improve 450ᵇ by omitting *in.* Whether the phrase *in helle* could be construed adjectively (= 'hellish') like the *on helle* of *Beow.* 101 (see Klaeber's Glossary under *on*) seems somewhat doubtful.

451. Cf. the thought of 115-7.

452-453. As Dietrich says, the *sense* of the MS. reading is complete. To bring the lines into some sort of metrical regularity with as little alteration as possible, I have ventured to print them as an expanded line, omitting the word *God,* which the scribe may have added unconsciously, and which in any case adds nothing to the meaning. The content of *seoððan . . . clom* is elevated enough for it to be treated as a *schwellvers.*

Cf. 281-2, 428-9.

453-456. The Blickling homilist (p. 87) makes Adam express a longing to be delivered 'ūt of þyssum bendum, and of þyses carcernes hūse, and of dēaþes scuan.'

Why Trautmann considers this passage faulty in meaning one cannot see ('Zum Altenglischen Versbau,' *Eng. Stud.* 44. 336). The metre of 455 is somewhat unusual, since the short foot *scuwa* does not follow a foot with a secondary accent ($- -$), but other cases of this scansion are to be found.

Cf. *Chr.* 118 (see also 257) : *deorc dēaþes sceadu drēogan sceoldan; Beow.* 160: *deorc dēaþscua.*

454a. The *atole* of the MS. might be an adverb, a weak adjective (acc. sing. neut., modifying *clom,* which some grammarians consider to be either masc. or neut. on occasion), or a neuter adjective used substantively in either the inst. sing. or acc. plur. Grein emended it to *atolne,* and it is also legitimate to emend to the substantive *atol* (see 395[b]). This substantive *atol* has seemed to be the best of the alternative constructions, because either some substantive or the colorless adverbial *eall,* referring to a preceding substantive, rather than a true adjective, is used with the phrase *tō æhte* in all the other cases; yet a hair will turn the scale.

454b. egsan gryre. So 728[b]. Schücking (*Bedeutungslehre,* p. 35) thinks this compound has here and in 728 developed a specifically Christian sense equivalent to 'qual,' 'verdamnis.' He compares *egsan þrēa, Chr.* 947, 1064, 1365. Yet *egsan gryre* surely did not become so concrete that the idea of 'terror' was much suppressed, not even in *Dan.* 467, where it is used as virtually a metaphor representing the fiery furnace.

455a. Cf. 105[a].

456. According to Schücking (*op. cit.,* p. 49), *gryre* here is nothing more than an intensive, as in 433.

457. Cf. *Nicod.* 24. 2 (Version A) : 'Et extendens Dominus manum suam fecit signum crucis super Adam et super omnes sanctos suos, et tenens dexteram Adæ ascendit ab inferis ; et omnes sancti secuti sunt eum.' The saints are then led to the *earthly* paradise. Turmel (*La*

Descente du Christ aux Enfers, pp. 53-7) states that Gregory is responsible for the idea of their going directly to heaven (i. e., on Ascension Day), instead of to the earthly paradise.

458a. So 506ᵃ. Concerning the orthodoxy of representing Christ as ascending to *heaven* at this time, see the note on 512ᵇ.

459b. Cf. 624ᵇ; *An.* 40, 287; *Dan.* 609; the phrase is used of heaven in *Ph.* 633.

460. *Him* adds nothing; but, on the other hand, it is not seriously 'disturbing' (see Graz).

Gregory makes a point of remarking that Christ, in his ascension from the Mount of Olives (and the same would apply to his ascension from hell), mounted up without the aid of the angels (*Hom. in Evang.* 29). Bede (quoted by Cook, *The Christ of Cynewulf,* p. 122) follows Gregory. Yet the conception of Christ's being aided by the accompanying host is also found. Cf. *Chr.* 517-9:

> Wē mid þyslice þrēate willað
> ofer heofona gehlidu Hlāford fergan
> tō þǣre beorhtan byrg mid þās blīðan gedry[h]t.

In the present case, however, in which the prophets, not the angels, are the spirits specifically mentioned, since practically all accounts of the Harrowing state that Christ takes Adam by the hand, and leads the company forth, it is not impossible that the MS. reading is not exact, and that the lines should be as follows:

> hōf hī[e] mid him handum hālige
> wītigan ūp tō ēðle, Abrahames cynn.

Compare 460 with the *hōfon hine hondum* of *Gu.* 702.

461b. Cf. *Ādāmes cyn,* 408.

462-463a. Cf. 404ᵇ-5ᵃ; *Hymn* 25: *Đū . . . fīond geflǣmdest; Gu.* 107: *fēond wæs geflȳmed.*

463b-464. It is altogether possible that there is a gap after *wolde,* in which some such line as that suggested by Ziegler once stood (see variants). The meaning would then be parallel to 401ᵇ-2. By this interpretation, the prophecies mentioned would be those of which so much is made in the *Gospel of Nicodemus.* Yet the line is intelligible as emended by either Bouterwek, Grein, or Graz. Grein's reading is very close to that of the MS., and may be scanned ××|-́-̀|-́ ×, *swā* bearing the alliteration.

466b. Cf. 380ᵃ.

467b-468a. Cf. 380ᵇ-1ᵃ, and especially *Harrowing* 34ᵇ-5ᵃ: *helle weallas forbrecan and forbȳgan.*

468b-469. Ettmüller seems to have been the only editor who has seen the drift of these lines; he says: 'de dæmonum et damnatorum ossibus poeta loquitur.' The translators all seem to be afraid of the word 'bones.' The poet is simply employing Scriptural phraseology. Cf. Ps. 101. 4: 'ossa mea sicut cremium aruerunt'; Prov. 17. 22: 'spiritus tristis exsiccat ossa'; Ezek. 37. 11: 'aruerunt ossa nostra'; *Nicod.* 1. 7.

471a. Cf. *An.* 733; *Rid.* 36. 13.

471b ff. Grüters (*Über einige Beziehungen zwischen Altsächsischer und Altenglischer Dichtung,* pp. 35 ff.) has already demonstrated a relation between this address of Christ to the patriarchs and his address to the sinner on Judgment Day in *Chr.* 1380 ff. In certain portions this relation is quite close. Cook indicated as the source of the passage in *Chr.* the homily included among the *Sermones Supposititii* of Augustine (CCXLVI), but assigned to Cæsarius of Arles (*Patr. Lat.* 39. 2207). The eighth Vercelli homily (folio 60ᵃ) also has a version of this address. There is no evidence of direct connection between *Sat.* 471 ff. and the Latin. Another somewhat similar speech of Christ to Adam is to be found at the end of the Paschal homily in which Epiphanius recounts the Descent (*Patr. Gr.* 43. 462).

Compare with this story of the fall of man the short accounts in the *Heliand,* 1032-9 and 3593-3606.

472. On Christ as creator, see the note to 9-10. Groschopp's objection (p. 253) to the shift in the person of the verbs and pronouns in Christ's speech (cf. 474, 482) is trivial. In 472 he is addressing the whole company of patriarchs; hence he naturally speaks of Adam and Eve in the third person. But since these two were present, and in the forefront of the assembly, the poet may certainly be allowed, without giving special notice, to represent Christ as turning to them (in 482) when his words have to do with their personal history in particular.

Cf. *Chr.* 1380: *Hwæt! ic þec, mon, hondum mīnum ǣrest geworhte.*

473. Cf. 20.

474a. On *begēton,* see Sievers, *Gram.* 109.

474-478. For the *menio,* cf. *Nicod.* 20: 'Tunc pater noster Adam intuens omnem illam multitudinem diligentius mirabatur si omnes ex eo procreati essent in seculum.'

In order that we may not make the poet guilty of dating the birth of Adam's forty children before the fall, as has been the custom of previous editors and translators, Thorpe excepted, it would seem justifiable to consider 474-480 as a parenthesis, in which Christ describes how the creation of man was extended. This parenthesis is a sort of introduction to the story of the fall. In 477-480 the poet states the common doctrine that men might have lived many, many years in paradise if they had not sinned. *Eorlas,* therefore, is simply a general term for men (i. e., the men whom the first parents would have brought forth in innocency). The idea, applied exclusively to Adam and Eve, is found in *Gu.* 803-816. *Gen. B* 786-8 also expresses it briefly: 'ac hīe wel meahton libban on þām lande, gif hīe wolden lāre Godes forweard fremman.' A paraphrase of 477-8 will bring out the poet's conception: 'It would have been possible for men to dwell in that homeland many, many years, until (or but) it afterwards befell, etc.'

474b. *On Godes willan* recalls the command of Gen. I. 28: 'multiplicamini, et replete terram.'

475a. In view of the fact that the number of Adam's children is a variable quantity in the works which mention the subject, it is hard to decide whether it is best to assume some undiscovered source for *fēowertig;* or to agree with Groschopp that the number arose through confusion (or, as seems just possible, through a conscious effort for parallelism) with the forty days intervening between the Resurrection and Ascension, and the forty days of Jesus' fast, which are both mentioned later; or, as a third possibility, to acquiesce in a suggestion which one of my colleagues offered, that 'forty' here is merely a good round number. Groschopp had also mentioned the possibility that *fēowertig* is used, similarly to other multiples of four, to denote an indefinitely large number. (See Wülker's *Altenglisches Lesebuch,* I, notes on selection 3, l. 232; 12. 172; and II, note on 5. 2.) Cf. also Klaeber's note on *Beow.* 147.

In the *Vita Adæ et Evæ* (24. 2) we are told that Adam 'begat thirty sons and thirty daughters; in all sixty-three children.' The *Apocalypse of Moses* (5. 1) does not count the first three sons separately, but mentions thirty sons and thirty daughters. The *Book of Jubilees* does not state the total, but, by adding up those referred to, we get fourteen. According to Charles (note on *Jubilees* 4. 10), Syncellus assigns Adam thirty-three sons and twenty-seven daughters.

476. [on] middangeard. It is better to assume that the scribe, because he had just finished writing the syllable *on* twice in *þonon,* omitted the preposition unconsciously, than to accept the Corrector's *middangearde.* Cf. the similar phrasing of 439-440. The cancelation point under the *e* of MS. *onweocon* is clearly by the scribe.

479-480. The MS. reads: *þæt hē āfyrhte eft / fēond in firenum / fāh is æghwǣr.* Dietrich has a long note on these lines, the upshot of which is that they should be printed as one, because there are several other lines in the poem which make sense, but appear metrically irregular. But 479-480, as Dietrich reads them, cannot be made to approximate the scansion of any known OE. line. The emendation he offered to make the passage intelligible is very ingenious. He believed that *eft* in the MS. reading of 479 was erroneously written for *ēst*, as an echo of *eft* in 478. *Āfyrhte* is a mistake for *āfyrde* (Ettmüller and Bouterwek had already suggested this last). Dietrich translates: 'bis alsdann es geschah dass er (Adam) die liebe entfernte: . . . ein hasser ist furchtbar feindlich überall.' The last clause is absurd, and, besides, such an indefinitely expressed reference to Adam is altogether out of harmony with the phrasing of the preceding lines, in which Adam has not been logically distinguished from Eve and their children. The obvious way of interpreting Dietrich's reading would be to construe *hē* merely as an anticipation of *fēond*, as the subject of *āfyrde*. The passage could then be translated: 'that the sinful fiend put away their favor' (i. e., removed God's favor from them).

Klaeber (*JEGP.* 12. 257-8) omits *eft*, reads *āfyrde* [*foldbūendum*] *fēond in firenum*, and translates: 'that he, the enemy, removed it (= *ēðel*) from men.' He compares *Ph.* 5-6. It seems to me that the sense of Klaeber's reading would be improved if Dietrich's *ēst* were retained as an explicit object of *āfyrde*, in place of the unexpressed *hine* (= *ēðel*). Cf. Grein's translation; also Kennedy's: 'until . . . the fiend . . . brought God's mercy to an end.'

The simplest method of treating the lines, and the one least disturbing to the text of the MS., is to omit *eft* (as a scribal dittograph), and print the words *þæt—ǣghwǣr* as one expanded line. Graz objected to assuming isolated expanded lines in *Sat.* However, as they are by no means a rare phenomenon in the other OE. poems, I have admitted a very few into *Sat.*, when such a pointing would allow us to keep close to the form of the MS., and give at the same time a possible scansion.

The use of *āfyrde* may be regarded as similar to that in 67. Of course, the fiend did not actually drive Adam and Eve from paradise, but it was through his activity that they were expelled. *Hē* may be construed as the Anglian form of *hīe*, which we have met before. (Cf. Bouterwek's translation: 'was sie hernach entfernte.') This *hē* may be responsible for much of the confusion in the MS. at this point.

Compare 479 with 128ᵃ.

481a. For the material on the derivation of *neorxnawong*, see Klaeber's bibliographical note in the *Later Genesis*, p. 53.

483a. On *æpla*, see Sievers, *Gram.* 273, n. 3.

484a. Barnouw (*Textkrit. Untersuch.*, p. 108) says: 'In der am wenigsten formelhaft aussehenden wendung *beorhtan blǣda* mag vom schreiber die urspr. starke endung in die schwache geändert sein, indem er das adv. *þā* für den bestimmten artikel hielt; oder ist dies *þā* etwa artikel?' He compares *Chr.* 694-5: *þā / gimmas.*

Cf. *Gen. A* 902: *þā blǣda ǣt.*

486a. On *oferhygdon*, see Sievers, *Gram.* 416, n. 4. Klaeber (*Later Gen.*, p. 55) thinks the construction of *oferhȳran* (see variants) with the acc. would be doubtful.

487a. Klaeber (*Anglia* 37. 541) illuminates this rather cryptic phrase by citing it in connection with *Gen. B* 717: 'Hē æt þām wīfe onfēng helle and hinnsīð'; and *Gen. A* 936-8:

> oðþæt þē tō heortan hearde grīpeð
> ādl unlīðe, þē þū on æple ǣr
> selfa forswulge.

He quotes from Hagenbach (*Dogmengeschichte*, § 63) Irenæus' statement that men 'simul enim cum esca [i. e., the apple] et mortem adsciverunt.'

A similar conception is to be found in *Gu.* 840-2, where death is called 'þone bitran drync, þone Ēve fyrn Ādāme geaf, byrelade brȳd geong.' This is expanded in *Gu.* 955-966. Cf. also *Gen. A* 893: 'ǣte þā unfreme.'

487b. As the *Heliand* puts it (3596), 'thō uuarð im the hatola te nāh.'

489-490. Cf. *Chr.* 1415-8:

> Ðā mec ongon hrēowan þæt mīn hondgeweorc
> on fēonda geweald fēran sceolde,
> moncynnes tuddor māncwealm sēon.

490. Cf. *clom and carcern*, 637; *Chr.* 734-5: *ligeð in carcerne, clommum gefæstnad; An.* 130, 1560.

Since the MS. has a metrical point after *carcernes,* and since *þæs* is a word which might easily drop out, I accept Graz's modification of Ettmüller's reading.

491-493. Cf. Ælfric, *Hom.* 2. 6: 'þā nolde hē āsendan tō ūre ālȳsednysse nāðor nē engel, nē hēahengel, nē wītegan, nē apostolas, ac sende se Fæder his āncennedan Sunu.'

494. Cf. *Chr.* 1601: *hwæt him se Waldend tō wrace gesette; El.* 495: *tō wræce ne sette.*

495. Cf. *Chr.* 443-4: 'þā se Ælmihtiga ācenned wearð þurh clǣnne hād.'

497. There is no sufficient reason for altering the MS. reading of this line further than by transposing *and* (so Thorpe). *Tintregan* is gen. sing. (weak) after *fela.* 'Much torment and great grief' has nothing suspicious about it. The only objection to Thorpe's reading, namely, anacrusis in the second hemistich, is unimportant.

498. Cf. *Ps.* 54. 18: 'forðon mē manige ymb mægene syrewað'; and *Bl. Hom.* 83: 'hēr manige sētunga and searwa ādrēag æt Iūdēum.'

499a. So *Gu.* 582; *Gen.* 2349; *Beow.* 2269; *Ph.* 147, 478; *El.* 198.

499b. Cf. *Gu.* 195, 830.

500a. *Bora* is never found alone save in the MS. reading of this line, whereas it occurs frequently as the second member of a compound. The adjective *rīce* is used in the poetry once with *rǣdbora* (*Pater Noster* 3. 38), and once with *rǣsbora* (*An.* 385); but since *rīces rǣdboran* is perfectly intelligible, Dietrich's emendation to *rīce* is unnecessary.

500b. *Hrefnan* is spelled thus with *h* in the Lindisfarne Matthew (6. 24). The word is used in a similar context in *Ph.* 641-2, but in a passive sense: 'þēah hē dēaþes cwealm on rōde trēow[e] ræfnan sceolde.' Translate the lines in *Sat.:* 'how they might bring to pass my death.'

501. So *Gen.* 1719.

503. Based on *Lk.* 3. 23. The first hemistich must be considered expanded, if *gēara* is retained. Cosijn refers to *An.* 157 for an instance of the omission of the unit of time measured.

504-506. The MS. reads: *gemunde ic ðæs mænego / and* (or *ond*) *þā minan hām / lange þæs ðe ic of hæftum / hām gelǣdde.* The form *lange* for *langie* is analogous to *folge,* which is found in the Rushworth gloss to Matthew. See Sievers, *Gram.* 412, n. 7; 416, n. 9. *Þæs ðe* is used after *langian* in *Soul's Address* 155, with the meaning 'because.' A clearer case of a genitive after *langian,* which will illustrate the construction and meaning of *þæs ðe* here, is *Bl. Hom.* 227. 1: 'Hē for ðǣm dēaþe ne forhtode, ah hine ðæs heardost langode hwanne hē of ðisse worlde mōste.' Since *þæs* for *þās* (see 504) is found in the plur. in *Met.* 20. 223, and elsewhere in *Boethius,* we may let stand this instance of *ðǣs,* construed as acc. sing. fem.

Thorpe, Grein, Dietrich, and Barnouw assume that the MS. reading *þā minan* is equivalent to German 'die Meinigen,' but the weak inflection of *mīn* never occurs elsewhere (nor for that matter the weak inflection of any of the possessives, except one very doubtful *ūran*). The Corrector hazarded *minnan* without fitting it into the context. Graz emended 504b to *in þām minnan hām,* and translated: 'da gedachte ich dieser menge in der verruchten heimat.' (The only pertinent parallel among those he cites is *in þone lāðan hām,* 178.) Graz, however, renders his interpretation impossible by canceling *lange,* because he thus leaves the construction of 505 uncertain. We may accept his emendation of 504[b] (inserting *on* for *in* as a more natural source of MS. 7 $=ond$), and by retaining *lange* obtain an intelligible text. Aside from the corrupt hemistich, 504[b], that which has caused the most confusion concerning the signification of the passage is the fact that the conjunction *þæt*, introducing the clause which is the object of *gemunde* (i. e., *ðæs mænego—earde*), has been left unexpressed. Dietrich pointed this out in his note. Grein followed Dietrich's suggestion in his translation.

The lines as restored run thus: 'I was mindful that this company in this wretched home were longing that I should lead them from their bonds [to their heavenly] home.'

There is some uncertainty about the meaning and derivation of *minnan*. The OE. dictionaries derive it from the same root as Goth. *miniza* and Lat. *minus*, and define it 'abjectus,' 'vilis,' 'mean,' 'vile,' whereas the *NED.* regards it as probably cognate with *mān*, and gives as the meaning 'wicked,' 'harmful.' Cosijn (*PBB.* 23. 118) having emended the two instances of *min* (or *minne*) in *Gu.* 622 and 881 to the required form of *mirc*, Holthausen proceeds to make away with the other instances which remain. He opines that *min* can be left out of the dictionaries, because the positive degree of this adjective is not found in other languages (see *Anglia Bb.* 16. 228). But it seems strange that, aside from the fact that some form of *min(ne)* is found three or four times in other OE. poems, the LWS. Corrector should have deliberately offered *minnan* as an emendation, if there were no such word. A mistake in spelling exactly like that of the MS. *minan* occurs in *mine, Gu.* 622.

The meaning of line 505 is intelligible without the expression of the object (i. e., *hēo*), and, since there are already five unaccented syllables in the first thesis, it is not advisable to add another (see variants).

Compare 505 with 553; also 506 with 554.

506b. The MS. reading of 554[b] is similarly incomplete in its metre. Holthausen's *sculon* (*sceolon* is the spelling used in *Sat.*) is to be accepted in both cases.

507a. So *Dan.* 32, 745. Cf. *Gloria* 47: *hāligdōmas.*

508. The verbs here change to the present, for the future.

Compare 508[a] with 556, 593; and 508[b] with 42.

509a $=$ 236[a], 569[a], 632[a].

509b. This is evidently a vague reminiscence of Jesus' prayer for his executioners in Lk. 23. 34.

510-511. See Jn. 19. 34.

511a. The plural *on galgum* is never used for 'on the cross.' *Galgum* is undoubtedly a slip for *galgan* (cf. 550), due either to the influence of the preceding *gārum,* or to a confusion in the number of vertical strokes which compose the ending (see p. 137).

511b. *Giunga* means 'young man' = 'soldier.'

512b. So *Dan.* 441^b.

The poet in 512-3 is following a chronology which is distinctly unorthodox. Something may possibly be omitted from the MS. after either 512 or 513, because Christ never alludes to the results of his being mindful of the saints in hell (i. e., his overthrow of Satan's power, and liberation of his faithful ones). Still, the poet may have considered that he had dwelt sufficiently on this theme, and that no further mention was necessary. At any rate, there can be no doubt but that 512 is in the right place, and that the poet intended to represent Christ as ascending to heaven immediately upon his crucifixion, and remaining there until early Sunday morning.

In the *Gospel of Nicodemus,* the impression is given that Christ came to harry hell immediately upon his giving up the ghost. Irenæus (*Hær.* 5. 31: *Patr. Gr.* 7. 1208) quotes numerous passages (among them that which Justin Martyr had accused the Jews of cutting out of Jeremiah) to prove that Christ's soul really went to the abode of the dead after the Crucifixion. Tertullian (*De Anima* 55: *Patr. Lat.* 2. 742) has the definite statement: 'Nec ante ascendit in sublimiora cœlorum, quam descendit in inferiora terrarum.' The Augustinian *Sermo CLX* (*Patr. Lat.* 39. 2061) reads thus: 'Mox ut spiritum redidit, unita suæ divinitati anima ad inferorum profunda descendit.' The same view is expressed by Dracontius (*Carm. de Deo* 528: *Patr. Lat.* 60. 812), and in OE. by the writer of the first Vercelli homily.

However, an interpretation which bears a distinct resemblance to that in *Sat.* is to be found in a sentence from Fulgentius Ruspensis, quoted by Monnier (p. 143, n. 1; the reference for a passage which he has just quoted is given as *Ad Trasimundum* 3. 34, but no separate reference is added for that which is of interest to us; as I was unable to locate the quotation in the vicinity of *Ad Trasim.* 3. 34, it must rest upon the authority of Monnier): 'Dominus ad Paradisum venit ut Adam a pœnis eriperetur; . . . prius Dominus cum latrone ad Paradisum quam pro Adam descendit ad Tartarum. Nam illum primo die descendens collocavit in requie, istum ascendens tertio die deduxit ad lucem.' Fulgentius here presupposes the belief held by some Fathers that the paradise to which the good thief and the patriarchs were led was not heaven, but the earthly paradise which Adam lost, and which was sometimes located underground, as here (*descendens*). Isidore mentions still another explanation. He says that some think that the 'limpidissimum subcœlestium spatiorum habitaculum,' whence the apostates fell (which must not be confused with the spiritual heaven), is reserved as a place of rest for the souls of the saints while they wait for the future resurrection, and that it was this paradise which Christ meant in his promise to the thief (*De Ord. Creat.: Patr. Lat.* 83. 926).

Some such ideas as these may be ultimately responsible for the poet's heresy in the present passage. Christ cannot correctly be thought to have ascended to his Father before the Resurrection, because of his words to Mary (Jn. 20. 17) : 'Noli me tangere, nondum enim ascendi ad Patrem meum.' Yet the poet is not wrong, in so far as he represents Christ as visiting some blissful place after his death, because this is implied in the definite promise to the thief in Lk. 23. 43.

The gap may be located after 513 as well as anywhere. *Tō,* then, will have the sense of 'from,' as in 686. Graz's division of the phrase, *tō . . . hāligum Drihtne,* to prevent *tō* from being anacrustic, is unnecessary, because prepositions are used as anacrusis occasionally.

514a. wuldres Weard. So *Gen.* 941; *Chr.* 527; *El.* 84. Compare 514 with 661.

515. Holthausen's transposition of *ǣr* gives a normal line.

516b. Cf. *Chr.* 467; *El.* 187. The Blickling homilist (89. 32) says : 'Mid þon þe Drihten þā þā herehȳhþ þe [? omit *þe*] on helle genumen hæfde, raþe hē lifgende ūt ēode of his byrgenne mid his āgenre mihte āweht.' Cf. also the Augustinian sermon (*Patr. Lat.* 39. 2061) : 'Facta præda in inferno vivus exiit de sepulchro; ipse se sua potentia suscitavit, etc.' Earlier accounts of the Harrowing, as noted above, conceived it as occurring on Friday afternoon, probably because of the influence of Mt. 27. 52. In considering the various chronological permutations and combinations in the accounts of the events subsequent to the Crucifixion, one should keep in mind the tendency, which the various writers exhibit, to follow the practise of Pseudo-Augustine, who introduces his version with the phrase, 'ut hæc breviter cuncta perstringam.'

517b. Grein's emendation is obviously correct.

521a. *On* is in later times a common colloquial or dialectal substitute for *of,* especially when used with *out;* i. e., *out on = out of.* One can never be sure when such expressions began to be used, and therefore *on* should be left in the text here. There are other somewhat similar cases in *Sat.,* where *on* is the preposition which governs the noun denoting the source whence something is taken, and which we must translate by 'from'; see, e. g., 417.

521b-522. Compare the spelling of *gefatian* with *fatas* (*Lind. Gosp.,* Lk. 20. 35) and *fatiga* (Wulfstan, *Hom.* 227. 8).

None of the cognates of *gefatian* ever seem to have the meaning 'bring news,' 'tell' (Kennedy), 'künden' (Grein), but, as Cosijn remarks, the verb is always transitive. It means either 'fetch' or 'summon,' always with the acc. Therefore the lines mean: 'He bade the shining angels summon his eleven followers.'

The MS. *winum* (or *sinum*) would upset the metre, and might be explained as merely a wild guess of the scribe at the signification of some gloss like *wine* or *winas,* which had crept into the text through conflation.

For the *englas eallbeorhte* see Lk. 24. 4; Jn. 20. 12; and, for their message to the eleven and Peter, Mk. 16. 7; 14. 28; also Mt. 28. 7; 26. 32. The spelling *andleofan* is not found elsewhere. The 7 in the MS. may well represent *ænd.* It is to be noted that in the Biblical accounts, the angels do not communicate their message directly to the disciples, but entrust it to the women to be delivered. The version of this incident in the *Heliand* (5834-43), though closer to the Bible, is very similar to that in *Sat.:*

Hiet sia eft thanan
fan them graƀe gangan endi faran te thēm iungrun Cristes,
seggian thēm is gisīthun suothun uuordun,
that irō Drohtin uuas fan dōðe astandan;
hiet ōc an sundron Sīmon Pētruse
uuillspell mikil uuordun cūthian,
cumi Drohtines, iac that Crist selƀo
uuas an Galilēo land, 'thār ina eft is iungron sculun
gisehan, is gisīthōs, sō hie im ēr selƀo gisprac
uuārun uuordun.'

522a. Cf. *Dan.* 337; *Chr.* 506, 548, 881, 1277.

525b. Cf. 117, 279.

527. gāstes blēd. Cf. 646.

529-531b. The MS. reads thus: *hāligne Godes Sunu / swā hēo gesēgon / hwǣr Sunu Meotodes / þā gingran on upp / stōd ēce Drihten.* These lines are in a badly confused state, and none of the attempts at restoration have been wholly successful. The *gingran* which stands before *on* in the MS. (530) begins a new page, and is probably anticipated from 531ᵇ. We need not suspect *þā,* the last word of the preceding page; it may be retained as an adv. The metre demands a light syllable between *upp* and *stōd,* and Holthausen's *gestōd* may be accepted provisionally. The best that can be done is to reproduce Wülker's pointing, with Holthausen's emendation.

The general drift of these and the following lines is clear enough. The incidents which the poet describes are told in Mt. 28. 16-7. *Upp* corresponds to the 'montem' of v. 16, and 533 renders v. 17: 'videntes eum, adoraverunt.' The importance of Peter's rôle in this passage is ultimately derived from Jn. 21. 1 ff., but Peter's actions and words in *Sat.* are in no way similar to what is recorded in the Gospel.

533a. Cf. 546ᵃ.

534a. Cf. *Gu.* 750: *þoncade þēodne.*

534b. Cf. 569ᵇ.

535b. Cf. 563ᵇ.

537a. 'Is it thou, Lord?'

537b = *Beow.* 1645ᵇ; cf. *Jud.* 300: *dōme gedȳrsod.*

538b. So *Met.* 9. 23.

539. Cf. this construction in *Rid.* 4. 13-5; 21. 29-30; *An.* 1192. The *c* of *þec* has a cancelation point under it in the MS. (put there probably by the Corrector). An accent above *e* has become blurred. These two facts show that either the scribe or the Corrector thought the pronoun emphatic enough to receive the metrical stress, and we may acquiesce in that opinion. In the MS., the cæsural point comes before *on.* Adverbial *on* is usually stressed; hence Bright locates the cæsura after *on,* and suggests for the b-verse *lāðe benda.* The MS. reading is perfectly clear, and, since an unaccented adverbial *on* is found in *Deor* 6ᵇ (followed, however, in that instance, immediately by the verb), there is no necessity of alteration.

Bl. Hom. 17. 1 mentions Christ's *heardan bendas.*

540a. The MS. form *hǣþenne* is probably due to the influence of *lāðne.* For another possible explanation, cf. Sievers, *Gram.* 231, n. 3.

540b. Cf. *Gen. B* 816, 819.

541a. *Endestæf* is found in *Beow.* 1753; *An.* 135; *Jul.* 610; *Fates of Men* 11.

542-545. This passage is both syntactically and logically incoherent. The poet began by following his chief source of lines 526-545, Mt. 28. (We are told in verse 17 that 'quidam autem dubitaverunt.' Cf. the WS. version: 'sume hīg twēonedon.) Then, of course, the story of doubting Thomas at once came to mind; this made him forget that he had begun his sentence in the plur., and he naturally used the sing. in the rest of the sentence, which refers to Thomas alone. (For the story of Thomas, see Jn. 20. 24-30.)

The lines might be explained in another way. *Genōm* might be a mistake for *genōmon.* *Hē* in the original might have been an Anglian nom. plur. By this interpretation, 543ᵇ would be merely parenthetical.

Mōd is an uninflected instrumental (found often enough in the prose), unless we may assume elision before *on-.* Compare the MS. reading of *Gen.* 1957.

543a. The hemistich certainly means: 'that it was the Dear One (i. e., Christ).' *Se dēora* has no point if applied to Didymus. Moreover, such an interpretation renders the sequence of the passage unintelligible. Compare with *se Dēora* the *Lēofne* of 155; *his se dēora Sunu*, 243; and *Harrowing* 70: *Dryhten mīn se dēora.* Groschopp (p. 254) and Barnouw (p. 105) suggested this interpretation of *se Dēora;* but the latter assumes a gap in the MS. after the phrase, which is wholly unnecessary. The only lacuna was in the poet's thought.

543b. Cf. Jn. 20. 24: 'qui dicitur Didymus.'

544. Cf. 680A.

546. Emendation here not only is not needed, but would actually obscure the true meaning of the line. Not one but two 'baths of baptism' are intended by the poet. His conception is based upon an interpretation of Jn. 19. 34 which was easily accessible to a mediæval writer, but one which was coming to be obscured by another that in time completely suppressed it (see Westcott in the *Bible Commentary, ad loc.*). The verse in St. John relates that after Jesus' death, one of the soldiers pierced his side with a lance. 'Et continuo exivit sanguis et aqua.' According to the dominant exegesis, the water and blood signify the sacraments of baptism and the eucharist. But a second theory existed alongside of this for centuries. Starting from such verses as Mk. 10. 38 and 1 Jn. 5. 6, certain Fathers regarded Christ's passion itself as a *second baptism* of martyrdom. The following passages will show the full development of this view. Cyril of Jerusalem writes (*Cat.* 3. 10, Lat. version, *Patr. Gr.* 33. 439): 'Latus transfixus sanguinem et aquam emisit: ut alii quidem pacis tempore per aquam, alii vero persecutionum temporibus propriis sanguinibus baptizentur.' Euthymius Zigabenus (*Comment. in Joan.*, Lat. version, *Patr. Gr.* 129. 1474) describes the water and blood as 'duo designans baptismata, unum quidem per sanguinis martyrium, alterum vero per aquæ regenerationem.' Tertullian (*De Pudic.* 22: *Patr. Lat.* 2. 1028) is still closer to the text of *Christ and Satan:* 'Hos duos baptismos de vulnere perfossi lateris emisit.' Rufinus (*Comment. in Symbolum Apost.: Patr. Lat.* 21. 361) speaks of the 'duplicem gratiam baptismi. Unam quæ datur per aquæ baptismum, aliam quæ per martyrium profusione sanguinis quæritur: utrumque enim baptismum nominatur.' Cf. also the lines in the 12th century hymn in Mone 1. 97:

lavans e tuo latere
nos munda vita vetere.

For interesting expositions of the more usual theory, see Prudentius, *Cathem.* 9. 85 (*Patr. Lat.* 59); and *Dittoch.* 165 (*Patr. Lat.* 60. 108); Sedulius, *Pasch. Carm.* 5. 287; and, in OE., Ælfric, *Hom.* 2. 260. The blood and water are mentioned in *Chr.* 1112-5; *Jul.* 292.

Bæðe may be considered either a scribal blunder for *baðu* or *baðe,* or merely a somewhat unusual form of the same. Cf. Sievers, *Gram.* 237, n. 5; 240.

545. Cf. *swāt forlǣtan* in a causative sense in *An.* 968-9; *Chr.* 1112.

546b. Cf. *An.* 1640; *El.* 490, 1033: *fulwihtes bæð.*

547-557. The tone of these lines recalls the hortatory passages of 1-365.

547. Frēodrihten. So 566.

549a. For the conception of Christ's 'ascending' the cross, cf. *Rood* 34, 40; *Chr.* 727, 1172.

549b. Cf. *An.* 1449b.

550b. Cf. *Chr.* 145, 319.

552b. In view of the word *secgan* in 552a, it is possible that Dietrich's *wordum* represents the original; yet the tautological phrase is perfectly clear, and it has been left undisturbed. Spelled as it is, *weorcum* could hardly be a *misreading,* although it might have been substituted for *wordum* through carelessness or a slip of memory in copying.

553-555. Cf. 402-3 and 361. The whole passage, 553-6, is so similar to 505b-8 that we are justified in accepting Holthausen's *sculon (sceolon)* and Bouterwek's restoration of 555. This permits us to reach 556 without a metrical gap. Graz's reduction of 556 to a line of normal length by reading *wunian in wynnum* would render the passage still more like 505b-8, and his theory that the omission of 555b might have caused a scribe to expand *wunian in wynnum* to two hemistichs (i. e., 556a as printed in the text) is ingenious. Line 556a as it stands is a slightly irregular expanded C-verse. Compare the rhythm of *Dan.* 455a.

556b-557a. Cf. 594; *Chr.* 1673; *Gu.* 457; *An.* 105; and especially *An.* 1611-2: *Ēow is wuldres lēoht torht ontȳned, gif gē teala hycgað.*

557b. Cf. *Wond. of Creat.* 20: *þencan forð teala; Dom.* 119: *sē nū wel þenceð.*

558-559. Cf. the specification of the length of the interval between the Resurrection and the Ascension in *Chr.* 466-7, and *Credo* 35-6.

559-560a. Kock (*Anglia* 44. 258-9) takes exception to the interpretation of *folgad folcum* as 'bedient von den völkern,' on the ground that *folgian* is an intransitive verb. He would simply remove *folgad* from the place where it does not fit, and put it in again after *mancynnes.* He translates the phrase: 'help of men.' This rendering he thinks justified by the facts that ON. *fylgð* sometimes means 'help,' and that God is *ealra cyninga help* in *Pater Noster* 3. 61-2. The only objection that could be offered is that there is no evidence that *folgad* could mean 'help' in OE., whereas in ON. this meaning is well attested. It seems not impossible that the poet in a special instance might lose sight of the fact that *folgian* is intransitive, and use *folgad* as we should in Mod. E., i. e., to mean 'followed' (of course, not 'served,' which in the context makes nonsense). Kock objected that Christ was not 'bedient von den völkern' for forty days. But *fēowertig daga* need not be applied more particularly to *folgad* than to *wæs on eorðan* or *gecȳðed;* and if we take a synthetic view of the Gospel passages dealing with the post-resurrection period, as the poet would certainly do, it becomes evident that in the trips to Galilee, back to Jerusalem, and out to Bethany, Christ was 'followed by people.' Since the laws of alliteration demand some change, I have accepted for the text Grein's suggestion that the order of the two hemistichs of 559, as they read in the MS., should be reversed.

Cosijn thought *folgad* to be a correction offered by the scribe for a dittograph of *folcum,* which stood in his copy. Cosijn therefore canceled it, printing 559-560ᵃ thus: *folcum gecȳðed fēowertig daga Meotod mancynnes.*

Shipley (*Gen. Case in A.-S. Poetry,* p. 65) believes that MS. *mancynnes* cannot be construed as gen. after *gecȳðed.* Wülker had connected the word with *folcum;* Shipley would refer it back to *ēce Drihten.* Grein's *mancynne* is preferable to such strained constructions.

560b. Cf. note on 139.

561a. *Burhlēod* occurs only in *Sat.* and *Jud.* 175, 187.

562a. Thorpe brings out the correct interpretation of 560ᵇ-2: 'ere he into the great creation . . . would bring his holy spirit to heaven's kingdom.' One is at a loss to make out what event or conception Bouterwek, Grein, and Kennedy think the poet is alluding to, when they render *hāligne gāst* by 'den heiligen Geist' and 'the Holy Spirit.' 560ᵇ-2 obviously introduce the account of the Ascension, not Pentecost.

For this mode of describing Christ's movements, cf. *Bl. Hom.* 85. 4: 'hē þā *onsende his* þone wuldorfæstan *gāst tō* helle grunde.'

563-569. Compare the version of the Ascension story in *Chr.* 458-532.

564b and 568-569b. Compare 564ᵇ with 403. The *swēg,* of course, comes from the angel hosts, not the clouds themselves. For the mention of clouds in connection with the Ascension, see Acts 1. 9.

Cf. *An.* 88-9: *cōm wuldres tācen hālig of heofenum; Gu.* 1256-7: *ðā cwōm lēohta mæst hālig of heofonum.* Note the description of the angel's music at the ascension of Guthlac's soul (*Gu.* 1288-90). For the angels cf. *Chr.* 491-5:

Ðā wearð semninga swēg on lyfte
hlūd gehȳred: heofonengla þrēat,
weorud wlitescȳne, wuldres āras,
cwōmun on corðre;

and also the description of the angel host at the Last Judgment, *Chr.*
928-9:

ond him on healfa gehwo[n]e heofonengla þrēat
ymbūtan farað.

See Cook's note on *Chr.* 494.

570a. Cf. 346[b].

570b. None of the proposed restorations of this line fit the context.
Christ was neither *mid niððum* (the reading proposed by Grein and
Holthausen) nor 'hienieder' (Grein's translation) during the ten days
between the Ascension and Pentecost. As a possibility, I suggest for
570[b], *nēosade weras* (or *wera*). The line with this reading would
mean: 'while yet Christ the Saviour visited mankind;' i. e., before
Christ's supernatural manifestations of himself to men were inter-
mitted. (Or should one say became very rare, since, because of the
universal belief in visions, no one in the Middle Ages could have
thought of them as ceasing entirely?) *Nēosian* is frequently used to
signify God's visitation to mankind, sometimes for the Lat. *visitare*.

571. Bright's note has completely elucidated this line, and must be
reproduced at least in part. After alluding to Holthausen's emendation of *twelf* to *endleofan*, which had been proposed in order to
restore the alliteration, and to bring the line into harmony with such
Biblical verses as Mt. 28. 16, Mk. 16. 14, and Lk. 24. 33, Bright continues: 'The passage surely relates to the Pentecostal gift of the
Spirit (*Gāstes gife*), which, of course, took place ten days after the
Ascension, the event spoken of in the immediately preceding lines
as having occurred forty days . . . after the Resurrection. Ælfric
is specific in saying that the Pentecostal gift was given *on þām end-
leoftan dæge Crīstes ūpāstīges* (*Hom.* I. 298), and the duration of
the period of waiting for the fulfillment of the promise is expressed
in *Christ* 542 by *tȳn niht.* [I may add that the eleventh Blickling
homily (117. 14) is still more explicit, and nearer to the text of *Sat.*
as well: 'ac nǣron hīe þā gȳt þā hālgan mid þon godcundan Gāste
swā getrymede, swā hīe sōna emb tēn niht wǣron;' (119. 13) 'hē þē
tēoþan dæge him þone Hālgan Gāst onsende;' see also the twelfth
homily, 131. 8.] The context therefore would require the same
specific designation of time, measured from the foregoing limit of
the 'forty days,' inasmuch as the poet is clearly following the record
of the beginning of the Acts. He puts appropriate stress upon such

details as the date of the gift of the Spirit (Acts 2. 1 . . .); the restored number of the disciples—restored to *twelve* by the election of Matthias [Acts 1. 16-26]; the defection of Judas, of which so much is said in the same connection (Acts 1. 16 ff.); and the great number of souls (*sāwla unrīm*) established in the new faith (vid. Ælfric, *Hom.* 1. 316). Moreover, to confirm this interpretation in a striking manner, it will be noticed that the poet, according to his original, Acts 1. 26, here names the disciples '*apostolas*' (cf. the only other occurrence of this name in the poetry, *Men.* 122: *Petrus and Paulus: hwæt, þā apostolas*). We therefore must conclude to read the line . . .: *þæt hē þæs ymb tȳn niht twelf apostolas.*'

Bright then proceeds to correct the metre 'by transposing the adverbial *þæs* to the emphatic position': *þæt hē ymb tȳn niht þæs* (cf. *Men.* 41, 131, 137, etc.). But this is to do unnecessary violence to the text. In a document for which an Anglian original may be so safely assumed, there can be no objection to accepting *tēne* for *tȳn*. The metre of the line then becomes almost identical with that of *Men.* 19. Moreover, *tēne* in OE. script would have been much more likely to be mistaken for *āne* than *tȳn*. If such a form as *tīne* should by any chance have been in the scribe's copy, the possibility of misreading would have been still greater. (*Tīn* and *tīene* are to be found, but not *tīne.*)

572a. gāstes gife. Cf. *An.* 530-1.

573. Cf. Acts 2. 41: 'et appositæ sunt in die illa animæ circiter tria millia.' *Gesette* looks like a translation, or possibly a mistranslation, of *appositæ sunt,* turned into the active voice.

575. Klaeber (*Anglia* 27. 258) compares this with *his frēond . . . on gold bebycgan,* which is found in Bede's *Hist. Eccl.* (130. 32). He describes it as 'a rare archaic construction,' as in *Beow.* 2799. Dietrich explains the idiom thus: '[In den] älteren dialecte[n] . . . [wird] das gut . . . in gelt verwandelt. . . . So im altn. *seldi hann iarðir sínar til silfrs.*'

Compare this reference to Judas with *Bl. Hom.* 63. 7; 69. 13.

576b. Cf. Verc. hom., fol. 114ᵇ: *him se rǣd ne gebāh.*

578b. Cf. 418.

579a. So 713ᵃ, etc.

580. Cf. Mk. 16. 19. See also 611; *Chr.* 531-2; *Hymn* 30-1.

Graz, in support of his omission of *hond,* cites several instances from the OE. *Psalms* in which *swīðre* is used alone to denote the right hand.

581-582. Cf. *Chr.* 427-8:

his forgifnesse gumum tō helpe
dǣleð dōgra gehwām, Dryhten weoroda.

For *help and hǣlo* see *Gu.* 655, 862; *Run.* 28.

583b. Cf. *Deor* 19: *þæt wæs monegum cūþ.*

584-585a. Cf. *An.* 325-6, 702-3: *Wealdend and Wyrhta wuldor-þrymmes, ān ēce God eallra gesceafta; Met.* 30. 14: *Waldend and Wyrhta weorulde gesceafta.* Cf. Wulfstan, *Hom.* 21. 19; 73. 6; 107. 32; 108. 5.

585b = 392[b].

586b. Cf. 81[b]. Dietrich remarks on 586[b]: 'Von Christus ausge-sagt verstösst die benennung "ein heiliger engel" gegen das bestimmt-este bewustsein des ganzen christlichen alterthums.' Yet the con-ception of Christ as an angel was not unknown, and may have found its way into the poem through a misunderstanding or confused recol-lection of some passage in which this heretical view was combated. Harnack (*Dogmengesch.* I. 204, n. 4) says: ' "Angelus" ist eine sehr alte bezeichnung für Christus (s. Justins Dialog), die sich bis zum nicänischen streit erhalten hat und z. b. noch in Novatians schrift de trinit. 11. 25 ff. ausdrücklich für ihn in anspruch genommen wird (ATliche stellen, die auf Christus bezogen wurden, schützten das wort). In der regel ist es aber nicht als bezeichnung des wesens (so jedoch bei Hermas: Jesus = Michael), sondern als solche des amtes Christi zu verstehen; . . . es gab Christen, die das wort als wesens-bezeichnung gebrauchten und von alten zeiten her findet sich ein widerspruch gegen diese auffassung.' See also Dorner, *Entwick-lungsgesch. der Lehre von der Person Christi* (2d ed. I. 568). Tertullian writes a long refutation of this doctrine as it was held by the Gnostics, Marcion and Apelles, in *De Carne Christi* 8 and 14 (*Patr. Lat.* 2. 769, 777). An interesting apocryphal passage relating to the Messiah is found in the Testament of Daniel (*Testam. Duodecem Patriarchorum*): 'Draw near unto God and to the Angel that intercedeth for you, for He is a mediator between God and man.'

In *Chr.* 104 the Saviour is called *engla beorhtast,* but we should be too rigid in our logic if we interpreted that to mean that Christ is *necessarily* to be included among the angels of which he is the brightest. But see Cook's note in his edition.

587a. For the association of the saints with Christ in the rule of the heavenly kingdom, cf. Rev. 3. 21: 'Qui vicerit, dabo ei sedere mecum in throno meo;' also Rev. 2. 26. In Rev. 20. 4 we are told that the righteous reigned with Christ a thousand years. See also Mt. 19. 28.

587b. Cf. *Gen.* 11[b].

588b. Sievers, in his collation, correctly deciphered the MS. as having originally read *swegl betalden.* The Corrector canceled the *t,* and wrote *he* above it. But *behealden* is, as Dietrich puts it, 'verwässert.' Junius, Dietrich, and Grein prefer *befalden,* and write the hemistich as one word. But an *f* was not nearly so likely to be mistaken for a *t* as an *o* for an *a*. *Betolden* gives every bit as good a sense as *befalden* (for which cf. *synnum bifealdne, Chr.* 117). A hemistich very similar to 588ᵇ occurs in *Ph.* 609ᵇ, where it is said that the righteous 'in wlite wuniað, wuldre bitolden.' Since such a verbal compound as *sweglbeteldan* (or *-befaldan* or *-behealdan*) is at least problematical, it is better to construe *swegl* as an uninflected instrumental. However, both modes of dealing with the word come to much the same thing. Translate: 'The Son of glory hath his dwelling enfolded in (or covered with) ether.' The metaphor is a bold one.

589-591. Cf. the phrasing of 361-2 and *Bl. Hom.* 7. 9: '[Israhela cyn] tō heofona rīce laþode.' *Lǣcedōm* is found elsewhere in the poetry only in *Chr.* 1573. Lines 589-597 form still another passage in the hortatory vein, like those in 1-365. On *laðað,* see the note to 632.

594b. Dietrich's *teala* restores the metre, and is supported by such phrases as: *þām ðe teala þenceð* (557); *An.* 1612: *gif gē teala hycgað;* and *Wonders of Creat.* 20: *þencan forð teala.*

595. Cf. 364, 645.

596a. Cf. *Gu.* 277.

596b-597. See the comparison in 213.

598. This formula meets us also in *Dom.* 5: 'Hafað him geþinged hider þēoden ūser on þām mǣstan dæge;' and in the homily written in the margin of MS. 41, Corpus Christi College, Cambridge (see *Mod. Phil.* 1. 611): 'Ūre Drihten hafað eft geþingod heder on þisne middangeard.' Cf. Wulfstan, *Hom.* 250. 16: 'hū hē him on ðās weoruld þingian ongan.'

The Last Judgment is described at some length in the following OE. poems: *Ex.* 539-547; *Chr.* 868 ff.; *Be Domes Dæge; El.* 1276 ff.; *Ph.* 491 ff.; *Soul's Address; Rood* 103-121. Two works which discuss the OE. treatments of this theme are: Deering's *Anglosaxon Poets on the Judgment Day,* and Grau's *Quellen und Verwandtschaften der Älteren Germanischen Darstellungen des Jüngsten Gerichtes.*

598b. Cf. *þēoden mǣra, Gen.* 2144.

600. Stoddard (*Anglia* 10. 162) calls attention to the repetition of *on,* which in the MS. is the last word on p. 226, and the first on p. 227, as final proof that Thorpe was wrong in assuming the loss of a leaf at this point.

601-603. See the blowing of the trumpets in *Chr.* 879-883 and *Dom.* 109-112; also Mt. 24. 31 ('Et mittet angelos suos cum tuba,

et voce magna; et congregabunt electos eius a quatuor ventis');
1 Cor. 15. 52; 1 Thess. 4. 15.

602b. So *Chr.* 1240ᵇ.

603. The parallel in *Chr.* 879 (*from fēowerum foldan scēatum*) makes Grein's emendation, as modified by Holthausen, a very appropriate correction.

605b. Cf. 232ᵇ.

606. Cf. the homily in MS. Hatton 116 (Förster, 130. 6): *þone langan dōmesdæg.* For the din of Doomsday, cf. *Chr.* 834-5, 931, 949, 954-5; *Dom.* 59.

607a. Cf. *Chr.* 492ᵃ.

608a. See Rev. 1. 7; Mt. 24. 30; Dan. 7. 13.

609a. Both metre and sense make *gescearian* preferable to the MS. *gescēawian.* With the latter the verse would have to be scanned ⏑×× | ×⏑ | ⏑×, with only the first word alliterating, an arrangement found nowhere else. *Gescēawian* would have to mean in this context 'make manifest,' 'exhibit.' But, since the poet is following Mt. 25. 31 ff. in the main outlines of his Judgment scene, it is better to accept *gescearian* as a rendering of the Lat. *separabit.*

Gescearian (for *gescirian*) is usually defined 'ordain,' 'allot,' 'assign,' 'number,' but there is no reason why the word may not have its radical sense of 'separate,' 'divide.' B.-T. Sup. cites one case of *gescirian* with this meaning, and *āscirian* has it almost exclusively. It is better to accept *gescearian* than Thorpe's *gescēadan.* Because of the similar appearance of OE. *w* and *r,* a scribe would be more likely to mistake the former word for *gescēawian* than the latter.

609b. Note the recurrence of the conception that righteousness is beautiful; cf. 211ᵇ.

611a. See Barnouw (*op. cit.,* p. 105) on this use of the weak adj.

611 ff. The dependence of this passage upon Mt. 25. 31 ff., which is the ultimate source, is only very general.

615. Cf. 360.

616a. Cf. 671ᵇ, 697ᵇ; *Gen.* 978; *Ex.* 420; *Chr.* 687; *An.* 1603.

616b. Cf. the phrasing of 627ᵇ.

617-619. Cf. Mt. 25. 34: 'Venite, benedicti Patris mei; possidete paratum vobis regnum a constitutione mundi.'

619. Cf. 362.

620-622. Cf. Verc. hom., fol. 21ᵃ: 'þonne standað forhte and āfærede þā þe ær wirigdon and unriht worhton, and swið betwyh him hēofað and wēpað hwylcne dōm him Dryhten dēman wille.' See also the fear of the wicked in *Chr.* 801, 921, 1230-2, 1560-2; *Jul.* 706-711 (cf. the fear of the angels in *Chr.* 1020). Since *forht* and *forworht* are both used in connection with Doomsday, it is natural that a scribe should have confused them, without taking notice of the metrical requirements. The confusion may have existed in the present scribe's copy, since the same mistake appears in the work of the man who wrote 1-125, viz., in 76.

Translate 621-2: 'They shall tremble for fear of the time when the Son of God will judge them.'

622b. Cf. *þurh þīnra dǣda spēd, Ps.* 118. 91.

623a = 109^b.

626. The original form in the MS. was probably *reodende, -ande,* or *-unde,* a mistake for *reordende, -ande,* or *-unde.* The Corrector changed this to *reordiende.* Thorpe's *rodera Waldend* is the best stop-gap for 626^b.

627. Compare the phrasing of 241. The Corrector thought *gecwæð* a mistake for *gecwyð,* and so it might be. The context demands the present. I leave *gecwæð* unchanged, because it could be a northern equivalent of *gecwyð;* see Sievers, *Gram.* 370, n. 7; 371; 391, n. 5.

628-629. Based on Mt. 25. 41. Cf. 691; *Gu.* 226; *Chr.* 1520; *wītehūs* occurs only in *Gen.* 39 and *Chr.* 1536.

629b. This recalls Mt. 25. 12.

630b. Cf. 126, 731; *Gen.* 90.

630-634. This incident is not to be found in Matthew's detailed account of the Judgment, but the poet was not drawing on his invention for it. In MS. B of the Ethiopic version of the *Book of Enoch* (62. 11) we are told that 'the angels of punishment shall take [the damned] in charge to execute vengeance upon them;' but these angels of punishment are not at all to be confused with devils. Ephraem Syrus (*Opera* 3. 133) describes how the soul of the evil man at his death 'abit, tractus ab angelis malis in locum supplicii.' According to the fifteenth Vercelli homily (Förster, 128. 3), after Christ's malediction of the wicked, 'þonne gesamniað ðā dīoflu hīe tōsomne, and hīe ðonne drīfað þā synfullan and þā cearfullan sāwla tō helle.' The homily in MS. 41, Corp. Chr. Coll. Cambr. (*Mod. Phil.* 1. 613), contains the same idea. There may be some connection between the OE. passages and Mt. 13. 49-50: 'Sic erit in consummatione sæculi: exibunt angeli, et separabunt malos de medio justorum; et mittent eos in caminum ignis.'

631. Cf. *Beow.* 163: *hwyder helrūnan hwyrftum scrīþað.* Schücking (*Eng. Stud.* 56. 171) says of *scrīðan* that if it meant 'schreiten,' 'gehen' primarily, we should expect to find it used occasionally of living human beings, but it is thus used only once, in *Wids.* 135 (for 'wander about'). Where it has been thought to mean 'schreiten,' 'gehen,' non-human beings are in question, as in *Sat.* 631, *Beow.* 163

and 703. It is probable that the word signifies a ghostly gliding movement. With this interpretation the phrase *hwyrftum scrīpað þūsendmǣlum* is highly poetic in the present context.

632. The scribe's original form *leaðað* was no error. The Corrector either did recognize *laðian* in this form, which has resulted from *o/a*-umlaut (Sievers, *Gram.* 160. 4; on the ending, see 412, n. 6), and thought it a mistake for *lēdað*, or he considered that his *lędað* suited the context better than *laðiað* (The latter alternative is certainly the true one, because the Corrector merely changed *leaðað* to *laðað* in 589, where *laðian* was obviously the right word.) It is, indeed, rather hard to believe that the poet did not write originally *lēdað*. Yet compare the homily on Doomsday in Assmann's *Homilien und Heiligenleben* (p. 167): 'God ūs laðaþ tō līfe, and dēofol ūs laðaþ tō wīte.' Some one has erased *he* before *þider*. This was very probably an acc. plur. pronoun, object of the verbs, which really need some such explicit word to govern.

634a. Cf. *Gen. B* 697[a]. The ᚦ of the MS. may be an error for *þone*.

634b. Cf. 377[b].

635. ūp þonan. Cf. 327.

636a. Cf. *wīte þolian* in *Gen. B* 323, 367; *Chr.* 1452.

636b. *Ph.* 644 supports Grein's emendation, which was proposed for the sake of the alliteration. Moreover, *þearlic* is really a more fitting adjective for *wīte*, because *earmlic* always in the poetry modifies a word connoting rather subjective suffering than objective torment.

636-638. Cf. *Chr.* 1514-5: 'þæs gē sceolon hearde ādrēogan wīte tō wīdan ealdre, wræc mid dēoflum geþolian.'

Sievers and Graz would render 638[b] a normal B-verse by reading *spel*.

639-641. on edwīt oft āsettað. Cf. *Gen.* 2728; *Gu.* 459. The object of *āsettað* in 639 is the clause introduced by *þær ðe*, which also stands in a sort of appositive relation to *fǣhðe and firne*. I construe the passage thus, because the phrase *settan on edwīt* in every instance has a direct as well as an indirect object, of which the former usually takes the shape of an object clause. *Stǣleð fǣhðe and firne*, then, is practically a parallel to *on edwīt āsettað*. Since it seems unlikely that such a period would be broken into by a change of number in the subject which would add nothing to, and would really weaken, the thought, I have proposed *fēondas* (parallel to *swearte sūslbonan*) as the subject of *stǣleð*. This completes line 640 more satisfactorily than *Sātān*, which would give a line with four alliterating *s*'s. The very uncommon alliteration *s, s : st* itself presents quite a sufficient amount of irregularity. On the possibility of a plural verb in *-eð*, see Sievers, *Gram.* 360, n. 2. Bouterwek (p. CCXXXIV) has already suggested that *stæleð* is written for *stælað*. The scribe is clearly hurrying and cramping his writing in this whole section, which increases the chances that he may have omitted such a word as *fēondas,* and left the sentence in confusion, because he did not stop to figure out its meaning.

Kock (*Anglia* 27. 229-233) was the first to explain completely the phrase, *stæleð fǣhðe and firne,* although Cosijn must be credited with the actual emendation. (The MS. reads *fǣhðe and in firne.*) According to Kock, '*(ge)stǣlan hwæt on hwone* means "lay something to somebody's charge," hence "call him to account for it," "avenge it on him." In the majority of sentences quoted by Bosworth-Toller, the idea of charging, or accusing, or upbraiding is quite distinct. . . . The object of the active (the subject of the passive) clause is in each case a real or imputed crime or injury.' Kock notes the presence of the formula *fǣhðe and firne* in *Beow.* 137, 879, 2480, and, reversed, in 153. For *stǣlan fǣhðe (fyrene)* see *Gen.* 1351; *Beow.* 1340; *Gu.* 1044; *Chr.* 1374.

Bright's assumption that *on* is accented is unwarranted (see variants for his alternative readings).

641. Cf. the first instance in which Grein's *Frēodrihten* restored the alliteration, 435, and see 547, 566.

643. Cf. 176, and especially *Father's Instruction* 63: *weoruda Scyppend hafa þē tō hyhte.*

There are two passages in the Vercelli homilies that are similar to 638-643. Both refer to the accusation of the wicked by devils on Doomsday before the final sentence is pronounced (not after, as here). In the first (fol. 66ᵇ-7ᵇ), the Devil addresses his accusation to God, and says: 'þīne sōðfæstan lāre hīe forgēaton;' and the homilist adds: '[Sātān] þā misdǣda stæleð on þā gǣstas.' Similarly, in the second (fol. 115ᵃ), men are enjoined to be mindful 'hū ðā dīoflu him on stǣlað ealle þā unrihtan weorc.'

644a-645. Cf. 594ᵇ-5. See also 183, 364.

646b. gāstes blēd. Cf. 527ᵇ.

648. The MS. *swegletorht* (or to be exact *swegle · torht*) might stand for a northern uninflected acc. sing. masc. *swegltorht,* modifying *sunu* (= Christ). See Carpenter, *Deklin. in . . . der Lindisf. Hs.,* p. 17. Grein, in a note, suggested *swegltorhtne.* The word is elsewhere applied only to the sun or stars, or to the heavenly home. I suspect that the scribe inadvertently inserted *torht* between *swegle* and *sunu,* through the influence of the common phrase, *swegltorht sunne,* which lingered in his mind. Grein had suggested by a query

in his note that *sunu* might bè nom. plur. He follows this up in the *Sprachschatz* by canceling *torht*. *Swegle* would then be the regular dat. (? inst.) object of *mid*, and would mean 'ether,' or possibly 'harmony,' 'music'; the *ēadige sunu* would be the same as the *ēadige bearn* of 144.

649. In Rev. 21. 21, the gates of the New Jerusalem are of pearl. Could this line be a reminiscence of *þā gyldnan geatu, Chr.* 251?

650b-651. Cf. 617ᵇ-8ᵃ.

652-653. Cf. 295-6, 307-9.

653-655. Thus in Assmann's *Ags. Homilien und Heiligenleben*, p. 166, there are enumerated among the dwellers in heaven, 'englas and hēahfædras, and wītegan, and ealle hālie.'

655b. Cf. 184, 305.

657a. Cf. 258; *Chr.* 578.

657b. So *Pater Noster* 3. 12ᵇ.

658-660. The fourth Vercelli homily (fol. 20ᵇ) contains a long address of praise and thanksgiving, which the redeemed soul makes to the Lord after it has been awarded everlasting bliss.

658b and 659a. Brown (*Lang. of Rushw. Gloss to Matt.* 2. 79-80) records three instances of weak nom. sing. masc. nouns in *-an*. However, the forms in the MS. of *Sat.* are probably mere errors.

660. See note on 678-680.

661. See Introduction, p. lv, n. 82.

661b. Cf. *Gen.* 2; *Beow.* 3176; *El.* 892.

662a. Cf. 155ᵃ; *An.* 871:

> Ūtan ymbe Æðelne englas stōdon,
> þegnas ymb þēoden þūsendmǣlum
> heredon on hēhðo hālgan stefne
> dryhtna Dryhten: drēam wæs on hyhte.

Cf. also *Sat.* 45-8.

662b. Cf. *Rood* 139: *þǣr is blis mycel.*

665-667. These lines are transitional, and introduce the account of the temptation. Bouterwek, indeed, groups them with the preceding passage. Line 669ᵇ also forms a connecting link between 665-733 and the rest of the poem.

665b-666a. Cf. *Bl. Hom.* 85. 2: 'dēað hē geþrōwode for ūs.'

666b. So 388ᵇ.

669-671. The text could be translated as it stands: 'Then it befell the accursed one who was formerly cast out of heaven that he dived into hell (or had to dive into hell) when he tempted (or after he had tempted) the King of Creation.' Thus the lines would refer to what happens in 690-733, and 672-689 would have to be considered as merely recounting the action of which we must be informed if we are to understand the subsequent matter, which is to be the central theme of the section. Judging from the portions of the two temptations which are extant, the account of the temptation *in toto* was not intended to be of equal length with that which follows, of the sentencing of Satan, and of his serving the sentence pronounced. Hence such an interpretation as that proposed above would not be inappropriate. The usual method of dealing with the passage is illustrated in Grein's translation: 'Da fiels dem Unhold ein, der einst geworfen aus den Himmeln ward, dass er zur Hölle tauchte, dass er den Wart aller Wesen wollte da versuchen, brachte ihm, etc.'

669b-670a. Cf. 181ᵃ: *āworpen of worulde.*

670b. Cf. 30; *Gu.* 555.

671b. Cf. 616ᵃ.

672 ff. The poet follows the order of Matthew (4. 1-11), the second temptation being either omitted or lost in course of transmission, almost certainly the latter.

672a. Cf. 153, 357.

672b. The qualification of *stānas* by *brāde* here was probably inspired by the fact that this adjective was used in a technical sense with *hlāf*, to signify *paximatium* (the overdone bread which served as part of the provisions on sea-voyages and military campaigns). Hence Satan is said to bring Christ broad, flat stones shaped like bread.

673a. for hungre. Kennedy: 'to stay his hunger;' cf. *Heliand* 1067: 'gehēli thīnan hungar.'

674. Cf. *Heliand* 1065 in exactly the same context: 'ef thu giuuald habes.' This corresponds, of course, to the Scriptural 'si Filius Dei es.'

675 = 690. So also *An.* 202, 343, 510 (*him þā* . . .).

676b. Cf. 'scriptum est,' Mt. 4. 4, etc.

677. Grein thought this fragment belonged to the answer to the first temptation. If so, the poet took as great liberties in his treatment of this answer as in that to the third. The phrase would fit more naturally into the third itself, as a rendering in the first person of the Lat. *illi soli servies* (v. 10), which may have been expanded by the poet so as to include allusion to the First Commandment: 'Non habebis deos alienos coram me.' Bouterwek is evidently thinking of this when he translates: '[Du sollst Niemand anbeten] ohne mich allein.'

678-680. As Kühn suspected (*Über die Angelsächsischen Gedichte von Christ und Satan,* p. 15), these lines are misplaced. They are clearly in the tone of the hymns of praise to the Saviour which occur

in both of the earlier sections of *Sat.*, and would fit especially well
(if *ac* be changed to *and*) after line 660. We may assume that the
scribe in his effort to conserve time and space, which an examination
of this page of the MS. discovers, omitted them, and inserted them
later at a point where it is very likely that there was a gap in his
copy.

678b. So *Chr.* 420, 513.

679b. būtan ende. So 379ᵃ.

680a. We may proceed on Graz's suggestion that the second hemistich of this line contained an object of *genōm*. Not that such an
object is absolutely necessary, however, because the *Drihten Hǣlend*
of 683 is near enough so that there can be no misunderstanding.
Graz's emendation, *hālig Scyppend,* is impossible, since grammar would
require *hāligne,* which would give us an expanded E-verse. For
hǣleða Scyppend, cf. *Hymn* 34 and *gāsta Scyppend, Sat.* 244.
Cf. *mid hondum Hǣlend genōm,* 544.

681. See Sievers, *Gram.* 221. 2, on the ecthlipsis of *h (esle)*.

682a. Cf. *blāc bealowes gāst,* 721.

683a. E. Meyer (p. 24) considers *on dūne* equivalent to an adv. =
'nieder'; but it is surely only a parallel to *on beorh.*

683b. So 219ᵃ, 576ᵃ.

684. Such a form as *-bēwende* could hardly be an error. It is
probably a spelling analogous to *getrēweð < getrēoweð,* parallel to
getrūweð (see Sievers, *Gram.* 156. 5).

685b. Manning (*Supplement* to Lye's *Dictionarium*) cleared the
way for an understanding of the MS. reading, *þines seoferdum,* by
suggesting that it is a mistake for *þines seolfes dōm,* 'in tui ipsius
potestatem.' Grein completed the emendation by prefixing *on,* so
that the phrase becomes similar to *Beow.* 2147ᵇ, *Gu.* 678ᵃ, *Minds of
Men* 64ᵇ, and *By.* 38ᵇ.

688b-689. 'If thou wilt be truly king of angels and men, as thou
didst intend (or hast purposed).' The devil implies that Christ's
ideas about his kingship will remain only ideas unless he accepts
power from the Prince of Evil. This clause need not be interpreted
(with Groschopp, p. 255) as rendering the 'si Filius Dei es' of the
original, and hence as belonging to the missing temptation. Satan is
merely putting into words the thoughts which he believes have been
in Christ's mind.

riht Cyning. Cf. 260A; *Gu.* 654; *An.* 120, 324, 700.

691 ff. The violence of the answer which Christ is here represented as making to Satan forms a striking contrast to the simplicity
of the Gospel story. Gregory, indeed, holds up the Saviour's mild-
ness as a model for all men to follow when under temptation. He

says: 'Ecce adversitatem diaboli Dominus pertulit, et nihil ei nisi mansuetudinis verba respondit' (*Hom. in Evang.* 16: *Patr. Lat.* 76. 1136). The only treatment of the temptation theme I was able to find which contained even a slight hint of the vivid passage in *Sat.* is in the Blickling homily for the First Sunday in Lent (31. 12). Christ's reply there is as follows: 'Gā þū on bæcling, and gemyne þē sylfne hū mycel yfel þē gelamp for þīnre gītsunga and oforhȳdo, and for þīnum īdlan gilpe; and forþon ic þē ne fylge, forþon on þyssum þrīm þū eart oforswīþed.' But later on the same homilist also follows Gregory in lauding the Lord's patience and meekness.

691. Cf. 628.

692a. Thus, in Mt. 4. 10, Christ signifies his recognition of the identity of the tempter ('Vade, *Satana*'), who is first described simply as 'tentator.'

692b-693. Compare the phrasing in 27-30, 41-3, 449-450. For a similar use of *weotod*, cf. *An.* 889, 951, 1365-6; *Rid.* 16. 6, 11.

693a. Cf. 287; *Dom.* 91, *gearwað tōgēanes; Sat.* 711. The Corrector gives the normal inflection, *gearo.* See Sievers, *Gram.* 300.

695 ff. Compare Satan's return to his 'crew' in *Paradise Regained* 4. 576-580:

> So strook with dread and anguish fell the Fiend,
> And to his crew, that sat consulting, brought
> Joyless triumphals of his hop't success,
> Ruin, and desperation, and dismay,
> Who durst so proudly tempt the Son of God.

696b. sorga mæste. Cf. *Chr.* 1082[b], 1209[a]; *Gen. B* 364[b].

700. Dietrich would relate the MS. reading, *helheoðo,* and the *heoðe* in the MS. of *Beow.* 404 to κύτος, which signifies various wide spaces, e. g., the hold of a ship, the cavity of the body, and the vault of heaven in κύτταρος. He translates it 'umbraculum' or 'höllenge-wölbe.' Scholars have tended on the whole to reject this explanation. Grein proposed *hel heorodrēorig* ('traurige' in the translation). Rendered by 'mournful,' 'sad,' as in *Ph.* 217, this reading offers the most satisfactory way out of the difficulty. Cosijn's *heaðodrēorig* seems possible, but is unsupported. Could we retain the compound substantive of the MS., interpreted as an error for *helhleoðo,* 'slopes' or 'promontories of hell'? (Cf. *Gen. B* 764, *sēcan helle gehliðo.*) *Drēorig* would then have to be construed as an uninflected adj. in the post-positive position.

700b. Cf. 706[b].

704. Cosijn's transposition of *sēo* neatly mends the rhythm. *Sēo* is dissyllabic.

Compare the *swartan mistas* of *Gen. B* 391. According to 2 Pet. 2. 17, the mist of darkness ('caligo tenebrarum') is reserved for the wicked.

705. Cf. Vercelli homily 21 (fol. 114ᵇ): 'Hīe wiston þē geornor, wītum besēne on þǣre byrnendan helle, wið hwǣne hīe winnan ongunnon.' For 705ᵃ, cf. *An.* 932ᵇ; *El.* 945ᵇ; *Beow.* 821ᵇ; for 705ᵇ, *Gen. A* 77; *Gen. B* 346; *Beow.* 113; *Ex.* 514; *Chr.* 1527.

707-708. The metre of the MS. reading could be improved by the simple expedient of transposing *sēo,* so that it would come after, instead of before, *grim grǣfhūs;* but 708ᵃ would then be an irregular E-verse. Indeed, it is practically impossible to restore the abnormal lines between this point and the end of the poem without creating at least one new difficulty for every old one which is removed. The clauses are fairly well connected and intelligible as far as the thought is concerned, but one cannot hope to construct perfect OE. verses out of them, at least not with any pretence of restoring the original. I think it quite probable that the MS. preserves for us just about what the poet wrote, and that we should not blame the scribe for the poor versification. These remaining lines are more like a rough draft, never worked up into final form, than a jumbled copy of finished work. At any rate, I have in general printed them almost as they stand in the MS., and shall merely try to interpret their contents. The attempts at reconstruction which various scholars have made are interesting, and sometimes suggestive. They will be found in the variants.

Sievers' emendation, *grimme,* is not quite satisfactory, because it would add another instance to the already long list of weak adjectives modifying substantives, without an accompanying article.

Tō is an adv., and 708ᵇ connects well with the two following lines; so no gap should be assumed.

709a. The *on* of *seondon* is clearly added by the Corrector, but we may admit it, to obtain a normal hemistich.

Kock's interpretation (*Jub. Jaunts,* p. 14) of *tīda* as 'seasons,' 'years,' is unnecessary. I see nothing preposterous in a spirit, who could post as swift as thought, being 'supposed to measure hell *wīd and sīd* in two hours.' Christ uses the adv. *ricene,* and the whole tone of his command implies the greatest speed. Moreover, in the sequel these points are to be noted: in 713-5 we learn that Satan 'now measured with his hands his woes and torments'; in 721, in compliance with Christ's words in 701ᵃ and 703ᵇ, he has reached hell's bottom. Thence it seemed to him that it was a hundred thousand miles to hell's doors. The poet then continues, 'thus (or as?) the Mighty One had commanded that he measure his torment,' and one may infer that Satan's calculations are approximately completed. Yet there is not the slightest hint that two years have elapsed. Poetical condensation might account for the omission of notice that two hours had passed meanwhile, but hardly for silence regarding the passing of two years. Moreover, for the poet to represent the Prince of Evil as forced to go over hell, measuring it span by span would be to introduce a ludicrous picture; and if one is inclined to be literal, one might think it rather doubtful whether Satan could have covered the hundred thousand miles to hell's doors alone in two years.

710. There are no traces discoverable of a verb *mercian* or *myrcian* from *myrce*, 'dark,' 'murky.' In spite of the fact that in *Dom.* 26 hell is called *þā mircan gesceaft*, it is preferable to derive *merced* from *mercian (mearcian)* 'mark,' 'design,' 'appoint.' Cf. *gemercade=designavit*, Lk. 10. 1 (Lind.). Bouterwek construes it as syntactically parallel to *āmeten* (in translating it 'berechnet'), but this is a doubtful construction.

Stoddard (*Anglia* 10. 162-3) thinks it possible that a folio is missing between 710 and 711, but if such is the case, judging from the context, it is extremely doubtful whether the leaf contained any writing.

711. For fem. nom. *wrece*, see Sievers, *Gram.* 253, n. 2.

712b. Cf. *Chr.* 1526: *sceolon raþe feallan on grimne grund*.

713. *Ǣglēce* is an Anglian nom., and need not be emended. Holthausen's *earmum* gives a line grotesque both in form and content.

715a. wēan and wītu. Cf. 185, 336.

715b. Cf. *wonna lēg, Bēow.* 3115.

716. læhte. Cf. the *lācende lēg* of *Dan.* 476; *Chr.* 1595; *El.* 580.

718a. hē. Nom. plur.

718b. So 390[b].

719. There is apparently a gap after this line. *Godes andsacan* may, as Holthausen concludes, be the last two words of the sentence which is broken by the gap, but it is unsafe to make final deductions from the metre in this passage.

721a. Cf. 682[a].

721b. According to Gregory, *Moral.* 26. 37, 'infernus vero recte fundum non habere creditur.'

723a. helle duru. Cf. 98, 380, 467.

723b. se Mihtiga. Cf. *Gen. B* 299; *Ex.* 484.

725a. Grein's *sīnne* for *synne* is very acceptable. It renders the hemistich a perfect parallel to 694[b], where Christ issues his commands to Satan *þurh þā hēhstan miht*. The new scribe, who had taken up his task only at 711, probably did not understand the reference of *sīnne*, and hence altered the *i* to *y*. If *synne* be retained, the phrase must mean 'by means of his sinful power'; it could hardly be equivalent to Kennedy's 'for his sin.'

726. Holthausen's *gēmde* restores the alliteration, and is a possible change. Cf. *Gen. B* 349: *Sātān . . . sceolde gīeman þæs grundes.* However, *gīeman* seems not to have been employed absolutely, in the sense of 'ponder,' 'meditate,' 'consider,' which the word must mean here, whereas *gemunan* is used thus several times.

727b. Cf. 26ᵇ, 73ᵇ, 129ᵃ.

728b. On *egsan gryre,* see note on 454ᵇ.

729. dēofla mænego. So 111ᵃ.

731. Cf. 80.

731b-732. Cf. *An.* 469: *Ongan ðā reordigan.* **wērigan gāstas.** Cf. *se wērega gāst,* 126. The words *on þa* in the MS. of 731 may be taken as a repetition of the two syllables preceding; or should we read: *ongunnon þā þā wērigan gāstas?*

I print Grein's reconstruction of lines 729-732 consecutively, for reference. It is no improvement on the original, but is of some interest, being the only attempt which has been made to render the passage unobjectionable in both form and content:

> oð þæt egsan gryre
> dēofla mænego [ādrēogan ne mihton];
> þonne ūp āstāg [earmra gedræg]
> wordum in wītum; ongunnon þā wērigan gāstas
> reordian and cweðan [wið heora rīces boran]:

This is translated in the *Dichtungen:*

> bis dass Angstgraus da
> der Teufel Menge tief erfasste:
> dann stieg auf allda der Elenden Geheul
> mit Worten in den Wehqualen; die verworfenen Geister
> begannen zu reden und zu rufen zu ihres Reiches Fürsten
> Da! nun sei im Uebel du! du wolltest eh nicht gut!

Grein's reading, besides being metrically incorrect, is not in perfect harmony with what would certainly have been the context if the end of the poem were more nearly complete. The poet is clearly reverting to the motive of Satan's being forced to endure the reproaches of his own followers. Hence Grein's interpretation of *egsan gryre,* and his phrase *earmra gedræg,* are rather out of place. *Gedræg* seems to mean 'sorrow,' 'lamentation,' and for this reason is not an appropriate word for a context in which reproaches and taunts are to be uttered.

The closing passage, though metrically impossible, makes fair sense: 'The perfidious and loathsome wight gazed through that wretched den until the dreadful multitude of devils arose: those malign spirits in their torments began to speak words and to say, "Oh! thus be thou in misery now henceforth: thou didst never desire that which was good." ' Cf. the devils' reproaches in 53-64.

Egsan gryre I take to mean not the terror which the fiends are suffering, but the terror which they inspire.

Finit Liber II. Amen.—a tantalizing rubric. What was *Liber I?* Junius (p. 91) explains the matter thus: 'Sequentia vero a pagina 213 usque ad finem . . . videntur . . . adjecta ab aliquo, qui (quemadmodum ex fine libri colligitur) hunc veluti librum Secundum prioribus putavit adjiciendum.' This would seem to be the correct explanation. Otherwise we should have to accept the improbable hypothesis that *Christ and Satan* is only a fragment or fragments of a long poem.

ADDITIONS TO VARIANTS

The following readings from Grein's 'Nachträgliche Verbesserungen' (*Bibl.* 2. 414) were omitted from the variants through oversight: 160 cwiðde, firena, herde (hirde) (?); 199 uppe (?); 376 into; 486 hige ofergymdon (?); 511 galgan; 634 nið *deorsum* (?).

BIBLIOGRAPHY

I. EDITIONS

(a) Complete:

FRANCIS JUNIUS, *Cædmonis Monachi Paraphrasis Poetica Genesios ac præcipuarum Sacræ paginæ Historiarum, abhinc annos MLXX. Anglo-Saxonicè conscripta, et nunc primùm edita.* . . . Amstelodami. . . . Typis et sumptibus Editoris. MDCLV.

BENJAMIN THORPE, *Cædmon's Metrical Paraphrase of parts of the Holy Scriptures in Anglo-Saxon.* London, 1832.

KARL W. BOUTERWEK, *Cædmon's des Angelsachsen Biblische Dichtungen.* Elberfeld, 1848-1854.

CHRISTIAN W. M. GREIN, *Bibliothek der Angelsächsischen Poesie.* Göttingen, 1857. (Vol. 1.)

RICHARD P. WÜLKER, *Bibliothek der Angelsächsischen Poesie.* Leipzig, 1894. (Vol. 2.)

(b) Partial:

LUDWIG ETTMÜLLER, *Engla and Seaxna Scopas and Boceras.* Quedlinburg and Leipzig, 1850. (Pp. 194 ff. contain 1-224, 366-513.)

MAX RIEGER, *Alt- und Angelsächsisches Lesebuch.* Giessen, 1861. (Pp. 115-6 contain 160-189.)

OWEN T. WILLIAMS, *Short Extracts from Old English Poetry.* Bangor [Wales], 1909. (Pp. 23-9 contain 75-125, 19-64, 385-436, 680A-725.)

FREDERICK KLAEBER, *The Later Genesis and other Old English and Old Saxon Texts relating to the Fall of Man.* Heidelberg, 1913. (Pp. 34-5 contain 410-421, 470-494.)

II. TRANSLATIONS

THORPE, as above.

BOUTERWEK, as above.

CHRISTIAN W. M. GREIN, *Dichtungen der Angelsachsen stabreimend übersetzt.* Göttingen, 1857. (Vol. 1.)

CHARLES W. KENNEDY, *The Cædmon Poems, translated into English Prose.* London and New York, 1916.

III. TEXTUAL STUDIES

Franz Dietrich, 'Zu Cädmon' (*Zeitschrift für Deutsches Altertum* 10. 310-311, 361-7).

Christian W. M. Grein, 'Zur Textkritik der Angelsächsischen Dichter' (*Germania* 10. 419-420).

Eduard Sievers, 'Collationen Angelsächsischer Gedichte' (*Zeitschrift für Deutsches Altertum* 15. 459-461, 456-7).

———, 'Zur Rhythmik des Germanischen Alliterationsverses' (*Beiträge zur Geschichte der Deutschen Sprache und Literatur* 10. 209-314; 12. 451-544).

Ferdinand Holthausen, 'Beiträge zur Erklärung und Textkritik Altenglischer Dichter' (*Indogermanische Forschungen* 4. 385 ff.).

———, Review of Wülker's text (*Anglia Beiblatt* 5. 232-4).

Friedrich Graz, *Die Metrik der sogennanten Cädmonschen Dichtungen, mit Berücksichtigung der Verfasserfrage.* Weimar, 1894. (Pp. 57-73.)

———, 'Beiträge zur Textkritik der sogennanten Cädmon'schen Dichtungen' (*Englische Studien* 21. 13-27).

Peter J. Cosijn, 'Anglosaxonica III' (*Beiträge zur Geschichte der Deutschen Sprache und Literatur* 21. 21-5).

James W. Bright, 'Jottings on the Cædmonian Christ and Satan' (*Modern Language Notes* 18. 129-131).

Ernst A. Kock, 'Interpretations and Emendations of Early English Texts' (*Anglia* 27. 229).

———, *Jubilee Jaunts and Jottings.* Leipzig, 1918. (*Lunds Universitets Årsskrift.*)

IV. CRITICISM, INTERPRETATION, SYNTAX, SOURCES, ETC.

George Hickes, *Thesaurus Linguarum Vett. Septentrionalium.* Oxford, 1705. (1. 133.)

Richard P. Wülker, *Das Evangelium Nicodemi in der Abendländischen Literatur.* Paderborn, 1872.

Frederik Hammerich, *Älteste Christliche Epik der Angelsachsen, Deutschen, und Nordländer.* (Translation by Michelsen. Gütersloh, 1874. Pp. 64-9.)

Robert S. Watson, *Cædmon, the First English Poet.* London, 1875. (Pp. 80-6.)

Bernhard Ten Brink, *Geschichte der Englischen Litteratur.* Berlin, 1877. (English translation: *Early English Literature.* London and New York, 1883; 1. 86-8, 375-6.)

Hugo Balg, *Der Dichter Cædmon und seine Werke*. Bonn, 1882.

Friedrich Groschopp, *Das Angelsächsische Gedicht 'Crist und Satan*. Halle, 1883. (Also in *Anglia* 6. 248-276.)

Albin Kühn, *Über die Angelsächsischen Gedichte von Christ und Satan*. Halle, 1883.

Heinrich Ziegler, *Der Poetische Sprachgebrauch in den sogennanten Cædmonschen Dichtungen*. Münster, 1883.

Oscar Hofer, *Der Syntaktische Gebrauch des Dativs und Instrumentals in den Cædmon beigelegten Dichtungen*. Halle, 1884.

Eduard Sievers, 'Zu Codex Junius XI' (*Beiträge zur Geschichte der Deutschen Sprache und Literatur* 10. 195-9).

Richard P. Wülker, *Grundriss zur Geschichte der Angelsächsischen Litteratur*. Leipzig, 1885. (Pp. 111-146.)

Adolf Ebert, *Allgemeine Geschichte der Literatur des Mittelalters im Abendlande*. Leipzig, 1887. (3. 255-6.)

Henry Morley, *English Writers*. London, 1888. (2. 95.)

Robert W. Deering, *The Anglosaxon Poets on the Judgment Day*. Halle, 1890.

Heinrich Ungemach, *Die Quellen der Fünf Ersten Chester Plays*. Erlangen and Leipzig, 1890.

Charles J. Abbey, *Religious Thought in Old English Verse*. London, 1892.

Stopford A. Brooke, *History of Early English Literature*. London, 1892. (Pp. 325-331.)

Ernest J. Becker, *A Contribution to the Comparative Study of the Mediæval Visions of Heaven and Hell*. Baltimore, 1899.

Adriaan J. Barnouw, *Textkritische Untersuchungen nach dem Gebrauch des Bestimmten Artikels und des Schwachen Adjectivs in der Altenglischen Poesie*. Leiden, 1902. (Pp. 101-8, 230.)

Robert T. Gaskin, *Cædmon, the First English Poet*. 3d ed. London, 1902.

Charles D. A. F. Abbetmeyer, *Old English Poetical Motives derived from the Doctrine of Sin*. Minncapolis, 1903.

Otto Grüters, *Über einige Beziehungen zwischen Altsächsischer und Altenglischer Dichtung*. *Bonner Beiträge zur Anglistik* 17. 1-50. 1905.

Francis A. Blackburn, *Exodus and Daniel*. Boston, 1907. (Introduction.)

Heinrich E. W. Meyer, *Darstellung der Syntaktischen Erscheinungen in dem Angelsächsischen Gedicht 'Christ und Satan.'* Rostock, 1907.

M. Bentinck Smith, in *The Cambridge History of English Literature*. London and New York, 1907. (1. 53-4.)

142   *Christ and Satan*

JOHANNES O. L. WALTER, *Der Syntaktische Gebrauch des Verbums in dem Angelsächsischen Gedichte 'Christ und Satan.'* Rostock, 1907.

RICHARD P. WÜLKER, *Geschichte der Englischen Litteratur.* Leipzig, 1896. (2d ed., 1907; I. 59, 61-3.)

MAX FÖRSTER, 'Altenglische Predigtquellen' (*Archiv für das Studium der Neueren Sprachen* 116. 301 ff.).

ALOIS BRANDL, *Englische Literatur.* 1908. (In Paul's *Grundriss der Germanischen Philologie,* 2d ed., 2. 1045-6.)

GUSTAV GRAU, *Quellen und Verwandtschaften der Älteren Germanischen Darstellungen des Jüngsten Gerichtes.* Halle, 1908.

CARL RICHTER, *Chronologische Studien zur Angelsächsischen Literatur.* Halle, 1910.

STEPHANIE VON GAJŠEK, *Caedmon und Milton.* Vienna, 1911.

THEODOR FRINGS, 'Christ und Satan' (*Zeitschrift für Deutsche Philologie* 45. 216-237).

REINHOLD WIENERS, *Zur Metrik des Codex Junius XI.* Bonn, 1913.

ADRIAAN J. BARNOUW, *Anglo-Saxon Christian Poetry* (translation by Louise Dudley). The Hague, 1914. (Pp. 24-6.)

GLOSSARY

The diphthong _æ_ follows _ad;_ _ð_ and _þ_ follow _t._ Roman numerals indicate the classes of ablaut verbs; W1., etc., those of weak verbs; red., the reduplicating verbs; prp., the preteritive presents; anv., the anomalous verbs. When the indication of mood and tense is omitted, supply 'ind. pres.' (unless some other designation has just preceded); when of mood only, supply 'ind.' When no form is printed before a reference, supply the headword. The asterisk distinguishes words found only in _Christ and Satan,_ according to the Grein-Köhler _Sprachschatz._
The glossary is intended to contain references to all the forms in the text.

A.

ā, adv., _ever, for ever, always:_ 315, 362, 398, 619. _See_ āwa.

ābelgan, III, _anger, offend, provoke:_ pret. 1s. ābealh, 410; opt. 3s. ābelige, 195.

ābēodan, II, _offer, announce:_ opt. 2s. ābēode, 695.

Abraham, pr. n.: gs. Abrahames, 461.

ac, _see_ ah.

ād, m., _flame, fire:_ as. 331.

Ādām, pr. n.: ns. 411; gs. Ādāmes, 408; as. Ādām, 20, 473.

ādrēogan, II, _bear, suffer, endure:_ inf. 638.

ādrīfan, I, _drive, expel:_ pret. 3s. ādrāf, 201; inf. 174, 187, 257.

ādwǣscan, W1., _extinguish, quench:_ inf. 306.

ǣfre, adv., _ever, for ever, always:_ 116, 142, 231, 277, 304, 390, 413, 597, 635; in a negative clause: 50, 140, 171, 267, 451.

æfter, prep., w. dat., _after:_ 26, 630.

ǣghwā, pron., _every one:_ ds. ǣghwǣm, 363.

ǣghwǣr, adv., _everywhere, in every respect:_ 342, 479.

ǣghwylc, pron., _each, every (one or thing):_ subst. w. gen., ns. 194; gs. ǣghwylces, 273; absol., dsm. ǣghwylcum, 265.

ǣglǣca, m., _wretch, demon, fiend:_ ns. 161, 579; āglǣca, 448; ǣglēce, 713; np. ǣglēcan, 73.

ǣht, f., _possession, heritage, power:_ ds. ǣhte, 87, 117, 254, 279, 454.

ǣlan, _see_ onǣlan.

ælmihtig, adj., _almighty:_ nsm. 599; nsm. wk. ælmihtiga, 288.

ǣne, adv., _once:_ 410.

ǣnig, pron., _any:_ dsf. ǣnigum, 146.

æpl, m., _apple:_ gs. eaples, 411; ap. æpla, 483.

ǣr, adv., _before, formerly, previously, erewhile, earlier, beforehand:_ 74, 117, 123, 255, 279, 290, 303, 366, 383, 390, 525, 689, 733; w. verbs in pret. expressing a pluperf. sense: 246, 494, 575, 669; _early,_ 515; comp. ǣrror, 151, 299; sup. ǣrest, _first:_ 20, 323, 473, 703.

ǽr, prep., w. dat., *before, ere:* 466.

ǽr, conj., *before, ere:* 409, 503, 544, 560, 709.

æt, prep., w. dat., *at, by, before, to:* 98, 338, 538, 663.

ætsomne, adv., *together, at once:* 41, 127, 526.

æðele, adj., *noble, excellent, glorious:* dsm. wk. æþelan, 239; asn. 20, 473; npm. æðele, 46 (here equivalent to *righteous*).

āfirran, W I., *remove, put away, expel:* pret. 3s. āfirde, 67; āfyrde, 479; opt. 3s. āfirre, 284.

āfyllan, W I., *fill:* pp. *āfylled*, 100.

āfyrhtan, W I., *frighten, terrify:* pp. npm. āfyrhte, 385.

āgan, prp., *have, possess, own, get possession of, obtain:* 3s. āh, 118; 3p. āgon, 361; pret. 1s. āhte, 107; 2s. āhtest, 55, 59; opt. pret. 1p. āhton, 414; inf. 86, 96, 122, 174, 176, 253, 314, 370, 506, 554; tō āgan, 147. Negative: nāgan: 1p. 101.

āgangan, red., *go by, pass:* pp. āgangen, 501; npf. āgongene, 709.

āgen, adj., *own:* nsn. 10.

agēn, adv., *again, anew:* 76.

āgend, m., *possessor, Lord:* ns. 678.

āgēotan, II, *pour out, shed:* pret. 3s. āgēat, 549.

ah, conj., *but:* 268, 292, 347, 450, 520, 636, 694, 696; ac: 30, 112, 125, 626, 678; almost = *and:* ah, 331.

āhebban, VI, *raise, lift:* 3s. āhefeð, 311; pret. 3s. āhōf, 681.

ālǽdan, W I., *lead, lead out:* pp. ālǽded, 178.

ald, adj., *old, ancient:* nsm. wk. alda, 34.

aldor, n., *age, life* (ā tō aldre, *for ever*): ds. aldre, 315, 362, 619.

aldor, m., *chief, prince:* ns. 76, 323, 664; ealdor, 373, 567.

aldorðægn, m., *chief, prince:* as. 66.

ālēfan, W I., *grant:* inf. 116, 278.

all, *see* **eall**.

alwihte, fp., *all creatures, all created things:* gp. alwihta, 616, 671, 697.

āmetan, V, *measure:* opt. 3s. āmǽte, 725; imp. 2s. āmet, 700, 703; pp. āmeten, 710; asn. āmetene, 706.

an (= **on**), adv., *to:* 66.

ān, num., *one, a certain, alone, only:* nsm. 26; dsm. ānum, 55; asm. ænne, 677; gpm. ānra (w. gehwylc = *every one, all*), 432; dpf. ānum, 147; wk. nsm. āna, 32, 249, 260A, 584.

and, *and:* 2, 4, 5, 6, 8, 11, 15, 16, 17, 19, 20, 32, 42, 48(2), 49, 52, 56, 60, 79, 83, 87, 89, 105, 12, 13, 19, 20, 32, 52, 74, 75, 85(2), 92, 207(2), 9, 14, 20, 21, 23, 26, 35, 39, 42, 43, 46, 48, 49, 71, 75, 89, 91, 98, 303, 21, 25, 32, 33, 34(2), 35, 36(2), 37(2), 40, 42, 48, 60, 65, 76, 77, 81, 98, 408, 20, 25, 26, 32, 45, 48, 54, 55, 58, 68, 73, 77, 83, 96, 97, 99, 503, 7, 12, 21, 23, 25, 33(2), 49, 52, 55, 56, 66, 82, 85, 600, 6, 9, 10, 15, 32, 34, 37(2), 38, 41, 52, 53, 56, 58, 59, 81, 82, 86, 87, 89, 99, 700, 3, 4, 7, 12, 15, 32 *And* in the MS. always occurs as ⁊ I expand this sign *and*, because, in general, spellings in *an, am* outnumber those in *on, om*. However, *ond* would correspond more exactly with the phonology of the Anglian original.

andfeng, m., *reception, receiver, or,* possibly, *defense, guardian:* ns. 245.

andleofan, num., *eleven:* 522.

andsaca, m., *adversary, enemy:* ns. 191, 280; np. andsacan, 340, 719; ap. andsacan, 269.

andswarian, W2., *answer, reply:* pret. 3s. andswarode, 675, 690; 3p. andsweradan, 51.

andwlita, m., *countenance:* as. andwlitan, 378.

ānforlǣtan, red., *abandon, forsake:* pp. ānforlǣten, 228.

anmēdla, see **on—**.

anwalda, m., *ruler, sovereign:* asm. anwaldan, 209, 642.

apostol, m., *apostle:* ap. apostolas, 571.

ār, f., *favor, mercy:* gp. āra, 209.

ārīman, W1., *count:* inf. 11.

ārīsan, I, *arise, rise, start up:* 3p. ārīsað, 605; pret. 3s. ārās, 238, 240, 432, 516.

āscēadan, red., *separate, exclude, cut off:* pp. āscēaden, 177.

āsecgan, W3., *declare, express:* inf. 351.

*****āsellan**, W1., *expel:* pp. āseald, 89.

āsettan, W1., *set, set down, plant:* 3p. āsettað, 639; pret. 1s. āsette, 481; 3s. 683.

āstīgan, I, *arise, ascend, mount; descend:* pret. 3s. āstāh, 549, 563, 682; āstāg, 717, 730; imp. 2p. āstīgað, 628.

atol, adj., *dire, fierce, horrible, loathsome* (as subst. equivalent to *devil, fiend*) : nsm. 161, 681, 728; wk. atola, 96, 413, 487; nsf. atol, 61; gsm. wk. atolan, 327; dsm. wk. 108; asm. wk. 718; asn.

wk. atole, 26, 73, 129; npm. atole, 51; wk. atolan, 448; dpm. wk. 383.

atol, n., *terror, horror:* as. 395, 454; is. atole, 137.

āttor, n., *poison:* ds. āttre, 163; is. 40, 129, 318; ātre, 79.

āwa, adv., *for ever:* 315.

āweorpan, III, *cast out, expel:* pp. āworpen, 181, 669.

āwrītan, I, *write:* pp. āwriten, 676.

āwyrged, adj., *accursed:* nsm. wk. āwyrgda, 316; gsm. wk. āwærgdan, 416; vsm. āwyrgda, 676, 691, 699; vpm. āwyrgde, 628.

B.

bæc, n., *back:* ds. bæce, 158.

bæcling, only in the adverbial phrase, on ~ , *back, backwards, behind:* 698.

bǣttra, see **gōd**.

bæð, n., *bath:* np. bæðe, 546.

balu, adj., *baleful, wicked, pernicious:* nsm. wk. balewa, 484; apm. balewe, 488.

bān, n., *bone:* np. 468.

be, prep., w. dat. and instr., *by, with:* 268, 545.

bealo, n., *bale, woe, evil:* gs. bealowes, 682, 721; as. 71; ap. beala, 274.

bēam, m., *tree, cross:* ds. bēame, 510, 549.

bearm, m., *lap, possession:* ds. bearme, 153, 357, 672.

bearn, n., *child, son:* ns. 10, 587, 622; as. 86, 195, 577; np. 144, 153; gp. bearna, 475; dp. bearnum, 400, 582. *See* **frēo-, frumbearn**.

bebycgan, W1., *sell:* pret. 3s. bebohte, 577.

146		*Christ and Satan*

becuman, IV, *come, arrive, come upon, attain to, obtain:* pret. 1s. becōm, 512; becwōm, 179; 3s. becōm, 245, 379, 387, 406, 466.
bedǣlan, W1., *deprive, free:* pret. 3s. bedēlde, 68; pp. bedǣled, 186; bedēled, 122; npm. bedǣlde, 344; npf. 296.
bedrīfan, I, *drive, force:* pret. 3s. bedrāf, 192.
befæðman, W1., *embrace:* 3s. befæðmeð, 310, 359; inf. 289.
beforan, adv., *before, present before:* 487.
beforan, prep., w. dat., *before:* 389.
bēgan, W1., *bend, bend down:* pret. 3s. bēgde, 381. *See* for-, gebēgan.
bēgen, num., *both:* d. bām, 488.
begitan, V, *beget, bring forth:* pret. 3p. begēton, 474.
*begrēosan, II, *render fearful, horrify:* pp. npm. begrorene, 52.
behōfian, W2., *need:* 3s. behōfað, 210.
belgan, *see* ābelgan.
bēme, f., *trumpet:* gs. bēman, 172, 238; ap. bēman, 602.
benǣman, W1., *deprive:* inf. 346; pp. benēmed, 121.
bend, m., *bond, fetter:* as. 539; dp. bendum, 49, 414.
bēodan, *see* ābēodan.
beofian, W2., *tremble:* pres. p. beofigende, 622.
beoran, IV, *bear:* opt. 1p. beoran, 206; pret. 3p. bǣron, 483; inf. 158. *See* lēohtberende.
beorh, m., *mountain:* as. 682.
beorht, adj., *bright, splendid, glorious, beautiful, clear:* asm. byrhtne, 363; asf. wk. beorhtan, 139; npm. beorhte, 295; apf. beorhte,

418; wk. beorhtan, 484; sup. gsf. wk. byrhtestan, 172. *See* eallbeorht.
beorhte, adv. *brightly:* 215 (? adj. npm.), 295.
beorn, m., *soldier:* np. beornas, 510.
beornan, III, *burn:* 3s. beorneð, 414; pres. p. beornende, 71, 158.
beran, *see* beoran.
bescyrian, W1., *deprive, separate from:* pp. npm. bescyrede, 343.
beteldan, III, *cover, surround, enfold:* pp. as adj. betolden, 588.
bewindan, III, *surround, encircle:* pp. bewunden, 650.
bīdan, I, *abide, dwell, endure:* inf. 27, 49. *See* gebīdan.
biddan, V, *ask, pray for, bid:* pret. 3s. bæd, 438, 673; inf. 209.
bilewit, adj., *mild, gentle, guileless:* asm. bilewitne, 242.
bindan, *see* gebindan.
biter, adj., *bitter, dire:* dsm. wk. bitran, 274; asm. wk. biteran, 149.
bitere, adv., *bitterly, cruelly:* 418.
bitung, *see* gristbitungc.
blāc, adj., *black* (? *pale, wan, livid*): nsm. blāc, 721; npm. blāce, 71; wk. blācan, 196.
blǣd, m., *prosperity, reward, blessedness, joy, honor:* ns. 363; blēd, 593; as. blǣd, 42, 414, 508; blēd, 527, 646.
blǣd, f., *fruit:* ap. blǣda, 418, 484.
blāwan, red., *blow, sound:* inf. 602.
blētsian, *see* geblētsian.
blis, f., *bliss, exultation, joy:* ns. 381.
blīðe, adj., *blithe, happy, glad; gentle, kind:* npm. 613; apm. 206.
blōd, n., *blood:* as. 549.

blondan, see **geblondan.**

blōstma, m., *flower, blossom:* gs. blōstman, 357.

bold, n., *dwelling, home, mansion, palace:* ds. bolde, 149; gp. bolda, 139; ap. bold, 687.

bona, see **sūslbona.**

-bora, see **rǣdbora.**

botm, m., *bottom:* ds. botme, 721.

brād, adj., *broad, spacious, flat:* nsn. wk. brāde, 215; apm. brāde, 672.

brecan, IV, *break, burst through:* pret. 3s. brǣc, 381. *See* **forbrecan.**

brēost, n., *breast:* dp. brēostum, 206.

*breoton, adj., *spacious:* apn. breotone, 687.

bringan, WI., *bring, lead, carry, profer:* 3p. bringaδ, 357; pret. 3s. brōhte, 672; 1p. brōhton, 153; inf. 149, 561.

brūcan, II, *possess, enjoy:* inf. 138.

bryne, m., *burning:* ds. 274.

brynewelm, m., *burning heat or surge:* is. brynewelme, 27.

brytta, m., *lord:* ns. 124; np. brytan, 23.

būend, see **eorδbūende, londbēwende.**

burh, f., *city, citadel:* ds. byrig, 624; as. burh, 459, 613, 687; gp. burga, 86, 139, 602; dp. burgum, 215. *See* **sceldburg.**

burhlēod, m., *citizen (of the heavenly city):* gp. burhlēoda, 561.

burhstyde, m., *city, citadel:* as. 363.

burhweall, m., *city-wall:* ap. burhweallas, 295.

būtan, prep., w. dat., *without:* 147, 679; būton, 315, 379.

būton, conj., *except, save:* 391.

bycgan, see **bebycgan.**

byrht, see **beorht.**

*byrhtword, adj., *clear-voiced, eloquent:* nsm. 238 [?].

bysen, f., *example (warning):* ds. bysne, 196.

C.

cald, adj., *cold:* asm. wk. caldan, 637.

carcern, n., *prison:* gs. carcernes, 490; as. 637.

ceald, n., *cold:* ns. 132.

cearig, adj., *sorrowful:* dp. cearium, 67. *See* **sorghceari.**

cēosan, II, *choose:* opt. 1p. cēosan, 203.

cerr, see **edcerr.**

cerran, WI., *turn, direct one's course:* imp. 2s. cer, 698; inf. 217.

cester, f., *city:* ds. cestre, 258, 657; as. cestre, 298.

clǣne, see **unclǣne.**

clēne, adv., *wholly, entirely, altogether:* 7, 18.

cleopian, W2., *cry:* 3s. cleopaδ, 34, 616.

clom, m., *bond, chain, bondage:* ns. (? n.) 103; as. 452, 490, 637; as. 157; ap. clomma, 444. *See* **fӯrclom.**

cnāwan, see **oncnāwan.**

costian, W2., *tempt:* pret. 3s. costode, 671.

crǣft, m., *power, might, cunning:* as. 200, 392, 585, 725.

crǣftig, adj., *ingenious:* nsm. 349.

Crīst, pr. n., *Christ:* ns. 67, 205, 570; ds. Crīste, 217, 596; as. 346.

-cuma, see **wilcuma.**

cuman, IV, *come:* 3s. cymeδ, 607; 3p. cumaδ, 146, 301, 356; pret.

1s. cōm, 110; 3s. cōm, 36, 323,
393, 403, 426, 457, 564. *See*
becuman.
cunnan, prp., *know, have knowledge
of, understand, be able, can:* 1s.
can, 250; con, 629; pret. 1s. cūðe,
142; opt. 2s. cunne, 702; 3s.
cunne, 17.
cūð, adj., *known, evident, sure, safe,
known to be excellent:* nsn. 258,
583; comp. nsn. cūðre, 596.
cwānian, W2., *bewail, lament:* pret.
3p. cwānedon, 320.
cwealm, m., *death, torment, pain:*
as. 499.
cwēman, W1., *please, serve:* 3p.
cwēmað 655; opt. 1p. cwēman,
596; inf. 184, 305.
cwēme, *see* **gecwēme.**
cweðan, V, *say, speak:* 3p. cweþað,
657; pret. 3s. cwæð, 229, 306,
409; inf. 732. *See* **gecweðan.**
cwide, m., *phrase, words:* dp. cwidum, 67. See sōð-, wom-, word-
cwide.
cwīðan, W1., *lament:* pret. 3s.
cwīðde, 160.
cyle, m., *cold:* as. 335.
cyn, n., *race, people, kin, tribe, family, progeny:* ns. cynn, 461; as.
20, 408; cynn, 134, 353. *Sec*
encgel-, moncyn.
cynestōl, m., *royal city* or *throne:*
as. 298.
cyning, m., *king:* ns. 260 A, 663,
688; cynincg, 616; ds. cyninge,
205; as. 258, 657, 671, 698; gp.
cyninga, 205. *See* **heofen-, wuldorcyning.**
cyrr, m., *occasion, time:* ds. cyrre,
538.
cȳðan, W1., *make known, proclaim:*
inf. cȳþan, 298. *See* **gecȳðan.**

D.
dǣd, f., *deed:* ns. 576; gp. dǣda,
623; ip. dǣdum, 156, 552. *See*
iūdǣd.
dæg, m., *day:* ns. 105; gs. dæges
(adverbial, *by day*),499; vs. 166;
gp. daga, 12, 559, 606, 667; dp.
dagum, 15. *See* **dōmdæg, fyrn-
dagas, gēardagas.**
dægrēd, n., *dawn, daybreak:* ds.
dægrēde, 466; as. 404.
dǣl, m., *portion, region, quarter:*
ap. dǣles, 16.
dǣlan, W1., *portion out, distribute:*
3s. dǣleð, 581. *See* be-, ge-
dǣlan.
dēad, adj., *dead:* npm. dēade, 605.
dēað, m., *death:* gs. dēaðes, 455,
499; ds. dēaðe, 516; as. 462, 665.
dēma, m., *judge:* ds. dēman, 380.
See **heofendēma.**
dēman, W1., *judge, adjudge, decree,
proclaim, extol:* opt. 1p. dēman,
299; inf. 109, 623.
dēofol, n., *devil:* gs. dēofles, 638;
np. dēofla, 319; gp. dēofla, 111,
729.
dēop, adj., *deep:* nsf. dēop, 707;
asm. dēopne, 7, 638; wk. dēopan,
30; asn. dēop, 344.
deorc, adj., *dark, gloomy:* asm.
deorcne, 455; npm. deorce, 105.
dēore, adj., *dear, beloved:* nsm. 82;
wk. dēora, 243, 543; dsm. wk.
dēoran, 219, 257.
derne, *see* **underne.**
Didimus, pr. n.: ns. 543.
dim, adj., *dim:* dsm. wk. dimman,
111; asm. dimne, 455; wk. dimman, 337; npm. dimme, 105.
dine, *see* **dyne.**
dōgor, m., *day:* gp. dōgra, 243, 581.

dohtor, f., *daughter:* ds. dohtor, 439.

dōm, m., *glory, majesty, praise, honor, dignity:* as. 685; is. dōme, 537; ap. dōmas, 507, 555.

dōmdæg, m., *doomsday, judgment-day:* ds. dōmdæge, 600.

dōmlēas, adj., *inglorious:* asn. wk. dōmlēase, 232.

dōn, anv., *do* (in every case representing a preceding verb) : pret. 3s. dyde, 117, 279, 525; 3p. dydon, 191, 625.

draca, m., *dragon:* np. dracan, 98; ap. dracan, 337.

drēam, m., *joy, bliss, rapture; melody, music:* ns. 79, 94; gs. drēames, 168, 174; drēamas, 182; as. 82, 122, 293, 314, 328, 354; vs. 166; gp. drēama, 314; ap. drēamas, 19, 44, 512, 680; ip. drēamum, 68, 344.

drēogan, II, *do, perform, commit, practise, bear, suffer, endure:* pret. 1p. drugon, 255; 3p. 74; inf. 185, 232. *See* ādrēogan.

drēorig, adj., *mournful:* nsm. wk. drēorga, 394. *See* heorodrēorig.

drīfan, *see* ā-, be-, in-, þorhdrīfan.

driht, f., *multitude, throng, train:* ds. 177.

drihten, m., *lord:* ns. 109, 219, 241, 261, 397, 404, 443, 452, 462, 516, 520, 530, 558, 581, 600, 627, 665, 675, 690; gs. drihtnes, 232, 507, 555, 605; drihtenes, 164; dryhtnes, 68; ds. drihtne, 156, 314, 394, 513, 552, 590; dryhtene, 44; dryhten, 82; as. drihten, 47, 174, 187, 198, 202, 222, 257, 576, 683; vs. drihten, 410, 439, 537. *See* frēodrihten.

dropa, m., *drop:* gp. dropena, 12.

dūfan, *see* gedūfan.

dugan, prp., *be good* or *virtuous:* pret. 3s. dēah, 283.

duguð, f., *men, people, host; prosperity, glory, power:* gs. duguðe, 507, 555; gp. duguða, 164; ap. duguðe, 19; ip. duguðum, 122.

dūn, f., *mountain:* as. dūne, 683.

duru, f., *door, gate:* ds. 98, 723; ap. 380, 467.

dūst, n., *dust:* ds. dūste, 605.

dwǣscan, *see* ādwǣscan.

dyne, m., *din:* ns. 380, 394, 404, 466; gp. dinna, 606.

E.

ēac, adv., *also, furthermore:* 699; ēc, 326.

ēadig, adj., *happy, blessed, prosperous, rich:* nsm. 304; gsm. ēadiges, 93; dsm. wk. ēadigan, 660; asm. ēadigne, 293, 354; npm. ēadige, 647; wk. ēadigan, 356; npf. ēadige, 267, 653; npn. ēadige, 144; gpm. ēadigre, 221; apf. ēadige, 407.

ēage, n., *eye:* ip. ēagum, 140, 170, 390, 718; ēgum, 728.

ēalā, interj., *O, alas:* 164(2), 165(2), 166(2), 167(2), 168, 316.

eald, *see* ald.

eall, adj., *all* (often equivalent to *everything* or *wholly:* nsm. 137, 518; nsn. 226, 322, 465; gsn. ealles, 107, 168; alles, 55, 118, 182, 330; asm. alne, 8, 702; asf. ealle, 255; asn. eall, 87, 254; npm. ealle, 150, 154, 197, 385, 434, 532, 657; alle, 61; npn. ealle, 144; gpm. ealra, 205; gpf. ealra, 224, 442, 584; gpn. ealra, 664; alra, 60; dpm. eallum, 245, 249; apm.

ealle, 527, 616, 627; alle, 93; apf.
alla, 203; apn. ealle, 127; eall,
393.

eallbeorht, adj., *all-bright, most
brilliant or splendid:* apm. eallbeorhte, 522.

eapl, *see* æpl.

eard, m., *land, country, home, fa-
therland:* ds. earde, 93, 231, 458,
506; as. 116, 203; gp. earda, 113.

eardian, W2., *dwell:* 3s. eardaȝ,
592; 3p. eardigaȝ, 98.

ēare, n., *ear:* ip. ēarum, 171.

earfoȝe, n., *affliction, trouble:* ap.
earfoȝo, 127.

earm, m., *arm:* as. 432.

earm, adj., *miserable, wretched,
wicked:* nsm. 120, 448, 579, 713;
wk. earme, 87; npm. earme, 73.

ēc, *see* ēac.

ēce, adj., *eternal, everlasting:* nsm.
18, 241, 261, 442, 443, 530, 558,
627, 675, 690; wk. ēca, 276, 458,
532; gsm. wk. ēcan, 168, 182;
dsm. ēcan, 373; dsf. ēcan, 664;
asm. ēcne, 118, 199, 203, 525, 642;
wk. ēcan, 46, 378; asf. ēce, 619;
vsm. 410; apm. 512.

ēce, adv., *eternally, perpetually:* 98.

edcerr, m., *return:* gs. *edcerres*, 451.

edwīt, n., *reproach, scorn, mockery:*
as. 639, 681.

Ēfe, prn., *Eve:* n. 408.

eft, adv., *again, afterwards, hereafter:* 21, 75, 212, 229, 374, 478,
512, 541.

ēge, *see* ēage.

egeslic, adj., *terrible:* nsm. 434.

egsa, m., *terror* (? *torment*): ns.
379, 393, 406; gs. egsan, 454, 728;
is. egsan, 385; ap. egsan, 487.

*eisig, adj., *terrible, dreadful:* isf.
eisegan, 36.

encgelcyn, n., *order of angels:* ns.
366.

ende, m., *end, period:* ns. 40; ds.
315, 379, 679.

*enderīm, n., *number* (? *total*) : as.
12.

endestæf, m., *end:* as. 541.

engel, m., *angel:* ns. ængel, 81;
encgel, 586; np. englas, 60, 354;
gp. engla, 21, 36, 95, 167, 199,
221, 239, 302, 388, 397, 403, 424,
491, 520, 535, 563, 568, 653, 659,
666, 689; dp. englum, 123, 142,
249, 288, 293, 330, 391, 591, 625;
ap. englas, 522. *See* hēhengel.

eorl, m., *man:* np. eorlas, 478.

eorre, adj., nsm. 261, 429.

eorȝbūende, mp., *dwellers on, or
inhabitants of, the earth:* dp.
eorȝbūendum, 1.

eorȝe, f., *earth:* gs. eorȝan, 16, 56,
659; ds. eorȝan, 146, 246, 290,
299, 303, 356, 496, 558, 597;
eorþan, 267; as. eorȝan, 5.

esl, f., *shoulder:* as. esle, 681.

etan, V, *eat:* pret. 2p. æton, 483;
æten, 487.

ēȝel, m., *hereditary home, country,
land:* gs. ēȝles, 327; ds. ēȝle,
403, 461, 478, 496, 554; eȝele,
108; as. ēȝel, 117, 279.

ęȝm, m., *vapor:* ns. 704.

F.

fācne, adj., *wicked, factious:* ip.
fācnum, 65.

fæder, m., *father:* ns. 310, 359; gs.
308; fæderes, 580; ds. fæder, 318.
See hēhfæder.

fægen, adj., *glad, elated:* npm.
fægen, 435.

fæger, adj., *fair, beautiful, sweet:*
nsm. 79; nsn. 457, 547; asm.
fægerne, 329; comp. nsn. fægere,
389; asn. fægere, 213.

fægre, adv., *beautifully, elegantly:*
308.

fæhðe, f., *feud, hostility, enmity:*
ns. 405; as. 641.

fæmne, f., *virgin:* gs. fæmnan, 495.

fæst, adj., *fast, firmly fastened:* ip.
fæstum, 39. *See* sōðfæst.

fæstan, W1., *fast:* pret. 3s. fæste,
667. *See* oðfæstan.

fæste, adv., *fast, firmly:* 324; feste,
58; fęste, 104.

fæsten, n., *prison, sepulchre;* ds.
fæstenne, 521.

fæstlic, adj., *firm, perpetual:* nsm.
325.

fæstnian, *see* gefæstnian.

fæðman, *see* befæðman.

fāh, adj., *guilty, hostile:* nsm. 97,
128, 156, 186, 479; dsm. fāgum,
110.

fāh, adj., *stained, spotted:* nsm. 180.

faran, VI, *go, proceed, come:* 3s.
færeð, 608; inf. 407, 443.

fatian, *see* gefatian.

-fēa, *see* gefēa.

feallan, red., *fall, fall down:* pret.
3p. fēollon, 533, 546. *See* gefeallan.

fela, n. indecl., *many, much:* 402,
497; feola, 477; feolo, 421; adverbial: feola, 160.

fēlan, *see* gefēlan.

feng, *see* andˌfeng.

feohtan, *see* oferfeohtan.

fēond, m., *fiend, devil:* ns. 479; as.
225, 405, 463; npm. 104, 196;
fēondas, 640; gp. fēonda, 76; dp.
fēondum, 445.

feor, adv., *far away, distant:* 40.

fēower, num., *four:* 603.

fēowertig, num., *forty:* 475, 559,
667.

fēran, W1., *go, journey:* 3s. fēreð,
389; 3p. fērað, 654; pret. 3s.
fērde, 495; inf. 110. *See* gefēran.

ferian, *see* geferian.

ferð, *see* wīdeferð.

feste, *see* fæste.

fēða, m., *band, host, company:* ns.
457; ds. fēþan, 324; np. fēðan,
221.

firen, f., *sin, crime, iniquity, torment:* as. firne, 641; gp. firna,
160; dp. firenum, 479; firnum,
435; fyrnum, 128.

firenfull, adj., *sinful, wicked:* npm.
firenfulle, 65.

firnian, W2., *sin:* pret. 3p. firnedon,
620.

firran, *see* āfirran.

flēman, *see* geflēman.

flēogan, II, *fly:* pret. 3s. flēah, 162;
inf. 264. *See* ymbflēogan.

flōr, m., *floor, ground:* ns. 39, 318;
ds. flōra, 110; ap. flōras, 70.

flyge, m., *flight:* ds. 112.

flyht, m., *flight:* ds. flyhte, 112.

folc, n., *people, multitude:* as. folc,
686; ip. folcum, 559.

folde, f., *earth, ground:* ns. 213; gs.
foldan, 3, 603; ds. foldan, 495,
546; as. foldan, 264, 533, 686.

folgað, m., *service:* as. 329.

folgian, W2., *follow, attend:* pp.
folgad, 559.

folm, *palm, hand:* ip. folmum, 713.

fōn, red., *receive:* imp. 2s. fōh, 686.
See on-, ymbfōn.

for, prep., w. dat., *before, in the*

646; as. 14, 562; np. gāstas, 51, 630, 653, 732; gp. gāsta, 244; vp. gāstas, 471.

gāstlice, adv., *spiritually:* 301.

gēar, n., *year:* gp. gēara, 503.

geara, adj., *prepared, ready:* nsf. geara, 693.

gēara, *see* ungēara.

geard, *see* middangeard.

gēardagas, mp., *the olden days, days of yore:* dp. gēardagum, 368.

gearwian, W2., *make ready, prepare:* opt. 1p. gearwian, 287.

geat, n., *gate:* ns. 649.

gebēgan, W1., *depress, abase, crush:* pp. gebēged, 446.

gebīdan, I, *abide, await, endure:* pret. 1s. gebād, 496; inf. 108.

gebindan, III, *bind, fasten, secure:* pp. gebunden, 38, 58, 104, 324.

geblētsian, W2., *bless:* pret. 3s. geblētsode, 242.

geblondan, red., *mingle, mix:* pp. geblonden, 129.

gecwēme, adj., *pleasing, acceptable:* gpm. gecwēmra, 217.

gecweðan, V, *speak, say:* pres. 3s. gecwæð[?], 627; pret. 1s. gecwæð, 123.

gecȳðan, W1., *reveal, show, prove:* pret. 3s. gecȳdde, 200; pp. gecȳðed, 560.

gedēlan, W1., *distribute, allot, give out:* pret. 3s. gedēlde, 19.

gedūfan, II, *dive, plunge, sink:* pret. 3s. gedēaf, 670; inf. 30.

gefæstnian, W2., *fix, set firmly, establish:* pret. 3s. gefestnade, 3; pp. gefæstnod, 517.

gefatian, W1., *fetch, summon:* inf. 521.

gefēa, m., *joy:* as. gefēan, 199.

gefeallan, red., *fall, plunge:* pret. 3s. gefēol, 712.

gefēlan, W1., *feel:* pret. 3s. gefēlde, 77.

gefēran, W1., *fare:* pp. gefēred, 62.

geferian, W1., *carry, lead, bring:* inf. 148; pp. geferde, 92.

geflēman, W1., *put to flight:* pp. geflēmed, 463.

gefrætwian, W2., *adorn:* pp. gefrætewod, 308, 649.

gefrignan, III, *learn, hear:* pret. 1s. gefregn, 526; gefregen, 225.

gefylled, *see* fyllan.

*geglidan, I, *slip, fall:* inf. 376.

gehealdan, red., *keep, retain possession of:* pret. 3s. gehēold, 347.

*gehēaw, n., *gnashing:* ns. 339.

gehēnan, W1., *humble, overthrow:* pp. gehēned, 190.

gehēran, W1., *hear:* 1s. gehēre, 133; pret. 1p. gehērdon, 237; inf. 171, 328, 338, pp. gehēred, 333, 607.

gehrēowan, red., *grieve, cause to rue* or *repent:* pret. 3s. gehrēaw, 374; gerēaw, 489; inf. 540.

gehrīnan, I, *touch, lay hold of:* inf. gerīnan, 267.

gehwā, pron., *each, every:* ism, gehwǣm, 581.

gehwylc, pron., *each, every, every one:* nsm. 285, 432 (ānra gehwylc, *every one, all*); asm. gehwilcne, 243; gehwelcne, 12; isn. gehwylce, 551.

gehycgan, W3., *consider, be mindful, take heed, conceive, understand:* inf. 194, 283; gehicgan, 179.

gehȳdan, W1., *hide, conceal:* inf., 101.

gehygd, n., *thought, plan:* as. 344.

gesittan, V, *sit, lean*: pret. 3s. gesǽt,
432, 470.

gestīgan, I, *ascend to, mount up to*:
3p. gestīgaᵭ, 612.

gestondan, VI, *stand*: pret. 3s.
gestōd, 241, 530.

gestrēonan, WI., *obtain*: inf. 597.

geswīᵭan, WI., *strengthen*: pret. 3s.
geswīᵭde, 572.

gēt, *see* gȳt.

getenge, adj., *near, at hand, press-
ing hard*: nsf. 711.

geþencan, WI., *be mindful of, consider, reflect upon, resolve*: 1p.
geþencaᵭ, 290; pret. 1s. geþōhte,
187; 3s. geþōhte, 316, 371; inf.
644.

geþēode, n., *tongue, people*: ap. 19.

geþēon, I, *thrive, profit*: pret. 3s.
geþēah, 576.

geþingian, W2., *promise* (literally,
agree to, settle) : pp. geþingod,
598.

geþōht, m., *thought*: ap. geþōhtas,
206, 284, 488.

geþolian, W2., w. acc., *suffer, endure, bear*: 1p. geþoliaᵭ, 399; inf.
636; w. gen., *suffer loss* or *lack
of, forfeit*: inf. 273.

geþrōwian, W2., *suffer*: pret. 3s.
geþrōwode, 548, 666.

gewald, n., *power, control, dominion, possession*: ds. gewalde, 415;
gewealde, 687; as. 55, 86, 107,
118, 174.

geweorᵭan, III, *become, please
(seem good)*: pret. 3s. gewearᵭ,
256, 261, 669.

gewinn, n., *struggle, war* (? *distress, tribulation*) : as. 232.

gewītan, I, *depart*: imp. 2s. gewīt,
691.

geworden, *see* weorᵭan.

gewundod, *see* wundian.

gewunian, W2., *dwell in, inhabit*:
inf. 326; pp. npm. gewunade, 103.

gewunnon, *see* winnan.

gewyrcan, WI., *make, create, earn,
deserve*: 1p. gewyrcaᵭ, 303; pret.
1s. geworhte, 472.

gif, conj., *if*: 251, 290, 302, 674, 688.

gifan, *see* forgifan.

gīfre, adj., *greedy, rapacious*: npm.
32, 192.

gifu, f., *gift, grace*: as. gife, 646;
is. gife, 572.

gildan, *see* forgildan.

gim, m., *gem, jewel*: ip. gimmum,
649.

gin, *see* ongin.

gingra, m., *vassal, follower, disciple*: np. gingran, 191, 531; ap.
gingran, 522, 526, 572.

ginnan, *see* onginnan.

gitan, *see* be-, forgitan, ongeotan.

giunga, adj., *young*: nsm. wk.
giunga, 511.

glēaw, adj., *sagacious, discerning*:
nsm. 350.

glīdan, *see* geglīdan.

gnornian, W2., *grieve, bewail, lament, murmur*: pret. 3s. gnor-
nede, 280; inf. 274; pres. p. apm.
gnorncndc, 134.

gnornungc, f., *wailing, lamentation*:
ns. 334.

God, m., *God*: ns. 18, 32, 56, 109,
192, 244, 260, 281, 288, 350, 355,
430, 441, 493, 516, 531, 550, 574,
599; gs. Godes 10, 166, 191, 269,
280, 289, 340, 358, 368, 470, 474,
528, 565, 614, 622, 646, 651, 693,
719; ds. Gode, 82, 234, 314; as.
97, 524, 705.

gōd, adj., *good:* comp. asm. bæt-
    tran, 49; ipf. sēlrum, 45.
gōd, n., *good, blessing, benefit:* gp.
    gōda, 186, 331.
gongan, red., *go:* imp. 2s. gong,
    708; gang, 701; inf. 526, 614, 651.
    See āgangan.
grǣdig, adj., *greedy:* npm. grǣdige,
    192; grēdige, 32.
*grǣfhūs, n., *house of the dead:* ns.
    708.
grēne, adj., *green, fair, pleasant:*
    asf. 287.
grēosan, *see* begrēosan.
grim, adj., *grim, dire, horrible:* nsn.
    708; apm. grimme, 260.
grīpan, I, *seize, take hold of, snatch,*
    carry off: imp. 2s. grīp, 701; inf.
    269.
*gristbitungc, f., *gnashing of teeth:*
    ns. 334.
grund, m., *bottom, deep, depth,*
    abyss: gs. grundes, 701; ds.
    grunde, 269, 633, 703, 726; as. 31,
    91, 149, 450, 456, 485, 637; ap.
    grundas, 10, 134, 260.
*grynde, n., *abyss:* gs. gryndes, 331.
gryre, m., *terror:* ns. 433; as. 454,
    ns. (? is.) 728. *See* hinsīðgryre.
gylden, adj., *golden:* nsn. 649.
gylp, n., *pride, vaunt, boasting:* ns.
    254.
gȳt, adv., *yet, still, yet again:* 160,
    405, 408, 570; gēt, 225.

H.

habban, W3., *have, possess, hold,*
    keep, get: 1s. hebbe, 88, 92; 2s.
    hafast, 678, 706; hafus, 64; 3s.
    hafað, 587, 598; 1p. habbað 61;
    2p. habbað, 618; 3p. habbað, 144,
    354, 508; pret. 1s. hefde, 82; 3s.
    hæfde, 2, 200, 226, 404, 444, 462,

573; hefde, 33; 1p. hæfdon, 151;
    hefdon, 44; 2p. hæfdon, 485; 3p.
    hæfdon, 68, 70, 329, 527, 719; opt.
    2s. hæbbe, 674, 710; inf. 29, 37,
    43, 450, 591, 643. Negative: 1p.
    nabbað, 335. *See* wiðhabban.
hād, m., *nature, condition, relation:*
    as. 438, 495.
hæft, m., *captive, servant:* np. hæf-
    tas, 631; dp. hæftum, 319; ap.
    hæftas, 202, 717.
hæft, m., *bond, fetter, captivity:* dp.
    hæftum, 92, 148, 505, 553; ip.
    hæftum, 427.
Hǣlend, m., *Saviour* (= both
    Christ and *God*): ns. 219, 281,
    493, 607; gs. Hǣlendes, 153, 382,
    426, 486, 648; Hēlendes, 86; ds.
    Hǣlende, 364, 595, 645; Hēlende,
    54; as. 544, 576, 683.
hæleð, m., *man, hero, warrior:* np.
    heleð, 47; gp. hæleða, 194, 270,
    400, 680A, 658; hæleþa, 582.
hǣlo, f., *health, well-being, salva-*
    tion: as. 582.
hǣðen, adj., *heathen:* npm. hǣþene,
    540; gpm. hǣþenre, 268.
haldan, red., *hold, keep, retain:* 3s.
    haldeð, 260A.
hālig, adj., *holy:* nsm. 56, 81, 565,
    586, 592; dsm. hāligum, 513; wk.
    hālgan, 234, 291, 567; dsn. wk.
    hālgan, 417; asm. hāligne, 328,
    415, 528, 562; wk. hālgan, 202;
    asn. wk. hālige, 348; npm. 222,
    460; apm. hālige, 680; ipf. hāl-
    gum, 656.
hālsian, W2., *beseech, adjure:* 1s.
    hālsige, 422.
hām, m., *home, abode, dwelling:* ns.
    38, 96, 100, 216; gs. hāmes, 138;
    ds. hām, 111, 219, 257, 504, 567,

660; as. 25, 49, 178, 276, 278, 294, 337, 345, 362, 415; adverbial accus. hām, 88, 92, 148, 427, 431, 505, 553.

hand, *see* hond.

handgeweorc, n., *work of the hands, handiwork:* ns. 489.

*handþegen, m., *servant:* ns. 485.

hāt, adj., *hot:* nsm. 159, 281, 319; asm. hātne, 456, 485; asn. wk. hāte, 193, 419; npm. hāte, 99.

hāt, n., *heat:* ns. 132; as. 335.

hātan, red., *bid, command, name:* 1s. hāte, 694; 3s. hāteð, 601; pret. 3s. hēt, 484, 521, 523, 724; pp. hāten, 367, 543.

hāte, adv., *hotly:* 341.

hē, pron., *he:* nsm. 3, 4, 9, 11, 13, 19, 33, 77, 78(2), 80, 117, 147, 163, 190, 195, 200(2), 201, 212, 218, 260A, 265, 266, 279, 284, 292, 306, 317, 347, 369, 370, 372, 375, 380, 464, 467, 518, 520, 524, 525, 544, 545, 549, 553, 560, 571, 577, 584, 667, 670, 680A, 716, 721, 726(2); nsf. hēo, 409; nsn. hit, 22, 125, 396, 534, 569; gsm. his, 6, 13, 14, 127, 191, 243, 283, 326, 360, 376, 392, 545, 549, 550, 572, 580, 585, 588, 589, 592, 615, 623, 668; dsm. him. 51, 118, 125, 196, 211, 226, 235, 260, 281, 284, 374, 389, 428, 448, 568, 576, 578, 586, 611, 672, 673, 675, 690, 722; asm. hine, 154, 246, 376, 460, 566, 724; np. hīe, 23, 74, 346, 469, 474, 542, 635, 639, 641, 643; hī, 361, 378, 382, 451, 535; hēo, 25, 27, 99, 297, 312, 329, 345, 499, 506, 529, 541, 624; hē, 335, 718; gp. heora, 66, 223, 308, 323, 373; dp. him, 22, 24, 240, 249, 342, 379, 436, 452(2),

458, 460, 540, 622, 626, 639, 643, 696; hym, 70; ap. hīe, 359, 360; hēo, 67, 310, 445, 615; hē, 192, 479.

hēafod, n., *head:* as. 382.

hēah, adj., *high, deep:* nsf. hēh, 707; dsn. wk. hēan, 202; asm. hēanne, 17; sup. asf. hēhstan, 694.

hēahgetimber, n., *lofty building:* ap. hēahgetimbra, 29.

healdan, *see* ge-, ymbhealdan.

healf, f., *side:* ap. healfe, 610.

hēan, adj., *depressed, miserable:* nsm. 120.

hēap, m., *company, band, host:* ns. 87, 394; as. 242.

hēaw, *see* gehēaw.

hēawan, red., *strike, cut:* pret. 3s. hēow, 511.

hebban, VI, *raise, lift, bear up:* pret. 1p. hōfan, 154; 3p. hōfon, 460. *See* āhebban.

hēhengel, m., *archangel:* ap. hēhenglas, 601.

hēhfæder, m., *patriarch:* np. 656.

hēhseld, n., *throne, lofty hall:* ds. hēhselde, 208; as. 47, 372; gp. hēhselda, 43.

hēhsetl, n., *throne:* as. 220.

Hēlend, *see* Hǣlend.

heleð, *see* hæleð.

hell, hyll, f., *hell:* ns. hell, 707; hel, 193, 700; gs. helle, 70, 98, 133, 456, 467, 485, 631, 723; hylle, 433; ds. helle, 34, 88, 159, 161, 190, 281, 375, 380, 400, 427, 450, 579; hylle, 338, 717; as. helle, 25, 341, 436, 670.

*hellescealc, m., *retainer of hell, devil:* ap. hellescealcas, 133.

hellwaran, mp., *the inhabitants of*

158   *Christ and Satan*

hell: d. hellwarum, 695; helwa-
rum, 431.
helm, m., *helmet, protector:* ns. 658;
as. 252; vs. 164.
help, f., *help, aid, support:* ds. helpe,
436, 440; as. helpe, 291; help,
582.
helpan, III, *help:* inf. 99, 493.
hēnan, *see* gehēnan.
hēnðo, f., *humiliation, disgrace:* as.
399; inðo, 376.
hēofan, II, *lament, bewail:* pret. 3p.
hēofon, 344.
heofencyning, m., *king of heaven:*
ds. heofencyninge, 183, 317, 437.
*heofendēma, m., *heavenly judge:*
ns. 658.
*heofenþrēat, m., *heavenly band:*
np. heofenþrēatas, 222.
heofon, m., *heaven:* gs. heofones,
311; heofnes, 56; as. 169, 415;
gp. heofona, 278, 348, 618;
heofna, 567; dp. heofonum, 16,
151, 276, 328, 345, 372, 467, 563,
565, 670; heofnum, 29, 37, 43, 81,
586. *See* ūpheofon.
heofonrīce, n., *kingdom of heaven:*
gs. heofenrīces, 422; ds. heofonrīce, 216, 562, 680.
heolstor, n., *place of concealment,
retreat:* gs. heolstres, 101.
heonon, adv., *hence:* 424, 654;
heonan, 397.
heorodrēorig, adj., *mournful, sad:*
nsf. 700.
heorte, f., *heart:* ns. 283.
hēr, adv., *here:* 93, 102, 105, 132,
210, 262, 273.
hēran, W1., *obey:* opt. 1p. hēran,
595; inf. 54, 183, 234, 317, 364,
645. *See* gehēran.
herde, m., *keeper, lord:* ns. 160.

hereweorc, n., *warlike deed, fight:*
gs. hereweorces, 399.
herian, W1., *praise:* 3p. herigað,
47, 222, 656, 661.
herm, adj., *malicious:* nsm. 682.
hider, adv., *hither:* 423, 686.
hiht, *see* hyht.
*hinsīðgryre, m., *terror of death:*
as. insīðgryre, 456.
hīred, m., *household, company,
train:* ns. 376, 592; ds. hīrede,
423; as. 348.
hlāf, m., *loaf:* ap. hlāfas, 673.
hleonian, W2., *lean, recline:* pret.
3s. hleonade, 433.
hlūd, adj., *loud:* nsm. 467, 607; nsn.
wk. lūde, 340 (? adv.); isf.
hlūddre, 601.
hnīgan, I, *bend, bow down, sink:*
pret. 3p. hnigon, 533; hnigan,
240; inf. 375; nīgan, 208.
hof, n., *hall, dwelling:* as. 193.
hōfian, *see* behōfian.
holdlice, adv., *graciously, kindly:*
311.
holm, m., *sea:* as. holm, 17.
hond, f., *hand:* ns. 565; ds. handa,
433; as. 580, 611; is. hond, 360,
615; ip. hondum, 268, 460, 540,
544, 680A, 700; handum, 169,
417, 437, 706.
hraðe, adv., *straightway:* 229.
hrēam, m., *cry, clamor:* ns. rēam,
717.
hrefnan, *see* refnan.
hrēowan, *see* gehrēowan.
hreðer, m., *breast, interior:* ds.
reðre, 99.
hrīnan, *see* gehrīnan.
hrōpan, red., *cry out, scream:* pret.
3p. hrēopan, 319.

hū, conj., *how:* 33, 179, 196, 352, 499, 639, 647, 699, 704, 707.

hund, n., *hundred:* ns. 723.

hungor, m., *hunger:* ds. hungre, 673.

hūru, adv., *even, especially:* 171, 523.

hūs, n., *house:* as. 710. *See* græf-, wītehūs.

hwā, pron., *who, what:* nsm. hwā, 17; asn. hwæt, 109. *See* æg-, gehwā.

hwær, conj., adv., *where, whither:* 36, 529. *See* æghwær.

hwæt, interj., *lo:* 44, 132, 233, 439; adv., *how:* 316.

hwæðer, conj., used as an interr. part. introducing a direct question: 277.

hwearfian, W2., *wander about:* pret. 3p. hwearfedon, 72.

hweorfan, III, *turn, depart, go, wander* or *roam about:* pret. 3s. hwearf, 190, 400; 3p. hworfon, 71; hweorfan, 341; inf. 120, 270, 419.

hwīl, f., *time:* as. hwīle, 255; ip. hwīlum, as adv., *sometimes:* 132; correlative, *sometimes . . . sometimes, now . . . now:* 133, 135, 713, 715, 716, 717.

hwīt, adj., *white:* npm. hwīte, 220.

hwonne, conj., *when:* 622.

hwylc, *see* æg-, gehwylc.

hwyrft, m., *course:* ip. hwyrftum, 631 (? *wheeling, circling*). *See* ymbhwyrft.

hycgan, W3., *think, take heed, purpose:* pret. 1s. hogade, 84; inf. 594. *See* ge-, oferhycgan.

hȳdan, *see* gehȳdan.

hygd, *see* ge-, oferhygd.

hyht, m., *hope, expectation, joy:* ds.

hyhte, 70, 335; hihte, 176, 643; as. hyht, 695.

hyhtlic, adj., *joyous:* comp. nsm. hyhtlicra, 216; gsm. hihtlicran, 138.

*hyhtwilla, m., *hope of joy:* gs. hyhtwillan, 159.

hyll, *see* hell.

I.

ic, pron., *I:* ns. 48, 81, 84, 85, 88, 89, 92, 97, 108, 110, 112, 120, 123, 124, 130(2), 133, 138, 140, 141, 145, 148, 156, 168, 169, 173, 176, 177, 179(2), 181, 184, 187, 225, 248, 250, 268, 273, 275, 276, 410, 422, 424, 472, 481, 503, 504, 505, 509, 512, 526, 629, 685, 694; ds. mē, 49, 82, 86, 109, 141, 174, 175, 499, 686; as. mē, 489, 498, 510, 677; np. wē, 37, 41, 44, 54, 60, 61, 95, 101(2), 115, 150, 151, 154, 202, 208, 230, 233, 234, 236, 255, 256, 290, 299, 383, 390, 391, 398, 538, 554, 556, 590, 595, 597, 645; dp. ūs, 63, 99, 115, 198, 203, 241, 253, 261, 277, 294, 430, 556, 598, 665; ūsic, 256; ap. ūs, 53, 101, 287, 289, 291, 292, 301, 553, 589; dual n. wit, 411, 412, 414, 416, 419; d. unc, 418; a. unc, 413.

īdel, adj., *empty, vain:* nsn. 254.

ilca, pron., *same, very:* asn. ilce, 591.

in, prep., w. dat., *in, within, on:* 10, 29, 43, 48, 49, 58, 80, 81, 84, 102, 108, 128, 151, 158, 179, 203, 216, 219, 233, 274, 308, 309, 328, 368, 369, 380, 409, 435, 450, 463, 479, 508, 524, 531, 556, 593, 657, 664, 717, 731; w. accus., *in, into, to:* 25, 26, 30, 31, 91, 149, 178, 180, 193, 311, 376, 378, 419, 440, 446,

459, 560, 608, 613, 614, 617, 628,
633., 634, 650, 670, 691.
*indrīfan, I, *utter:* pret. 3s. indrāf,
80[?].
inneweard, adj., *inside, within:* 137,
707.
innon, prep., w. dat., *in, within:* 579.
insīðgryre, *see* hinsīðgryre.
īnðo, *see* hēnðo.
īren, n., *iron:* is. īrne, 518.
irnan, III, *run:* pret. 3s. ran, 712;
3p. urnon, 532.
iū, adv., *formerly, once:* 44, 81, 151.
iūdǣd, m., *former deed:* ip. iūdǣdum, 186.
Iūdas, pr. n., *Judas:* ns. 574.

L.

lā, interj., *oh, ah, indeed:* 457, 464,
644, 733. *See* ēalā.
lǣca, lēca, *see* ǣglǣca.
*lǣcan, WI., *spring* or *flare up:*
pret. 3s. lǣhte, 716.
lǣcedōm, m., *healing:* as. 589.
lǣdan, WI., *lead:* 3s. lǣdað, 361;
pret. 2s. lǣddest, 423; 3s. lǣdde,
566; inf. 398. *See* ā-, gelǣdan.
lǣran, WI., *teach, show, give:* inf.
250. *See* gelǣran.
lǣtan, red., *let, suffer; regard as:*
pret. 3s. lēt, 407, 443; opt. 3s.
lǣte, 196. *See* anfor-, forlǣtan.
land, *see* lond.
lang, adj., *long:* sup. nsm. lengust,
606.
langian, W2., impersonal, *long for,
desire:* opt. 3s. lange, 505.
langsum, adj., *enduring, sound:*
asm. langsumne, 250.
lāst, *see* wrǣclāst.
lāð, adj., *evil, grievous, hateful,
loathed, loathsome, hostile:* gsm.

wk. lāþan, 716; asm. lāðne, 539;
wk. lāðan, 178; asn. wk. lāðe,
727; apm. lāðe, 285.
laðian, W2., *invite, call:* 3s. laðað,
589; 3p. leaðað, 632.
leahtor, m., *sin, disgrace, infamy:*
dp. leahtrum, 263; ap. leahtras,
285.
lēan, n., *reward:* as. 679.
lēas, adj., *destitute of, deprived of;
false, perfidious:* nsm. 159, 168,
182; nsf. 727; npm. lēase, 331.
See dōmlēas.
lēasung, f., *lie, lying:* dp. lēasungum, 62.
lecgan, *see* gelecgan.
lēfan, *see* ā-, gelēfan.
lēg, *see* līg.
lēod, *see* burhlēod.
lēof, adj., *dear, beloved:* asm. lēofne,
155.
lēoht, līht, n., *light:* ns. lēoht, 106,
389, 556; ds. lēohte, 178, 589;
līhte, 361; as. lēoht, 28, 141, 253,
311, 449, 591, 617, 658; līht, 68,
679.
lēoht, adj., *bright, brilliant:* asm.
lēohtne, 469; vsm. wk. lēohta,
166.
*lēohtberende, m., *light-bearer:* ns.
367.
lēoma, m., *light, radiance, splendor:*
as. lēoman, 85, 351, 469. *See*
fȳrlēoma.
-līc, *see* ge-, ungelīc.
licgan, V, *lie:* inf. 263, 716.
līf, n., *life:* ns. 596; as. 212, 292, 361.
lifian, W3., *live:* pres. p. ns. lifigende, 574; npm. as subst. lifigend, 299; gp. lifigendra, 285;
dp. lifigendum, 679.

līg, m., *flame:* ns. lēg, 715; is. līge, 325.

līht, see lēoht.

līhtan, see gelīhtan.

lim, n., *limb, member:* np. leomu, 155.

limpan, see gelimpan.

*limwæstm, m., *size of limb, stature:* ip. limwæstmum, 130.

list, m., f., *art, skill:* ip. listum, 300.

loca, see fȳrloca.

*locen, n., *secret, mystery:* as. 300.

lōcian, W2., *look, gaze:* pret. 3s. lōcade, 727; imp. 2s. lōca, 684; inf. 170.

lofsong, m., *song of praise, hymn:* gp. lofsonga, 155.

lond, n., *land:* ns. 215; land, 213; as. land, 270.

londbēwende, m., *inhabitant of earth:* ap. 684.

lūcan, see onlūcan.

*Lūcifer, pr. n., ns. 367.

lūd, see hlūd.

lūtian, see gelūtian.

lyft, m., *air:* as. 263.

lyge, m., *lie, deceit:* as. 53.

lȳhtan, W1., *give light:* 3s. lȳhteð, 105.

lyt, see ymblyt.

lȳðre, adv., *miserably, wretchedly:* 62.

M.

mā, n., *more (others):* n. 113.

mā, adv., *more, again:* 140.

mægen, n., *might, strength, power:* ns. 491; ds. mægne, 519; as. mægen, 550.

mægð, f., *race, progeny, tribe:* ds. mægðe, 425; dp. mægðum, 272.

mæl, n., *time, appointed time:* gs.

mæles, 501; gp. mæla, 551. *See* þūsendmælum.

mænan, W1., *lament, mourn:* pret. 3p. mændon, 386; inf. 134.

mænego, see menego.

mære, adj., *great, illustrious, noble, splendid:* nsm. wk. mæra, 598; dsf. wk. mæran, 624; asf. wk. mæran, 459, 560; asn. wk. mære, 353.

mæst, see micel.

magan, prp., *can, be able, may:* 1s. mæg, 130, 169, 179; 2s. miht, 696; 3s. mæg, 9, 11, 283, 540; 1p. magon, 101; 3p. magon, 99; pret. 3s. mihte, 338, 493, 519; 3p. mihton, 542; opt. 1s. mæge, 425; 3s. mæge, 351; 1p. mægen, 597; pret. 3s. mihte, 22; 3p. mihten, 500.

man, see mon.

mān, n., *sin, crime, guilt; punishment, pain:* as. 305, 321.

māra, see micel.

Maria, pr. n., *Mary:* gs. Marian, 438.

martire, m., *martyr:* np. martiras, 655.

mearc, f., *limit, period:* ns. 501.

mecg, m., *man:* gp. mecga, 334.

mēdla, see onmēdla.

mencgan, W1., *mingle:* 3p. mencgað, 132.

menego, f. indecl., *multitude:* ns. 83, 262; mænego, 729 (? gs.); menio, 476; ds. 321; as. mænego, 201, 504; is. menego, 111.

Meotod, m., *Creator, God, Christ:* ns. 2, 8, 64, 262, 401, 459, 515; Metod, 668; gs. Meotodes, 143, 165, 173, 286, 353, 529; ds.

Meotode, 83, 184, 305, 655; as.
438, 697.

mercian, W2., *design, appoint:* pp.
merced, 710. *See* gemercian.

metan, V, *measure:* pret. 3s. mæt,
713. *See* āmetan.

mētan, *see* gemētan.

micel, adj., *great:* nsm. 662; dsn.
wk. miclan, 519; asm. micelne,
83, 497; wk. micclan, 252; asf.
micle, 674; ipf. miclum, 629; apf.
miccle, 201; comp. asn. māre, 64;
sup. nsm. mǣst, 606; asf. mǣste,
696.

mid, prep., w. dat., *with, together
with, along with:* 82, 123, 142, 205,
224, 293, 312, 314, 330, 373, 388,
391, 425, 448, 458, 460, 470, 482,
587, 590, 591, 608, 648; w. accus.,
with, together with: 60, 203, 376,
612; w. instr., *with, by, through:*
145, 157, 169, 170, 171, 300, 360,
385, 417, 437, 518, 540, 544, 572,
615, 680A, 700, 713, 728.

mid, adv., *with, by* (= *present,
there*): 565.

middangeard, -eard, m., *earth,
world:* as. middangeard, 8, 440,
476, 583; middaneard, 272; vs.
middaneard, 165.

miht, f., *might, power:* ds. mihte,
251; as. 2, 6, 13, 605, 694; is.
mihte, 353; vs. 165; dp. mihtum,
8; ap. mihte, 401, 472, 674; mihta,
201; ip. mihtum, 232, 262.

mihtig, adj., *mighty, powerful:* nsm.
wk. mihtiga, 724.   *See* ælmihtig.

***mīl,** f., *mile:* gp. mīla, 724; ip.
mīlum, 339.

milds, f., *mercy, favor, kindness:*
gs. miltse, 438; gp. mildsa, 668.

mīn, poss. pron., *my:* nsn. 489; dsf.

mīnre, 425; mīre, 251, 439; dsn.
mīnum, 84, 158; apf. mīne, 472.

min (*or* **minne?**), adj., *mean,
wretched:* dsm. wk. minnan, 504

mōd, n., *mind, heart:* ds. mōde, 22,
84, 286; is. mōd, 542. *See*
stīðmōd.

molde, f., *earth:* ds. moldan, 604.

mon, m., *man:* np. men, 307, 551,
604; gp. monna, 272, 491, 689;
manna, 401; dp. monnum, 381;
mannum, 440; ap. men, 135.

mōna, m., *moon:* as. mōnan, 4.

moncyn, n., *mankind:* gs. moncynnes, 64, 515, 698; mancynnes,
310, 359, 459, 668; ds. mancynne,
560.

monig, adj., *many:* npm. monige,
498; dp. monegum, 583.

morgen, m., *morning:* as. 515.

morður, n., *torment:* as. 321; morðer, 184.

mōtan, anv., *may, must:* 1s. mōt,
138, 140, 145, 148, 170, 268; 3s.
mōt, 266, 365; 1p. mōton, 259,
302, 556, 590; mōten, 96; 3p.
mōton, 312, 450, 451, 613, 635;
mōten, 297, 332, 651; pret. 1s.
mōste, 108, 176; 3s. mōste, 408,
524; 1p. mōston, 233; 3p. mōston,
477; mōsten, 378; opt. 1s. mōte,
425; 3p. mōten, 624.

munan, *see* gemunan.

mynt, *see* weorðmynt.

myntan, W1., *think, intend:* pret.
2s. myntest, 689.

N.

nā, nō, adv., *not, never:* nā, 412;
nō, 292, 377, 634.

nabban, *see* habban.

nacod, adj., *naked:* apm. nacode, 135.

nǣddre, f., *serpent, snake:* gs. nǣddran, 412; nēdran, 102; ap. nǣddran, 337.
nǣman, *see* benǣman.
nǣnig, pron., *none, no:* nsm. 349;
  asm. nǣnigne, 122.
nǣre, næs, *see* wesan.
nǣss, *see* ness.
nāgan, *see* āgan.
nalles, adv., *not, by no means:* 42,
  327, 449, 693; nales, 28.
nama, m., *name:* ns. 193.
nān, adj., *no:* nsm. 517.
ne, adv., *not:* 50, 54, 79, 99, 105, 115,
  130, 138, 140, 145, 169, 170, 171,
  179, 183, 195, 266, 317, 332, 408,
  412, 542, 576, 629, 695; nē, conj.,
  nor, 94, 95(2), 139(2), 145, 170,
  171, 349, 350, 451, 491, 492(2).
nearu, adj., *narrow, close, oppres-
  sive:* asn. nearwe, 634.
nearwe, adv., *closely, oppressively:*
  446.
nēddre, *see* nǣddre.
nēh, adv., *near:* 339.
nemnan, W1., *name, call:* pret. 1p.
  nemdon, 383; pp. genemned, 205;
  366 (possibly the meaning here
  is *mention*).
neoman, *see* niman.
neorxnawong, m., *paradise:* ds.
  neorxnawonge, 481.
nēosan, W1., *seek, visit:* inf. 113.
neowol, adj., *deep, profound:* dsn.
  wk. neowlan, 102; asm. wk.
  neowlan, 31, 91; asn. wk. neowle,
  180, 446.
nergan, W1., *save:* pres. p. nsm.
  nergende, 570; asm. nergendne,
  346.
Nergend, m., *Saviour:* gs. Nergendes, 377.

ness, m., *ground, earth, chasm:* dp.
  næssum, 135; ap. nessas, 31, 91.
nīgan, *see* hnīgan.
niht, f., *night:* gs. nihtes (adverbial,
  by night), 499; ap. 426, 571.
niman, IV, *take, choose:* pret. 1p.
  nāmon, 417; opt. 1p. neoman, 198.
  See geniman.
nis, *see* wesan.
nīð, m., *enmity, hatred, spite, malice;
  affliction, tribulation:* as. 377, 412,
  634 (? n. here).
nīðer, adv., *down:* 91, 135; nīðær,
  31.
*nīðsyn, f., *grievous sin:* ip. nīðsynnum, 180.
nīwe, adj., *new:* asn. 481.
nō, *see* nā.
nū, adv., *now, just now, but now,
  immediately, now henceforth:* 40,
  46, 57, 64, 92, 107, 141, 156, 157,
  177, 181, 188, 230, 231, 262, 392,
  395, 413, 422, 427, 441, 447, 580,
  592, 598, 628, 629, 684, 733.
nū, conj., *now that, since:* 110, 387,
  393.
nymðe, conj., *except, save:* 18;
  nimðe, 493; nymþe, 331, 335, 350,
  677.

O.

of, prep., w. dat., *of, from, out of:*
  34, 93, 146, 161, 173, 181, 187, 202,
  257, 258, 267, 356, 467, 505, 516,
  553, 565, 604, 605, 670.
of, adv., *off, absent:* 574.
ofer, prep., w. dat., *over, above:* 215,
  241; w. accus., *over, above,* 264,
  602, 616, 627, 684.
oferfeohtan, III, *conquer, vanquish:*
  pp. oferfohten, 405.
oferhycgan, W3., *contemn, scorn,*

renounce: pret. 2p. oferhygdon, 486; inf. 252; oferhycgen, 305.

oferhygd, n., *pride:* gs. oferhȳdes, 114; dp. oferhygdum, 50, 69, 197; oferhigdum, 228; ap. oferhȳda, 370.

oferwinnan, III, *overcome, vanquish:* pp. oferwunnen, 462.

ofost, f., *haste:* ip. ofostum, 629.

oft, adv., *oft, often:* 152, 271, 329, 639, 642.

ofþyncan, Wı., *mislike, displease, be an offence to:* pret. 3s. ofþūhte, 247.

on, prep., w. dat., *on, in, into, for, from:* 5, 8, 15, 22, 37, 39, 45, 67, 99, 110, 112(2), 131, 143, 159, 206, 231, 237, 246, 263, 265, 276, 278, 281, 286, 290, 299, 303, 324, 345, 368, 372, 414, 417, 478, 481, 496, 502, 504, 510, 511, 521, 549, 550, 558, 563, 575, 586, 597, 600, 680, 712, 721, 726, 733; w. acc., *on, upon, into, to, by, for:* 89, 139, 263, 347, 404, 406, 465, 474, 476, 515, 533, 539, 578, 580, 610, 611, 639, 681, 682, 683, 685, 698, 718.

on, adv., w. hwǣr forming a rel. adv., *whereon, where:* 530.

onǣlan, Wı., *kindle, burn, heat:* pp. onǣled, 40, 97, 322, 341, 421.

oncnāwan, red., *recognize, understand, believe:* inf. 542.

ondetan, Wı., *confess:* inf. 225.

onfōn, red., *receive:* pret. 3s. onfēng, 566.

ongēan, prep., w. dat., *towards, to meet:* 301.

ongeotan, V, *perceive, understand, conceive:* opt. 1p. ongeotan, 301.

ongin, n., *action, undertaking:* ns. 547.

onginnan, III, *begin* (often periphrastic): pret. 3s. ongan, 78, 248; 3p. ongunnon, 731; opt. 1p. onginnen, 645.

onlūcan, II, *unlock, disclose, reveal:* opt. 1p. onlūcan, 300.

onmēdla, m., *pride, presumption:* ds. onmǣdlan, 429; anmēdlan, 74.

onsēon, f., *sight, appearance:* ns. 61.

onstellan, Wı., *institute, be the author of:* 3s. onstalde, 369; 2p. onstaldon, 114.

onstyrian, W2., *stir up:* inf. 271.

ontȳnan, Wı., *disclose, reveal:* pp. ontȳned, 557, 594.

onwacan *or* onwǣcnan, red., *spring, be born:* pret. 2s. onwōce, 439; 3p. onwōcon, 476.

onwald, m., *power:* as. 60, 118.

onwecnan, Wı., *awake:* 3p. onwecnaðˇ, 604.

open, adj., *revealed, opened:* nsf. 406.

ord, m., *beginning:* as. 114.

ordfruma, m., *source, author, creator, prince, chief:* ns. 239, 374, 442, 659; ap. ordfruman, 21.

orðonc, n., *art, skill, invention:* as. 18.

ōðˇr, pron., *other, another, second:* asn. 212; ism. ōðˇre, 75; isn. ōðˇre, 229; npm. ōðˇre, 625; dpm. ōðˇrum, 26.

oðˇfæstan, Wı., *fasten on:* pp. oðˇfæsted, 445.

oðˇðˇæt, conj., *until:* 478, 702, 728.

P.

Pētrus, pr. n., *Peter:* ns. 536; ds. Pētre, 523.

R.

rǣcan, WI., *reach:* pret. 3s. rǣhte, 437. *See* gerǣcan.

rǣd, m., *advice, counsel:* as. 250.

rǣdbora, m., *counselor:* np. rǣdboran, 500.

rægn, m., *rain:* gs. rægnas, 11.

rēam, *see* hrēam.

rēd, *see* dægrēd.

refnan, WI., *carry out, bring to pass:* inf. hrefnan, 500.

reord, f., *speech, language:* as. reorde, 35.

reordian, W2., *speak:* pret. 3s. reordade, 75; 3p. reordadon, 66; inf. 732; pres. p. nsm. reordende(?), 626.

rest, f., *rest, place of rest:* as. reste, 612, 619.

rēðe, adj., *fierce, savage:* npm. 104. reðer, *see* hreðer.

rīce, n., *rule, dominion, kingdom:* ns. 693; gs. rīces, 347, 500, 688; ds. 278, 308, 368, 618, 651; as. 260A, 614. *See* heofonrīce.

ricene, adv., *quickly, straightway:* 708.

riht, n., *justice, right:* as. 207, 347.

riht, adj., *regular, true, real:* nsm. 260A, 688.

rīm, n., *number, multitude:* as. 401, 420. *See* ende-, ge-, unrīm.

rīman, *see* āriman.

rinnan, *see* irnan.

rīsan, *see* ārīsan.

rodor, m., *heaven:* gp. rodora, 688; rodera, 347, 612.

S.

saca, *see* andsaca.

sǣ, m., f., *sea:* ds. 5; as. 9.

sǣlig, *see* gesǣlig.

sanct, m., *saint:* np. sanctas, 240, 355.

sang, m., *song, singing:* ns. 663; as. 235; song, 45, 143; is. sange, 145. *See* lofsong.

sār, adj., *grievous:* gsf. wk. sāran, 28.

Sātān, Sātānus, pr. n., *Satan:* ns. Sātān, 712; Sātānus, 371, 447; vs. Sātānus, 692.

sāwol, f., *soul:* np. sāwla, 653; sāwle, 296; gp. sāwla, 573; dp. sāwlum, 145, 266; ap. sāwla, 398; sāwle, 407.

scacan, VI, *hurry, speed:* inf. 263.

scēadan, *see* āscēadan.

-sceaft, *see* gesceaft.

scealc, *see* hellescealc.

scealu, f., *throng, multitude:* as. sceale, 268.

scearian, *see* gescearian.

scēat, m., *corner, region, surface:* ap. scēatas, 3, 603.

sceaða, m., *criminal, wretch, fiend:* np. sceaðan, 72; gp. sceaðena, 633; sceaðana, 57.

scēawian, W2., *see, behold:* pret. 3p. scēawodon, 535; inf. 524. *See* gescēawian.

sced, n., *shade, darkness:* gs. scedes, 106.

sceldburg, f., *fortress, city of refuge:* ds. sceldbyrig, 309.

Sceppend, *see* Scyppend.

sceððan, VI, *hurt, harm:* inf. 146.

scima, m., *light, splendor:* ns. 352; *gloom:* ds. scīman, 106.

scīnan, I, *shine, gleam, glitter, be bright:* 3s. scīneð, 223, 352; 3p. scīnað, 214, 295, 309, 652; opt. 3s. scīne, 211.

scinna, m., *demon, evil spirit:* np. scinnan, 72.

scīr, adj., *bright, resplendent:* dsf. wk. scīran, 177.

scræf, n., *cavern, hollow, den:* as. 129, 419, 633, 727; scref, 26, 73. *See* **wītescræf**.

scrīðan, I, *glide in:* 3p. scrīþað, 631.

scrīfan, *see* **forscrīfan**.

scūfan, II, *shove, thrust:* 3p. scūfað, 633; pret. 3s. scēaf, 445.

sculan, prp., *must, have to, be destined to, shall, should, ought:* 1s. sceal, 48, 112, 120, 157, 171, 184, 188, 273; 3s. sceal, 194, 262, 394; 1p. sceolon, 231, 554; sceolun, 41; 3p. sceolôn, 270, 506, 551, 636; sceolun, 30; pret. 3s. sceolde, 375; 1p. sceoldon, 235, 412, 419; sceoldan, 37; scealdon, 54; 3p. sceoldon, 326, 643; sceolden, 27.

scūra, m., *shower:* ap. scūran, 11.

scuwp, m., *shadow:* as. scuwan, 455.

scyldig, adj., *guilty:* asn. wk. scyldige, 33.

scyppan, *see* **forscyppan**.

Scyppend, m., *Creator:* ns. 244, 563; Scypend, 57; Sceppend, 309; gs. Sceppendes, 106; as. 535, 680A.

scyrian, *see* **bescyrian**.

se, sē, demon. pron., demon. adj., defin. art., *that, the, he, she, it;* rel. *who, which, that:* nsm. 14, 34, 126, 183, 205, 210, 243, 247, 277, 283, 288, 294, 304(2), 316, 338, 355, 396, 406, 413(2), 457, 458, 466, 484, 487, 488, 494, 511, 532, 543, 575, 665(2), 704, 715, 724; nsf. sēo, 405, 576; nsn. þæt, 1, 17, 21, 322, 325, 355, 358, 366, 373, 374, 457, 493, 540, 547,

583, 606, 665; gsm. þæs, 174, 701; ðæs, 416, 531; þes, 716; ðes, 114; gsf. þære, 172; gsn. þæs, 231, 330, 399, 418, 434, 490, 501, 571; ðæs, 101, 247; ðes, 77; ðęs, 115; *see also* þæs, conj.; dsm. þæm, 239, 364; ðæm, 179, 219, 274; þam, 257, 291, 365, 373, 504, 557, 567, 711; ðam, 74; þan, 423; dsf. þære, 177, 470, 624; ðære, 321, 664; dsn. þæm, 521; ðæm, 202; þam, 193, 417, 519; asm. þone, 149, 178, 202, 209, 252, 332, 337, 378, 637, 643, 669, 702, 718; ðone, 30, 31, 46, 91; asf. þā, 139, 201, 459, 560, 580, 611, 694; asn. þæt, 20, 26, 33, 73, 89, 129, 179, 184, 193, 200, 220, 255, 290, 298, 303, 348, 353, 365, 446, 463, 473, 494, 578, 591, 628, 633, 634, 691, 727; isn. ðȳ, 120; þē, 705; np. þā, 196, 356, 448, 611, 613, 620(2), 654, 731; ðā, 482; dp. þæm, 630, 650; þam, 145, 147, 266, 383; ap. þā, 148, 487, 603, 652, 663.

sēcan, W1., *seek, go, proceed:* 3p. sēcað, 266. *See* **gesēcan**.

secg, m., *man:* np. secgas, 498.

secgan, W3., *say, tell, relate, announce, give (thanks, praise), sing:* pret. 2s. segdest, 63, 430; 3s. sæde, 126, 471, 514; 1p. sædon, 156; 3p. 464; inf. 235, 523, 552, 696. *See* **āsecgan**.

segnian, *see* **gesegnian**.

seld, n., *seat, hall, home, throne:* ds. sęlde, 173, 187, 202, 663; as. 235, 348, 588. *See* **hēhseld**.

sele, m., *hall, dwelling:* ns. 136; ds. 131; as. 332. *See* **wīn-**, **windsele**.

sēlra, see gōd.

-sēne, see gesēne.

seolf, pron., *self, very, own:* nsm.
309, 404, 462; sylf, 663; wk.
seolfa, 4, 57, 124, 244, 260, 275,
350, 355, 396, 430, 600; seolua,
13, 712; selfa, 9; sylfa, 218, 306,
441; gsm. seolfes, 588, 685; asm.
sylfne, 545; vs. seolf, 692; npm.
seolfe, 23, 590; selfe, 648; seolfa,
145.

seolfor, n., *silver:* gs. seolfres, 578.

sēon, V, *look:* inf. 378. *See* ge-,
onsēon.

seoðða̅n, adv., *afterwards, thereafter, henceforth:* 377, 398, 420,
634.

seoðða̅n, conj., *after, since:* 77, 452,
706.

serwan, WI., *plan, devise, plot
against:* pret. 3s. serede, 15; 3p.
seredon, 498.

setl, see hēhsetl.

settan, WI., *set up, establish, fix,
trace, travel:* pret. 3s. sette, 15;
inf. 189. *See* ā-, gesettan.

sibb, f., *friendliness, kindness:* as.
sibbe, 207. *See* unsib.

sīc, adj., *sick at heart, sad:* nsm.
275.

sīd, adj., *broad, wide, spacious:*
nsm., 704; nsf. 699; dsm. wk.
sīdan, 131.

sīde, f., *side:* ds. sīdan, 545.

*sigetorht, adj., *glorious in victory:*
ns. 240.

sigor, m., *victory:* gs. sigores, 678;
gp. sigora, 218.

Sīmon, pr. n.: ns. 536; ds. 523.

sīn, poss. pron., *his:* asm. sīnne, 725.

sinc, n., *treasure:* as. 578.

singan, III, *sing:* 3p. singað, 355.

sittan, V, *sit, dwell:* 3s. siteð, 580,
586; sit, 218; 3p. sittað, 647; inf.
590. *See* gesittan.

sīð, m., *journey, time:* is. sīðe, 75;
ap. sīðas, 189.

six, num., *six:* 15.

snotor, adj., *wise:* nsm. 349; vpm.
snotre, 471.

snytero, f., *wisdom:* ns. 492; as.
207.

some, adv., *likewise:* 83.

-somne, see ætsomne.

sōna, adv., *soon, forthwith:* 536,
630.

song, see sang.

sorg, f., *sorrow, grief, affliction:*
gs. sorge, 28; gp. sorga, 696; ip.
sorgum, 296.

sorghceari, adj., *sad, sorrowful:*
nsm. 189.

sorhful, adj., *sorrowful:* nsm. 275.

sōð, n., *truth:* as. 207; ds. (tō)
sōðe: *truly, as a fact, really:* 63,
430.

sōð, adj., *true:* asf. wk. sōðan, 13.

sōðcwide, m., *true words, truthful
speech:* ip. sōðcwidum, 471.

sōðfæst, adj., *righteous, just:* npm.
sōðfæste, 307; wk. soðfæstan,
611.

*spearca, m., *spark:* ip. spearcum,
162.

*spearcian, W2., *emit sparks:* pret.
3s. spearcade, 78.

spēd, f., *success, might, abundance:*
as. 623, 668.

*spellung, f., *talk, conversation:* as.
spellunge, 638.

spreocan, V, *speak, say:* pret. 1s.
spræc, 249; 3s. spræc, 536; inf.
78.

stæf, see endestæf.

stǣlan, W1., *lay to one's charge,
    accuse of, reproach, taunt with:*
    3p. stǣleð, 640.
stān, m., *stone:* ns. 517; ap. stānas,
    5, 672.
standan, *see* **stondan**.
starian, W2., *look, gaze:* inf. 140.
staðelian, W2., *establish, set up,
    take up (abode,* hām st- *some-
    times* = *dwell):* pret. 1s. staðe-
    lode, 276; 3p. staðeledon, 25;
    staðelodon, 345.
stefn, f., *voice, sound:* as. stefne,
    172, 238; is. stefne, 36, 601; ip.
    stefnum, 656.
stellan, *see* **onstellan**.
stenc, m., *fragrance, odor:* ap.
    stences, 357.
steppan, VI, *step:* inf. 248.
stician, W2., *pierce:* pret. 3p. stice-
    don, 510.
stīgan, *see* **ā-, gestīgan**.
stīðmōd, adj., *stern:* nsm. 248.
stōl, *see* **cynestōl**.
stondan, VI, *stand, be:* 3p. stondað,
    46, 620; standað, 220; pret. 3s.
    stōd, 128, 721, 726. *See* ge-
    stondan.
storm, m., *uproar, tumult:* ns. 387.
strǣt, f., *road, way:* as. strǣte, 287.
strang, *see* **strong**.
strēam, m., *current, stream:* as. 5.
strengðo, f., *strength, power:* as. 2,
    286.
strēonan, *see* **gestrēonan**.
strong, adj., *strong, severe, hard,
    stern, fast, close:* nsm. 427;
    strang, 248; nsn. 322; strang,
    226.
stronglic, adj., *firm, severe:* nsm.
    517; nsn. 387.
styde, *see* **burhstyde**.

styrian, *see* **onstyrian**.
sum, pron., *some, one:* ns. 57; npm.
    sume, 263, 270, 542; dsm. sumum,
    538.
-sum, *see* **lang-, wynsum**.
sunne, f., *sun:* ds. sunnan, 307; as.
    sunnan, 4.
sunu, m., *son:* ns. 63, 119, 243, 396,
    529, 580; as. 143, 173, 529; np.
    648.
sūsl, n., *torment:* ns. 692; ds. sūsle,
    712; as. sūsel, 41, 64; sūsle, 725;
    is. sūsle, 52.
***sūslbona**, m., *devil of torment:*
    np. sūslbonan, 640.
sutol, adj., *clear, plain:* asn. 89.
swā, adv., *so, thus, likewise, such:*
    14, 22, 61, 65, 83, 126, 191, 256,
    280, 349(2), 350, 464, 469, 514,
    529, 661, 674, 701.
swā, conj., *as:* 117, 279, 306, 412,
    484, 525, 625, 689, 724.
swarian, *see* **andswarian**.
swart, adj., *black, dark:* nsm. wk.
    swarta, 704; npm. swarte, 52, 640.
swāt, m., *blood:* as. 545.
swearte, adv., *darkly, dismally,
    wickedly:* 371, 447, 578.
swēg, m., *sound, noise, hissing,
    music:* ns. 102, 403, 564; as. 152,
    237.
swegl, n., *sky, heaven, ether:* gs.
    swegles, 23, 28, 124, 351; ds.
    swegle, 45, 143; is. swegl, 588;
    ds. (? is.) swegle, 648 (? =
    harmony, music).
swilc, pron., *such, so great:* nsm.
    262; swelc, 79.
swīð, adj., *right:* comp. asf. wk.
    swīðran, 580, 611; isf. wk. swī-
    ðran, 360, 615.
swīðan, *see* **geswīðan**.

swylce, adv., *also, thus, so, in such manner:* 322, 428, 667.

syllan, WI., *give:* 3s. syleð, 292; pret. 3s. sealde, 452. See ā-, gesellan.

symle, adv., *ever, always, continually:* 286.

syn, f., *sin:* as. synne, 306; ip. synnum, 131. See nīðsyn.

synfull, adj., *sinful:* npm. synfulle, 52.

syngian, W2., *sin:* pret. 1p. syngodon, 230.

T.

tācen, n., *sign:* as. 89.

tǣcan, WI., *show:* 3s. tǣceð, 294.

tān, m., *branch:* np. tānas, 482.

teala, adv., *well, rightly, righteously:* 557, 594, 733.

teldan, see beteldan.

telga, m., *bough:* dp. telgum, 482.

tēne, num., *ten:* 571.

-tenge, see getenge.

tēona, m., *injury, abuse, trouble:* as. tēonan, 497.

tīd, f., *time, hour:* np. tīda, 709; ip. tīdum, 45.

tīfer, n., *victim, sacrifice:* ds. tīfre, 575.

til, adj., *good:* apm. tile, 610.

timber, see hēahgetimber.

tintrega, m., *torment:* gs. tintregan, 497.

tīr, m., *honor, glory:* ns. 93.

tō, prep., w. dat., *to, into, towards, at, for, as:* 63, 70, 87, 88, 92, 111, 117, 148, 149, 153, 176, 190, 196, 198, 208, 239, 249, 254, 269, 279, 288, 291, 315, 335, 357, 361, 362, 375, 400, 403, 415, 427, 430, 436, 437, 440, 454, 458, 461, 494, 495, 506, 527, 533, 546, 554, 562, 567, 589, 598, 618, 619, 624, 625, 633, 643, 651, 660, 672, 686, 687, 703, 723; *from:* 513, 686; w. gen., *to:* 531; w. inf. 147.

tō, adv., *to, thither:* 708.

tōgegnes, prep., w. dat. obj. *preceding, for, in readiness for:* 693; tōgēnes, 287.

torht, adj., *bright, splendid, glorious:* nsm. 594; wk. torhta, 294; nsn. 557; asm. torhtne, 575. See sigetorht.

tōð, m., *tooth:* gp. tōða, 339.

tōweorpan, III, *overthrow, destroy, put an end to:* inf. 393; tōwerpan, 85.

trēow, n., *tree:* ds. trēo, 417; as. 482.

trum, adj., *strong, well:* asm. trumne, 525.

*trumlic, adj., *firm, stable:* asm. trumlicne, 294.

tūdor, n., *offspring, family:* as. 659.

twēgen, num., *two:* nf. twā, 411, 709; af. twā, 610.

twelf, num., *twelve:* 339, 571.

tȳnan, see ontȳnan.

þ.

þā, adv., *then:* 76, 84, 160, 181, 190, 225, 247, 248, 330, 369, 371, 379, 385, 400, 403, 405, 407, 408, 416, 432, 437, 443, 462, 470, 474, 483, 489, 501, 526, 530, 536, 558, 564, 569, 573, 574, 669, 675, 680A, 690, 711, 722; ða, 51, 256, 491, 726.

þā, conj., *when:* 89, 190, 192, 201, 236, 345, 375, 380, 382, 391, 406, 411, 419, 467, 469, 510, 570, 671, 726; ða, 3, 25.

þǣr, adv., *there, thither, in that:* 175, 215, 236, 266, 309, 321, 326,

352, 354, 511, 596, 636, 647, 649, 655, 662; ðær, 24, 245, 323, 339.

þǣr, conj., *where, whilst, whereas, in that:* 27, 46, 108, 143, 154, 218, 288, 297, 312, 329, 333, 361, 447, 532, 545, 554, 590, 592, 593, 618, 641; *if:* 234.

þæs, adv., *so:* 350, 517.

þæs, conj., *because, that, from the time that, after:* 187, 275, 486, 505, 516, 553, 577; ðæs, 173; þęs, 123.

þæt, conj., *that, so that, in order that, until:* 2, 22, 23, 41, 54, 55, 63, 85, 101, 115, 124, 130, 141, 168, 169, 182, 195, 200, 211, 230, 247, 256, 259, 284, 317, 339, 346, 351, 370, 372, 378, 414, 424, 435, 441, 457, 464, 466, 475, 479, 482, 489, 502, 506, 519, 524, 534, 535, 543, 547, 571, 584, 595, 624, 635, 645, 670, 676, 695, 697, 705, 710, 721, 722, 725; ðæt, 59.

þætte, conj., *that:* 430.

þanc, m., *thanks:* as. 552. *See* orðonc.

þancian, W2., *thank:* pret. 3p. þanceden, 534.

þanon, adv., *thence, from there:* 327, 722; þonan, 635; þonon, 475.

þe, rel. particle, indecl., *who, which, that:* 21, 37, 74, 88, 114, 147, 245, 261, 266, 323, 356, 383, 423, 643, 650, 669; ðe, 17, 146, 183, 210, 283, 304, 338, 364, 365, 413, 557, 575, 620, 654, 665; with þæs, þǣr, þonne, as conjunctions, *when:* 151, 516; *because:* ðe, 123, 187, 553, 641; *that:* 505.

þeah, conj., *though, although:* 433, 518; þǣh, 265.

þearle, adv., *severely, terribly, firmly, tightly:* 38, 421.

þearlic, adj., *violent, severe:* asn. 636.

þegen, m., *thane, servant, follower, disciple, warrior:* ns. 388, 426; np. þegnas, 326, 662. *See* hand-, aldorðægn.

þencan, W1., *think, consider, mean, intend:* 3s. þenceð, 183, 364, 557; 1p. þencað, 208. *See* geþencan.

-þeode, *see* geþeode.

þeoden, m., *prince, king:* ns. 247, 388, 548, 598, 666; ds. þeodne, 534; as. 662.

þeon, *see* geþeon.

þeostre, adj., *dark:* nsm. wk. ðeostræ, 38.

þes, pron., *this:* nsm. 136, 387, 394; ðes, 87, 96, 100, 303; ðis, 103; nsf. þeos, 213, 262; ðeos, 83; nsn. þis, 38, 254, 387, 465, 537; dsm. þissum, 660; ðissum, 111; þyssum, 131; ðeossum, 108; dsf. þisse, 604; dsn. ðissum, 102; asm. þysne, 157; asf. þas, 608, 644; ðæs, 504; asn. þis, 180, 253, 419.

þicgan, V (w. an occasional wk. pret., as here), *eat:* pret. 1p. þigdon (w. gen.), 411.

þider, adv., *thither:* 217, 302, 531, 589, 632.

þin, poss. pron., *thy, thine:* nsm. ðin, 63; nsf. 61; gsm. þines, 685; asm. ðinne, 53; dpf. ðinum, 62.

þing, n., *thing:* gp. þinga, 273.

þingian, W2., *plead, supplicate, sue, intercede:* 3s. þingað, 447; pret. 1s. þingade, 509. *See* geþingian.

þoht, *see* geþoht.

þolian, *see* geþolian.

þonne, adv., *then:* 210, 292, 323, 356, 359, 383, 604, 609, 613, 620, 701, 705, 706, 730; ðonne, 34.

þonne, conj., *when:* 163, 208, 212, 276, 541, 607; ðonne, 78, 80, 718; *than:* 176, 213, 390, 597; *than when:* 151.

þorhdrīfan, I, *drive* or *hurl forth:* pret. 3s. þorhdrāf, 163.

þrāg, f., ip. ðrāgum, *sometimes, from time to time:* 112.

þrēat, m., *troop, throng, swarm:* ns. ðrēat, 95; ds. þrēate, 388; as. 336; vs. 167; np. þrēatas, 568; ap. þrēatas, 424; *oppression, punishment:* ns. 325. *See* heofen-þrēat.

þrēo, num., *three:* af. 426; an. 503.

þrītig, num., *thirty:* an. 503.

þrōwian, W2., *suffer, endure:* pret. 1s. þrōwode, 503; 3s. ðrōwade, 490; inf. 41, 395. *See* geþrōwian.

þrym, m., *glory, magnificence:* ns. 662; ðrym, 36; as. 507, 555; vs. 164.

þū, pron., *thou:* ns. 53, 59, 439, 537, 658, 674, 676, 688, 691, 696, 699, 702, 705(2), 706; ðū, 55, 59, 423, 441, 689, 695, 697, 710; tū, 57, 64; ds. þē, 55, 685; as. þē, 410, 422, 692, 694; ðē, 538, 698; as. þec, 539; ðec, 60; np. gē, 251, 617, 618; gp. ēower, 113; dp. ēow, 493, 509; ap. ēow, 92, 250, 472, 629; dual n. git, 483, 486; d. inc. 488; a. inc. 484.

þurfan, prep., *need, have reason to ·* 1p. ðurfon, 115.

þurh, prep., w. accus., *through, by, by virtue of, in, because of, for:* 13, 14, 392, 401, 412, 438, 472, 495, 550, 585, 589, 605, 623, 646, 668, 681, 694, 725; ðurh, 6, 53, 59.

þus, adv., *thus, so:* 534, 569, 657, 733.

þūsend, n., *thousand:* ns. 302; gp. þūsenda, 402, 421, 723.

þūsendmǣlum, adv. (ip.), *in* or *by thousands:* 236, 509, 569, 632.

þyncan, W1., *seem, appear:* pret. 3s. þūhte, 434, 722; ðūhte, 22, 55. *See* ofþyncan.

U.

ufan, adv., *from above, down, above:* 69, 342, 496, 703.

ūhte, f., *dawn:* as. ūhtan, 406, 465.

unclǣne, adj., *unclean, foul, impure:* apm. 609.

under, prep., *under:* w. dat., 135, 319; w. accus., 91; undẹr, 31.

underne, adj., *revealed, manifest, clear:* nsn. 1.

ungēara, adv., *before long, soon:* 395.

ungelīc, adj., *unlike, different:* npm. ungelīce, 150.

unrīm, n., *a countless number:* as. 573.

unsib, f., *enmity, strife, discord:* as. unsibbe, 271.

ūp, upp, adv., *up, above, upward, on high:* ūp, 170, 245, 266, 288, 327, 403, 407, 424, 443, 458, 461, 482, 506, 512, 554, 563, 625, 635, 660, 730; upp, 530.

ūpheofon, m., *upper heaven, the heavens:* as. 16, 95; vs. ūpheofen, 167.

ūplic, adj., *on high, heavenly:* asm. ūplicne, 362.

uppe, adv., *up, above, on high:* 123, 142, 199, 231, 265, 293, 330, 373, 391, 397, 591, 647.

ūre, poss. pron., *our:* nsm. 548; apn.
392.

ūt, adv., *out, forth, outside:* 5, 34,
161, 163, 520.

ūtan, adv., *without, on the outside:*
342; w. ymb, *about, round:* 154.
See ymbūtan.

uton (1p. opt. of wītan), interj., w.
infin., *let us:* 298, 594, 644; uta,
217, 252.

W.

wā, adv., *woe:* 342.

wacan, *or* wæcnan, *see* on-.

wadan, VI, *go, travel:* inf. 121.

wælm, m., *surging flame:* ds. welme,
39; as. 30.

wærgðu, f., indecl., *condemnation,
punishment:* as. 89.

wæstm, m., *fruit:* np. wæstmas, 214.
See limwæstm.

wæter, n., *water:* as. 6.

-wald, *see* ge-, onwald.

walda, *see* anwalda.

waldend, m., *ruler, sovereign, lord:*
ns. 218, 564, 585, 587, 608;
wealdend, 125; gs. waldendes,
119, 195, 300, 396; wealdendes,
577; as. 188, 199, 253; np. 24.

*wālic, adj., *woeful, wretched:* nsm.
wk. wālica, 100.

waran, *see* hellwaran.

wēa, m., *woe, affliction:* as. wēan,
42, 185, 336, 715; wēa, 320.

wealdan, red., *possess:* pret. 1s.
wēold, 275.

weall, m., *wall:* ap. weallas, 652.
See burhweall.

weallan, red., *well, surge, boil:* pret.
3s. wēol, 318.

weard, m., *guardian, lord:* ns. 514;
as. 612, 661; vs. 422.

-weard, *see* inneweard.

wecnan, *see* onwecnan.

wel, adv., *well:* 365.

welm, *see* brynewelm.

wēnan, W1., *ween, suppose, imag-
ine, believe; hope* or *look for,
expect:* 1s. wēne, 50, 89; 3p.
wēnað, 624; pret. 2s. wēndest,
676; wēndes, 59; inf. 115, 451.

weorc, n., *work, deed:* ns. (? p.)
492; ip. weorcum, 223, 552; wercum, 48. *See* handge-, hereweorc.

weornian, W2., *wither, fail:* pret.
3p. weornodon, 468.

weorod, n., *host, multitude:* as.
werud, 33; gp. weoroda, 188, 198,
564, 581; weroda, 253.

weorpan, *see* ā-, tōweorpan.

weorðan, III, *become, be, befall,
take place:* pret. 3s. wearð, 1,
381, 711; pp. geworden, 282, 429,
452, 465. *See* for-, geweorðan.

weorðmynt, m., *honor, glory:* as.
152.

weotod, adj. (pp.), *appointed:* nsm.
692.

wer, m., *man:* gp. wera, 492.

*wērgu, f., indecl., *misery:* as. 42.

werig, adj., *weary, wretched, miserable; evil, malign* (? in 126, 332,
630, 669, 711, 732, wĕrig, and =
accursed; on the whole question
see Sievers, *Indog. Forsch. 26.*
225-35, and Klaeber's note on
Beow. 133): nsm. 162, 428; wk.
wērega, 126; dsm. wk. wĕrga,
711; asm. wk. wērigan, 332;
wēregan, 669; asf. wk. wēregan,
35; npm. wĕrige, 343, 449, 630;
wk. wērigan, 731.

wesan, anv., *be:* 1s. eom, 97, 130,
156, 177; eam, 168; 2s. eart, 57,

Glossary 173

441, 537, 658; 3s. is, 17, 38, 39,
61, 96, 100, 102, 103, 136, 141,
193, 205, 214, 215, 230, 254, 258,
260A, 288, 333, 355, 365, 387, 396,
427, 441, 479, 556, 583, 584, 593,
596, 649, 662, 663, 665, 692; biδ,
79, 182, 264, 304, 363, 606, 626;
1p. syndon, 150; 2p. sind, 617;
3p. synd, 358; seondon, 104, 709;
bēoð, 356, 613, 622; pret. 1s.
wæs, 81; wes, 89; 3s. wæs, 76,
190, 226, 244, 247, 281, 321, 322,
323, 325, 338, 339, 342, 366, 373,
383, 405, 452, 457, 465, 487, 501,
502, 532, 543(2), 547, 558, 565,
574, 669; 1p. wæron, 236, 391;
3p. wæron, 330, 385, 434; opt.
2s. sēo, 688; 3s. 213, 265, 704,
707; pret. 1s. wære, 124; 2s.
wære, 56; 3s. wære, 63, 518, 722;
3p. wēron, 23; imp. 2s. bēo, 733.
Negative: 3s. nis, 40, 93, 349;
pret. 3s. næs, 491, 517; opt. pret.
3s. nære, 676.
wid, adj., *wide, broad, long:* nsf.
699; apm. wīde, 189.
wide, adv., *widely, far:* 258, 320,
333, 386, 684; comp. wīdor, 120.
wideferð, adv., *forever:* 297.
wif, n., *woman:* as. 473.
wiht, f., n., *creature, wight:* ns. 727;
gp. wihta, 125. *See* **alwihte.**
wilcuma, m., *welcome guest:* npm.
wilcuman, 617.
willa, m., *will, command:* as. willan,
474. *See* **hyhtwilla.**
willan, anv., *will, intend, be willing,
wish, desire; shall, will:* 3s. wile,
289, 304, 392, 397, 609; 2p. willað, 251; pret. 1s. wolde, 173; 3s.
wolde, 401, 431, 436, 464, 561; 1p.
woldon, 234, 256; 3p. woldon,

346; opt. 3s. wille, 109, 116, 277,
623; pret. 1s. wolde, 85; 3s. 317,
370, 372. Negative: 3s. nyle,
147; pret. 2s. noldæs, 733.
windan, III, *wind, coil:* 3p. windað,
136. *See* **bewindan.**
windig, adj., *windy:* nsm. wk. windiga, 136.
*windsele (? wīnsele), m., *windy
hall:* as. 320, 386.
-winn, *see* **gewinn.**
winnan, III, *struggle, strive, fight:*
pret. 2s. wunne, 705; pp. gewun-
non, 719. *See* **oferwinnan.**
wīnsele, m., *wine or banquet hall:*
ns. 94.
winter, m., *winter, year:* gp. wintra,
420, 477, 502.
wirsa, *see* **yfel.**
witan, prp., *know:* 1s. wāt, 181; 2s.
wāst, 705; 3s. wāt, 32; imp. 2s.
wite, 699.
wītan, *see* **gewītan.**
wīte, n., *punishment, torment, tor-
ture:* gs. wītes, 77, 100, 103, 157,
444, 452; ds. 48; as. 494, 636; np.
wītu, 226; gp. wīta, 119; dp.
wītum, 80, 731; ap. wītu, 185, 336,
392, 715; ip. wītum, 162, 343, 428,
449.
wītega, m., *prophet:* np. wītegan,
464; wītigan, 461; gp. wītegena,
492; dp. wītegum, 587.
wītehūs, n., *house of torment:* asn.
628.
*witescræf, n., *cavern or den of torment:* as. 691.
wið, prep., w. gen., *towards, at:*
701, 716; w. dat., *over, against,
before, against:* 249, 433; w.
accus., *against, toward:* 97, 432,
705.

wiðhabban, W3., *withstand:* inf.
519.
wlita, *see* andwlita.
wlītan, I, *look, gaze:* inf. 409.
See geondwlītan.
wlite, m., *face, countenance, beauty:*
ns. 223; ds. 233; as. 152; is. 211.
wlitig, adj., *beautiful, fair:* nsn.
214; npm. wlitige, 652; apm.
wlitige, 609.
wlonc, adj., *rich:* gp. wloncra, 94.
wolcn, n., *cloud:* gp. wolcna, 564;
dp. wolcnum, 608; ap. wolcn, 6.
wom, m., n., *stain, spot, sin:* ns.
226; ip. wommum, 157.
*wōm, m., *wailing, lamentation* (?
noise) : ns. 333.
womcwide, m., *evil word* or *speech,
blasphemy:* dp. womcwidum, 282.
won, adj., *dark, lurid:* nsm. wk.
wonna, 715.
wong, *see* neorxnawong.
wōp, m., *wailing, weeping:* ns. 333.
word, n., *word, speech:* ns. 162; is.
worde, 80, 229; np. 358; dp.
wordum, 416, 630; ap. 155, 486;
ip. wordum, 48, 65, 126, 223, 386,
409, 514, 661, 731. *See* byrhtword.
wordcwide, m., *words, speech:* ap.
wordcwedas, 35.
worn m., *magnitude:* as. 77.
woruld, f., *world, universe, age:* gs.
worulde, 94; weorulde, 211; ds.
worulde, 181, 502; as. worulde,
644; woruld, 59, 224, 608; gp.
worulda, 224.
wracu, f., *misery, retribution, vengeance:* ns. wrece, 711; ds. wrece,
494; as. wrace, 185.
wræclāst, m., *exile-path* or *journey:*

ap. wræclāstas, 121; wreclāstas,
188, 259.
wrāð, adj., *angry:* nsm. 282, 452.
wrāðe, adv., *perversely, wickedly:*
316.
wrecan, V, *utter:* 3s. wriceð, 35.
wrec-, *see* wrac-, wræc-.
wrītan, *see* āwrītan.
wrōht, f., *strife:* as. wrōht, 369.
wuldor, n., *glory, heaven:* gs. wuldres, 14, 24, 107, 119, 141, 152,
175, 233, 237, 253, 343, 392, 449,
508, 514, 556, 585, 587, 593, 617,
650, 661; wulres, 42, 85; ds.
wuldre, 203, 369, 409; as. wuldor,
59; is. wuldre, 121, 444.
wuldorcyning, m., *king of glory:*
ns. 115, 428; ds. wuldorcyninge,
224, 312; as. 226.
wundian, W2., *wound:* pp. gewundod, 157. *See* forwundian.
wundor, n., *wonder:* gp. wundra, 6.
wunian, W2., *dwell, live, inhabit,
remain:* 3s. wunað, 210, 593; 3p.
wuniað, 508; pret. 1p. wunodon,
237; inf. 233, 259, 297, 312, 332,
420, 477, 556. *See* gewunian.
wurðian, W2., *honor:* pp. gewurðad, 537.
wyn, f., *delight, pleasure, joy:* gs.
wynne, 175; ds. wynne, 198; as.
43; dp. wynnum, 237, 508, 555,
593; ip. wynnum, 211, 650.
wynsum, adj., *pleasant:* nsn. 214;
apf. wynsume, 357.
wyrcan, W1., *make, build, accomplish, attain:* inf. 365, 372, 673.
See gewyrcan.
wyrged, *see* āwyrged.
wyrhta, m., *maker, creator:* ns. 14,
585.

wyrm, m., *serpent:* np. wyrmas, 103; gp. wyrma, 336; ap. wyrmas, 136.

wyrsa, *see* **yfel.**

wyrt, f., *plant:* ap. wyrta, 358.

Y.

yfel, n., *evil, misery:* gs. yfeles, 374; ds. yfele, 733.

yfel, adj., *evil, wicked, bad:* ap. yfle, 610; comp. nsn. wyrse, 125, 175; wirse, 24; wyrsa, 141.

ymb, prep., w. accus., *around, round, about:* 46, 47, 136, 154, 155, 220,

235, 498, 652, 662; temporal, *after:* 571; *before:* 426.

*ymbfleogan, II, *fly around:* pret. 3p. ymbflugon, 568.

ymbfon, red., *surround, circle:* pp. ymbfangen, 144, 518.

*ymbhaldan, red., *encompass, embrace:* 3s. ymbhaldeð, 7.

ymbhwyrft, m., *circuit, extent:* as. 702.

*ymblyt, m., *expanse, circuit:* as. 7.

ymbūtan, adv., *about, around:* 264, 352.